THE BOOK OF
SPARKWELL
WITH HEMERDON & LEE MILL

A PARISH PORTRAIT
PAM JAMES

HALSGROVE

First published in Great Britain in 2001

British Library Cataloguing-in-Publication Data
A CIP record for this title is available from the British Library

ISBN 1 84114 1127

HALSGROVE
PUBLISHING, MEDIA AND DISTRIBUTION

Halsgrove House
Lower Moor Way
Tiverton, Devon EX16 6SS
Tel: 01884 243242
Fax: 01884 243325
email: sales@halsgrove.com
website: http://www.halsgrove.com

Frontispiece photograph: *The Treby Arms, 1922.*

Printed and bound in Great Britain by Bookcraft Ltd, Midsomer Norton.

CONTENTS

Young community members cut the first turf for the new village hall in 1983.
Left to right: Neil Elford, Nigel Denny, Sally Cooper, Bernard Chudley, Lynne Denny.
Next to Lynne is Mrs K. Colborne-Mackrell.

The opening of the village hall in 1984. It was opened by
Major D. Ruttledge MBE on 3 November and was built on
land given by the late fourth Baron Seaton of Beechwood.
The architect was Edwin T. Ansted ARIBA and the builder
was F.G. Conybeare & Son. The formal naming of the hall
took place on 3 November 1984 by Lt Col the Earl of
Morley, HM Lord Lieutenant of Devon.

ACKNOWLEDGEMENTS

This book has been made possible with the help, enthusiasm and support of Sparkwell Parish. Thanks to those who have lent photographs, memorabilia and shared their memories of by-gone days. Special thanks to my husband Tony and my friends Dave and Glenys Wickstead for their patience, help with collating and logging material – and sorting out the computer! Thank you to Sparkwell Parish Council and to the Sparkwell Parish Trust for donating sums of money for basic costs.

Researchers include: Pam and Tony James, John Kingwell, Jean Newton, Brian and Susan Foster, John Colborne-Mackrell, Jim Woollcombe, Marjorie Serpell, Enid Hamlyn, Leo Harris, Jack and Heather Harvey, Gordon Chudley, Phyllis Long, Bill and Doreen Thorrington, Christine Hartley, Josh Dalton, Ann and Peter Tremain, Leo Harris, Dennis Root, Robert and Helen Wood, John Treneman, Ellis Daw, Lesley Masey.

Suppliers of memorabilia, photographs and memories include: Florrie Mudge, Enid Taylor, Reg, Charlie, John and Carol Serpell, Andrew and Hilda Wotton, John and Lorraine Denny, Rose Elliott, Fred Bennett, Harold Reed, Mary Chudley, Steve Hoskin, John and Dawn Evans, Nigel Tunnicliffe, Mrs Bunt, Lord Morley, Sheila Palmer, Ken and Deirdree Collings, Jill Phillips, Dave Barker, Jack Barker, Ethel Collier, Jean and Alan Jones, Jean Netherton, Geoff Perham, Gerald Tucker, Oxo and Monica Exworthy, Tom Weatherby, Gary Streeter, Dr and Mrs Gurrey, Dr Hooper, Edgar Clague, Yvonne Pinder.

Local families past and present who have been of much help include: Small, Stancombe, Sandover, Kitts, Clemo, Gulley, Conran, Seaton, Hill, Olver, Perraton, Perry, Rossiter, Mumford, Mortimer, Willcocks, Huxtable, Crowley, Abbot, Nelder. Apologies to anyone who has been overlooked.

Sadly, Andrew Wotton senr, Jack Lambshead and Ethel Collier died in 2001.

Site meeting, c.1930, of Plympton Rural District Council members on land at Birchland Farm approved for 40 Council houses, known as Birchland Road.

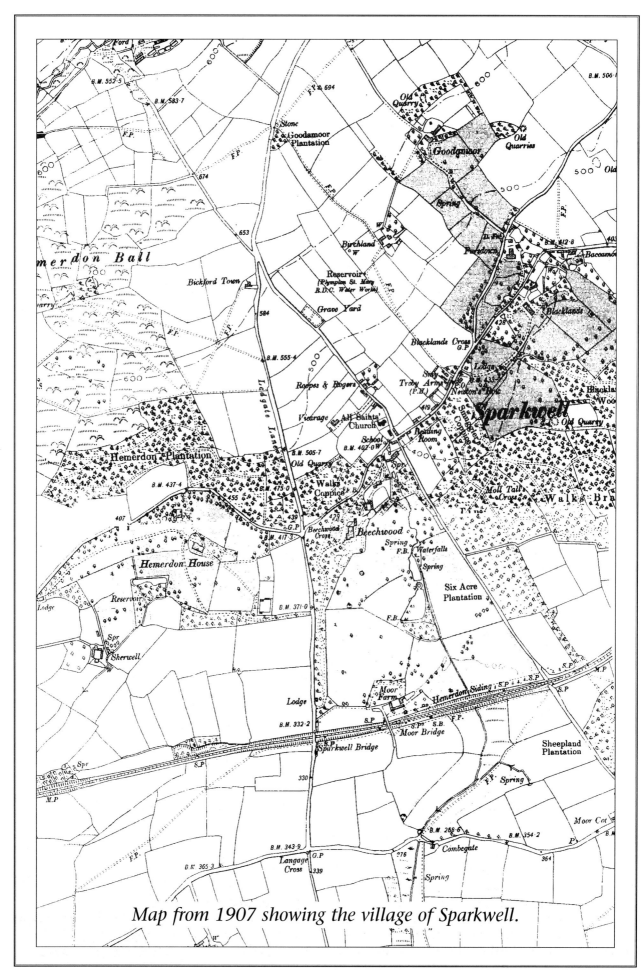

Map from 1907 showing the village of Sparkwell.

INTRODUCTION

Sparkwell is three miles east of Plympton and used to be in the eastern ward of Plympton St Mary Parish. No one knows for certain how the name originated but like so many places it could well be derived from a personal name. The family of Sperkwyll was mentioned several times as living in the neighbourhood in the early part of the 16th century. From 1536–37, William Sperkewyll was notorious, and countless times was placed before the courts to answer charges of ale-brewing and breaking the law! It is more than likely that 'going up to Sparkwell' became a slang saying for going for an illicit drink! Some locals, however, say that the village got its name from the wells in the area and that the water would 'sparkle'.

The parish of Sparkwell covers a large area and at its highest point is 628 feet above sea level – a fact which is announced on a stone erected at the 'Clump'. Large areas of the parish were either owned by local priories or prominent families; farms, cottages or smallholdings being worked or rented out by them. Originally the parish came under the control of Plympton Rural District Council until Plymouth took over and extended its control of Plympton and Plymstock in 1966. The arrival of the railway cut not only farms, but also the parish, in half.

The area of the parish includes three villages; Sparkwell, Hemerdon and Lee Mill, with hamlets Smithaleigh, Mount Pleasant, Venton, Lucas Wood, Drakelands and Elfordleigh also falling within its bounds. With the railway came boarding points, one at nearby Cornwood (station) and one at Venton (siding and halt), both for passengers and goods.

Farming and mining in various forms gave employment to most of the local population and work was also to be found in the mill at Lee Mill (now replaced with housing). Clay mining is still an important source of employment today. Sadly, farming has been in decline for some years and only a handful of farms still operate.

The arrival of the internal combustion engine meant that journeys to and from the area became easier and many locals opted to travel, taking up alternative forms of employment further afield. Deliveries to the area also became easier and tradespeople from further afield could deliver or sell where it had previously been impossible. Large multi-national stores opened up locally, selling not only foodstuffs, but also household goods and petrol. Local shops and garages could not compete and, after a long struggle to survive, had to admit defeat.

Lee Mill, always a main thoroughfare since stagecoach days, was eventually bypassed by the A38 (Parkway). No one seemed to have the foresight to realise that a large industrial estate and a substantial superstore would cause much more traffic, noise and danger than had existed there before. The Dartmoor National Park bounds the parish on one side so its area all told describes a stark transition from the bleak (on the side of the A38) to the beautiful (with the Park to the west).

One of the original approaches to Sparkwell was the old Cornwood road at the rear of Chaddlewood Garage, with a few houses on the left and a small gathering of houses and bungalows on the right. Further on just before Sandy Lane was Pellows Market Garden and just after the junction with Sandy Lane was Serpell's Market Garden run by Dennis Serpell. Opposite this was a black and white gatehouse which always had an immaculate garden. Further along the lane on the left were two cottages for workers employed by the West family. After passing these cottages, a short distance away was the entrance to Holland Farm fields – both sides of the road belonged to this farm. The next junction was a lane leading off to the right, to Lower and Higher Langage Farms. Unfortunately most of this has gone in the name of progress: Pellows has been replaced by housing, the gatehouse and Serpells are now the site of an office campus, Holland Farm and West Cottages are now an industrial estate, and Lower and Higher Langage Farms may soon disappear to make way for the site of a new power station and energy park.

Commemoration group of the Guardians of the Poor and chief officials of the Plympton St Mary Union, 7 March 1930, prior to the transfer of their duties to the Devon County Council under the Local Government Act of 1929.

Left to right, back row: Dr A Turner, Mr S.E. Paige, Mr J. King, Mr W.G. Rickard, Mr W.G. Triscott;

4th row: Mr J.H. Glover, Mr J. Davy, Mr J.J. Paull, Mr C. Hansford, paymaster Lt-Com. W.G. Abell, Mr S.E. Snawdon, Col W.F. Parker, Mr H. Felderman (relieving officer), Mr R.J. Townsend;

3rd row: Mr J.F. Ridler, Mr A.V. Tall, Mr T.A. Olver, Mr W.J.H. Ellis, Mr E.H.T. Lewis, Mr J. Atwill, Mr J. Hendy, Mr W.H. Elford;

2nd row: Mr W.J. Partington, Mr C.R.H. Selleck, Mr G. Dawe (master), Dr W.H. Trumper, Mr S.F. Lee, Mr H.J.P. Giles, Mr J. Cane, Mr W.J. Webber (relieving officer), Mr J.D. Hacker;

front: Mrs E.M. McArthur, Dr W.D. Stamp (medical officer), Mrs L. Dawe (matron), Mr H.G. Murdoch, Mr J.F. Hollow (Vice Chairman of the Board), Mr Leonard H. Hine (Chairman), Mr John W. Bickle (solicitor and clerk), Mr A.J. Edwards, Miss C. Hellings (matron of children's home), Mr W. B. Craig, Mrs E.M. Laws.

CHAPTER 1: CENSUS

The five schedules which survive for the parish of St Mary's deal chiefly with the farming population and date from c.1871. Three are listed here.

SCHEDULE 2: AREA COVERED BY THIS SCHEDULE

The Enumerators began with the National Schoolhouse at the top of Ridgeway, a building which had formerly been the Poorhouse for St Mary's parish. When the Union Workhouse was built in 1836 however, the inmates of the house at Higher Ridgeway were transferred to Underwood. Within a few years the premises were taken for school purposes. Such were the beginnings of public elementary education in Plympton. In 1857 the school was said to have 110 children on roll. The mistress, Mrs Mary J. Jenny of Fremley in Surrey, had lately lost her husband and lived at the Schoolhouse with her two sons, an assistant teacher named Elizabeth Bilbon (aged 15) and a nursemaid (aged 13).

The two adjoining houses were together known as the 'Police Station' and have since been incorporated into Elm Terrace. One was occupied by PC Thomas Froude with a wife and one son and the other by PC John Layers, who had living on the station along with his wife, three children, a lodger described as a 'watchman' and a prisoner from Brixton who happened to be locked up on the night of the census.

Mrs Millie Symons, aged 65, was the owner and occupier of Chaddlewood House and was the widow of Major W.A. Symons, 'lately deceased'. Her grown-up family had left home, but there were three visitors staying at Chaddlewood when the census was taken. The household staff included a butler, gardener, coachman, footman, page, lady's maid, cook, two housemaids and a dairymaid.

At Higher Chaddlewood, 54-year-old Aaron Andrews farmed 400 acres and employed six men. He had a wife and two sons (both working on the farm), two servant maids and five farm labourers living in.

At Holland George Dewdney farmed 140 acres and employed three men. His household consisted of himself, wife and four children, a brother helping on the farm, two maidservants and two labourers living in. At Higher Langage John Gardener farmed 100 acres with the help of just one man. The household consisted of himself, his wife, one married daughter, two grandchildren and one labourer. At Greater Langage Samuel Kingwell farmed 84 acres and employed one man. He had a wife, an unmarried daughter, two sons working on the farm and two farm boys living in.

At Coombe John Beer farmed 100 acres and employed one man. He had a wife, one daughter living at home, one maidservant, one labourer and a farm boy. At Mount Pleasant and Woodcock's Eye there were seven cottages all occupied by agricultural workers and their families. At Hitchcombe, Trobridge Horton, aged 68, farmed 170 acres and employed nine men. His grandson, aged 16, worked on the farm and there were also four labourers living in and two maidservants.

At Spurham, James Horton farmed 40 acres and employed three men, with his wife, six small children, a maidservant and one farm boy.

At Lee Mill Benjamin Holman, owner of the Paper Mills, was the principal employer. On the schedule he was described as 'Paper Manufacturer, age 56, born at Hatherleigh'. He had a wife, an unmarried daughter to help about the house, and a son, Francis, aged 15, who was 'employed in the Manufactory'. The Mills provided work for ten men. The village of Lee Mill appears to have consisted of 13 cottages occupied chiefly by farm workers, wheelwrights, carpenters, shoemakers and smiths. Ann Horton kept a general shop and Philip Abbott, blacksmith and victualler, kept the public house known until quite recently as the 'Blacksmith's Arms' (now Westward Inn).

At Challonsleigh, William Kingwell farmed 200 acres and employed five men. The household consisted of himself and wife, two sons working on the farm, a son-in-law and wife, a servant girl (aged 13) and three farm boys living in. The farm at Smithaleigh was likewise a family affair. George White, widower, farmed 128 acres and employed one labourer. His two sons worked on the farm and he had three daughters on household duties. In addition he kept a maidservant and one other farm boy. At Chokeford, Joseph Sercombe, widower, farmed 22 acres. He had two small boys at home, one labourer living in and a servant maid to keep house. At Collaford, William Wyatt, aged 61, farmed 35 acres. He had a wife and two sons (both working on the farm) and a daughter aged 17 also living at home.

At Ford, Edward Hosken farmed 109 acres and employed one labourer. He had four sons working on the farm and four younger children. He had one household servant. The three Ford Cottages beside the turnpike were occupied by a journeyman mason, a gamekeeper and a carpenter. At Applethorn Slade, William Phillips farmed 58 acres with the help of two grandsons.

At Voss, Henry Horton farmed 105 acres and employed one labourer. He lived at the farmhouse with his wife, a son aged 18 who worked on the farm, a niece helping in the house, three farm boys and a maidservant. Richard Pitt kept the Lyneham Inn.

At Battisford, James Doddridge, unmarried, farmed 211 acres with the help of two labourers, three farm boys and a maidservant. At Ley, Philip Sanders farmed 87 acres. He was a married man with five small children and two labourers living in. At Tuxton, Ambrose Willcox, unmarried, farmed 106 acres and lived with his widowed mother. He had two farm boys living in.

John Mead, wheelwright, lived at Lyneham Lodge – more often called Battisford Lodge – a rather picturesque little cottage which was pulled down shortly after work on the new bypass began (in 1969 or 1970). Then also there was a John Hamling, blacksmith, at Sandover's Shop. The old smithy has disappeared without trace but is believed to have stood a short distance along the road from the present Chaddlewood Garage at what used to be called Yealmpton Cross. A lane coming into the main road is still called Sandys Lane. At Yealmpton, Joseph Pearse farmed 240 acres and employed nine labourers. The household consisted of the farmer and his wife, a grown-up son and unmarried daughter, a maidservant and two farm boys.

At Lower Chaddlewood we complete the first circuit. Isaac Dewdney, aged 64, farmed 150 acres and employed four labourers. He lived on the farm with his wife and four children, a farm manager, one farm boy and two maidservants.

SCHEDULE 3: TAKING IN SPARKWELL, VENTON & OUTLYING PROPERTIES

Moor Farm is in the extreme south east of St Mary's parish, reaching almost into Cornwood. W.H. Beer, aged 38, farmed 100 acres and employed one man. He was married with four children, one maidservant and a farm boy.

James Yabsley, thatcher, lived at Beechwood Lodge. His wife is described in the schedule as a

Beechwood

'toll collector' and they had a lodger who was described as a 'rail policeman'. (In the early years of the South Devon Railway before mechanical signalling was introduced the traffic was controlled by men giving hand signals.)

Beechwood House was built in 1798 for the Plymouth banker, Mr Rosdew, whose wife belonged to the Mudge family. Following the death of Mrs Rosdew, widow, the estate was left to Lieut-Colonel Richard Zachary Mudge, R.E. (retired), whose name appears on the schedule. Then aged 60, he was farming 100 acres at Beechwood, employing four men and a boy. His wife's indoor staff consisted of a lady's maid, cook, housemaid and kitchen maid. The butler lived at Beechwood Farm.

The farm then known as Rooks and Rogers was held by a widower named R. Mumford who had a grown-up son employed on the farm and one boy. The village of Sparkwell included 21 occupied houses as well as one vacant one. The men of the village were employed in rural occupations – farmworkers, blacksmiths, wheelwrights, carpenters, shoemakers, etc., and the unmarried girls were nearly all in domestic service. There was a school in the village kept by Mr W. Giles (shoemaker) and his wife. John William Farley was listed as being a tin-miner.

Blacklands House was the home of two unmarried ladies of independent means – Miss Maria Braddon, aged 31, born in the East Indies and described as a 'landed proprietor', and her sister Miss Anne Braddon, aged 29. Their domestic staff consisted of a cook and undercook, upper housemaid and under housemaid, butler and coachman. At Baccamore Farm, Constantine Vawden, aged 67, farmed 184 acres and employed two labourers besides those living on the premises. He lived at the farm with Mary his wife, an unmarried daughter, a niece who did the cooking, one labourer, one waggoner, two farm boys, one kitchen maid and a general servant.

At Furzedon the family was away from home and the house was in the care of two female domestics and the gardener. Goodamore was the residence of the Treby family. The owner, Mr Paul Ourry Treby, aged 64, was described both as a 'Captain' in the East Devon Militia and as a 'landed proprietor'. Also living at Goodamore were Mr Henry Hele Treby, a younger brother of the former, and their two unmarried sisters, Miss Barbara Treby and Miss Blanche Treby. The house was staffed by two grooms, one stable boy, one errand boy (page), a cook, a lady's maid, housemaid, dairymaid and nurse.

At Birchland, William Head farmed the property with two sons and one labourer. At Houndall, Benjamin Corber farmed 56 acres with his two sons and one other boy.

At Great Stert Thomas Luscombe farmed 200 acres and employed three labourers. He had also the help of two sons, two daughters working indoors and three farm boys living in. At Graze Allers, 'landed proprietor' William Savery lived on the farm with his wife, one maidservant and one farm boy. Venton Village consisted of 14 occupied houses and three vacant houses. Here again the men and boys worked on neighbouring farms and the girls were in domestic service. Also at Venton the schedule records Mrs Mary Gulley, schoolmistress, with three children of her own described as 'scholars'.

In the same neighbourhood there were two 'smallholdings': 1. Mumford and Deadlake, 17 acres farmed by John Annis and boy; 2. Crees Venton, 36 acres farmed by Elias Rowe and one boy. At Venton Farm John Owen farmed 100 acres employing one man from outside. He lived in the farmhouse with his wife and brother, two labourers and a maidservant.

SCHEDULE 4: LOUGHTOR, NEWNHAM, BOTTLE HILL, HEMERDON DISTRICT

At Loughtor, the 53-year-old miller Andrew Moore had a 25-year-old son working with him in the mill. The family also included four daughters (two at school) and two boys (also at school). At the time of the census he also had a niece from London staying at the mill. He kept one maidservant and a serving-boy.

The ancient family of Strode lived at Newnham Park House. At the taking of the census the head of the household was Capt. George Strode, aged 71, born at North Huish, a retired Army officer and local magistrate. His wife, Mrs Dorothy Strode, was aged 60. Living at home were the two daughters, Miss Dorothy Strode (aged 27) and Miss Florence Strode (aged 25). Mr George Sidney Strode, son and heir to the Newnham estates, was 21 years of age and unmarried. The household staff consisted of seven female servants, the gardener and a footman named Luke O'Shannery who came from Ireland.

Bude Farm was divided into two parts each of 65 acres farmed by Benjamin Rowe and Joseph Rowe respectively. There follows in the schedule a list of cottages belonging to the Bottle Hill area:

At Bottle Hill, there were two cottages, one occupied, one vacant. Crownhill Down Cottage had six acres of land attached. Broomage consisted of three cottages. Smallhanger Farm had seven acres of land giving work for the farmer and son. There may have been some difficulty in differentiating between farmworkers and miners in this sort of country. Labouring men not wanted in the mine often turned to other work. John Farley, aged 47, living at Providence Cottage, belonged to a family connected with the Plympton mines for generations. At the taking of the census his sons James (aged 19) and George (aged 16) were also described as miners.

At Crownhill Down, William Burnell, miner, aged 43 and originally from Widecombe, had two sons (aged 15 and 13 respectively) working as mine labourers. John Tonkin from St Agnes, Cornwall, miner, lived at Hemerdon Ball. His wife was a dressmaker and their 16-year-old son also worked down the mine. George Gulley, mine labourer, lived at Drakeland Cottage. Little Drakeland was a farm of six acres. At Lobb Farm William Cose farmed 50 acres. He had four sons working on the farm. Stert's Farm consisted of 30 acres. William Dennis, aged 52, had three sons working on the farm together with one labourer from outside and two boys living in. At Windwhistle Richard Moore farmed 46 acres with the help of one labourer. At Sherwells John Sanders farmed 120 acres with two labourers and three others living in. At Old Newnham, ancestral home of the Strode family, the 31-year-old tenant farmer, George Coaker, lived with his wife and two small sons, farming 240 acres and employing ten labourers. There were five labourers living on the premises and two maidservants.

Hemerdon Village consisted of 22 households occupied mainly by miners or farmworkers. At Hemerdon Farm itself Richard Hillsdon worked 90 acres employing two men and two boys. On Hemerdon Ball there was a farm of 22 acres and Thomas Nicholls, widower, had a son working on the farm and two daughters at home.

At Hemerdon House, residence of the Woollcombe family, the parents appear to have been away from home at the time when the census was taken. The children registered were Robert Woollcoombe, aged 16, Caroline, aged 13, Sarah Maria, aged 11, and Edward, aged 8. They were apparently under the care of the governess, Ellen Daniel, of Lustleigh, aged 33. The household staff included William Giles, manservant, aged 65, and four maidservants.

A good day rabbiting. Ernest Wingett is on the far right.

Haymaking at Venton

THE CENSUS QUOTED ABOVE WAS TAKEN IN THE 1800S, WHEN SCHOOLS WERE SMALL AND EMPLOYMENT ON FARMS AND ESTATES ACCOUNTED FOR FAR MORE OF THE JOBS AVAILABLE LOCALLY. FROM THIS EARLY DATE WE WILL TAKE YOU ON A NOSTALGIC JOURNEY TO THE PRESENT DAY, HOPEFULLY SHOWING HOW PEOPLE'S LIFESTYLES AND LIVING CONDITIONS HAVE ALTERED.

BY-GONE DAYS

Bill Nelder with brother Norman (on pony).

Why do we miss those years gone by?
What wonders and pleasure, just gazing at the sky,
The wonder of looking at snails and slugs –
We had no telly or video to steal for drugs.
To watch the birds and other wildlife
No redundancies, take-overs or strikes –
It sure seemed an easier way of life.
Everyone now seeks thrills and pleasure;

A good old crop from the garden was a treasure.
To go to Plympton was a hike,
'cos we had no gears on our bikes.
People worked to rear calf or sow
Or others worked with horse and plough.

The children enjoying ice creams here include Sheila Long, Donald Hill, Valerie Netherton and Susan Rundle.

Some worked to extract the clay –
Very hard work for little pay.
Not this modern thing that if we want it just grab it –
Oh those days a man's dream was to catch a rabbit.
Not like today with all this HP,
But when something was wanted all the saving was down to me.

Roger Bennett helping to get the cows in for milking at Venton

Neighbours were friends and helped in any way.
A favour was a favour, no mention of pay.
People took care of clothes, shoes and rubber wellies
Now all they lust for is a digital telly.
When the only net to be scanned was on a fruit bush, so birds were banned,
When washing was done with a copper and stick
And today we have chemicals, so the fibres don't get thick.

Most of us attended school,
For those who did not could be the village fool.
Oh how I yearn for those days of old
When two people living together were held with a band of gold.
Those days are gone and will be no more
I must dash now to get to the Tesco store.

by Tony James

Top and above: *Sparkwell from the air without the village hall (c.1975) and with the new building. Eric Exworthy is to the left of the top photograph with his milk float.*

Chapter 2: Sparkwell Properties & Other Sites of Interest

Great Stert

Andrew Wotton senr moved into Great Stert Farm when he was only three years old in 1923. His father, Andrew Wotton, had farmed there before him and he (Andrew senr) carried on the tradition by in turn handing over to his son (also Andrew!). In 1966 the farm was under threat of being submerged if plans for a reservoir had gone ahead. The whole valley down in Lucas Wood would have been under 100 feet of water and hundreds of acres of agricultural land would have been lost. The magnificent gateway of Great Stert, dated 1674, would also have been lost. Luckily in the end the reservoir was built elsewhere.

Top: *Drew Wotton.*
Above: *William Wotton and John King.*
Left: *Left to right: Margaret, Andrew, Richard and Elsie Wotton.*

Top left: *Baccamore, October 1986.*
Above: *Evelyn King with her parents.*

Above: *Baccamore in the 1930s.*

Right: *Left to right at Baccamore: Jim Eggins, John King, Evelyn King, Jack King, ?.*

Below: *Steam thrasher at Baccamore, 1930s.*

BACCAMORE

Evidence exists that Saxons inhabited Baccamore prior to it being chronicled in the Devonshire section of the 1086 Domesday Book. Such inhabitants were referred to in the 823 Anglo Saxon Chronicle as Defras, a name derived from the Celtic tribe of the Dumnonii, who had settled in South-West England.

The Domesday entry refers to Baccamore as Pachemore/mora – one of 60 manors in Devonshire granted to the Norman lord Ralph (de Pomeroy) by King William following the Norman Conquest. Prior to this Baccamore had been part of land belonging to the Saxon, Ludhael of Totnes.

The post-Domesday description of the area is of Baccamore waste, on heathland. In 1986 to celebrate the 900th anniversary of the Domesday Book, Baccamore was used as a local example of a Domesday settlement in an exhibition staged by the Devon County Archivist in conjunction with the Post Office.

Sparkwell at the time of Domesday was known as Sperchewell/willa and was held by Richard from Baldwin the Sheriff. It subsequently became a tiny village.

Little is known of the earlier dwelling at Baccamore, although many fine dark granite carved stones have been excavated from its garden. Around 1950, W.G. Copeland, a local antiquarian, recorded the details of the house, then a farmhouse, describing the bulk of the ancient parts running alongside a public road. The present house has features surviving from an earlier, 16th-century dwelling, and a part of the property to the south is late-18th century. It was in this direction that the post-Domesday house may once have extended.

The 16th-century section of the house retains evidence of a more important apartment with a good granite mullion window, large granite fireplace and large chamfered wooden ceiling beam. At the east end of the house were the remains of a late-medieval kitchen next to the dairy. The roof space contains some old roof timbers with a crude finish and the main staircase of the house is late-18th century with two curved branching sections cantilevered off from the walls on either side and joined by a bridge of stairs.

The house is now a grade II listed building and is subject to continuing careful renovation. Outside there remains a cobbled farmyard and some ancient remnants of a shippen, with the garden ending in a 24-metre-diameter pond on its southern boundary.

Of the past inhabitants we know little, except for those details which can be gleaned from surviving title deeds/indentures which are available in their original form from 1390, 1598, 1690 and 1696 (and many more during the 18th century). These documents detail the lawful transactions between the incumbents and others involving land and property. For example, the 1696 indenture involves a sale of 22 acres of land together with a tenement called Backmore within the parish of Plympton St Mary by Suzanna Pearse a widow, mother of Richard Pearse, and another partner Charles Fortescue of St Budeaux to John Osborne of Churston. The sale cost was recorded as 'the sum of £250 of lawful money of England.'

Baccamore was bought in the mid-20th century by Mr Charles D. Serpell and managed by his son Reg. At that time the house was also home to Miss King and her many cats and Mr Stan Tall, who assisted on the farm. Stan Tall rented a room in the house.

Baccamore was subsequently bought by a local builder who set about its initial restoration but then sold it to Mr and Mrs Graham Adam in 1976 who continued the voyage of discovery and obtained the grade II listing. In 1985 the house was purchased by Dr and Mrs Geoffrey Perham and family who took on the task of the restoration to allow Baccamore to live on as a family home into the next millennium; hopefully its walls will continue to reveal as much to so many for centuries to come.

Baccamore in the 1930s.

Blacklands House.

BLACKLANDS

There is evidence of a house situated in the village of Sparkwell in 1480, although not until 1750 was land sold for 10 shillings to Samuel Brent to form an estate known as Blacklands (which at this point included farm buildings, cottages and orchards).

Blacklands House was built in 1849 by Isambard Kingdom Brunel and was a considerable time in the making. Its first owner was Judge William Bradden, who was attacked by two villains and died of his injuries within a year of the event. A charge of murder was subsequently brought against the perpetrators. In July 1859 the house was sold to William Conran for £6000 and handed down through his family for nearly 100 years. The Conrans spent a great deal of their time in Jamaica where they had a number of sugar plantations. Mrs Conran was terrified of staying in the house alone and in 1954 the Blacklands estate (which included the Lodge, orchards, walled gardens and an archery shoot) was sold for the same amount of money (£6000) to Dr Ted and Mrs Enid Hamlyn.

Dr Hamlyn became well known in the village and treated patients at his home. He was especially helpful during the hard winters when the villagers would assist him whenever he needed to dig his car out of the notorious snow drifts of the early 1960s in order to reach his surgery in Plymouth.

The house was used by the Hamlyn family until 1994 when it was sold to a business who have since changed the name to Welbeck Manor and now use the property as a hotel. The estate was converted into a golf course, used by many of the villagers, and although it is sad to see the farm and gardens converted, Blacklands is still being enjoyed by a great many people among the local community.

The gardeners at Blacklands were Mr Pring and later Mr Short and the grounds were beautifully laid out with fruit trees growing against the walls. Mr Short would grow white chrysanthemums and on All Saints Day would supply Sparkwell Church chancel with these flowers.

Jane, Claire and Paul Verran at Blacklands, c.1978.
Main: *Jane Conran and friends Mary, Maureen, Evelyn and Peggy at Blacklands, c.1930s.*

GOODAMOOR & THE TREBYS

Paul Treby Ourry Esq; later Paul Treby Esq; only son of Commander Paul Henry Ourry RN and Charity his wife, was born at Plympton St Maurice on 6 November 1758. On 14 June 1785, he married Letitia Anne, daughter of Sir William Trelawney, sixth Baronet and later the Captain RN Governor of Jamaica. At the time of their marriage he assumed the surname and coat of arms of the Treby family, and they moved to Goodamoor.

The Trebys were an influential and distinguished family, and a number lived and died at Goodamoor over a period of many years. The public house in the village of Sparkwell bears their name and coat of arms. The eldest son, Paul Ourry Treby, inherited Goodamoor and was a famous huntsman in his own right. He was forbidden by his father to fight in the Napoleonic Wars and in his preface to his *Hunting Chronicles* he wrote: 'Instead of shooting woodcocks at Cholwich Town I might have shot Frenchmen in Spain. This always I wished for, but the fates and my father forbad, so let it pass.' The *Hunting Chronicles* consisted of 22 volumes compiled over a number of years and collected and published by the author's great-grandnephew Captain H.P. Chichester Clark. Paul owned and ran the famous Black Pack Hounds of Goodamoor; 11 are buried at Goodamoor; the gravestones are still there and are maintained by the owner at the time of writing, Ellis Daw.

In the early 1880s Queen Victoria came down to Plymouth to perform the opening ceremony of the Royal William Yard in Devonport. Meanwhile her husband, Prince Albert, stayed with Paul Treby at Goodamoor, dividing his time between visiting Princetown on horseback, and hunting with the famous Black Pack hounds. Paul Treby used to often tell the story, with great gusto, that his whip, 'Short', told the Prince that he and Mr Treby lived so much together that they ate off the same plate and drank out of the same glass.

Henry Hele Treby, the second surviving son of Paul Treby Esq., was a churchwarden of Plympton St Mary for 24 years and during this time he presented a pair of bells – one to St Mary's and one to the new parish church which had been completed in his own village of Sparkwell not long before. He lived at Goodamoor, dying there unmarried on 9 April 1867.

Goodamoor was later occupied by the Martins family who owned the clay works on Headon Down at Lee Moor, then by the Naval Anstice family (in the days when Mr Lock was the gardener), and finally in 1948 by the Daw family.

The Daw family moved from a farm in Crabtree at Laira, in Plymouth, and occupied Goodamoor House in 1948. The family at that time consisted of Archie Daw and his wife Dorothy, her mother Selina, Ellis and his two sisters Margaret and Maureen, and old Charlie Colmer who was crippled by polio during the First World War.

It was farmed as a smallholding, and it was here that the famous Daw's clotted cream was produced for which Archie Daw was well known throughout the West Country. Archie had built and run Daw's Creameries in the 1930s in Saltash, which in time became Unigate. On the site of the old factory in Saltash on the waterfront under the Tamar Bridge stands Daw's Court, a block of luxury apartments named in his honour for the business and employment that he brought to Saltash. In the 1950s and '60s smallholdings became less economically viable as tractors began to enjoy wider use and acreage became the important factor, so Archie gradually stepped back and let his son, Ellis, take over and run the farm.

On 27 July 1954, Ellis attended his first stock car race at Pennycross, an event which ignited a passion for the sport which would continue for many years to come. Most of his races took place in Plymouth and St Austell, but some took him as far as Arlington near Newcastle, and all over the country between. Ellis qualified for the world final at Ringwood Stadium in Hampshire and came in fourth in the final at Bellevue in Manchester. By the middle of his career he had established a continuous run of wins and was then asked to become Captain of the Devon Stock Car Racing Team, a position which he accepted.

At the same time Ellis operated a stunt team called the Hellfire Stunt Drivers with his sister Maureen. At the age of 18 she provided the glamour and Ellis was the hard man. One stunt involved driving through a wall of fire with Maureen lying on the bonnet, and another often used for the finale involved driving up a large ramp and crashing through a double-decker bus or furniture lorry, which they sometimes set on fire for good measure. Ellis emerged from this career relatively unscathed with only cuts, bruises and a few broken ribs.

To help support Goodamoor and the farm, Ellis started a timber business that bought local woods and felled the timber to go to the timber mills in Dartington and Plymouth. He also purchased articulated lorries to transport wood for pulp to make paper at Sudbrooke Mill in South Wales. Ellis and his family would sell fire logs three days a week in Plymouth, and the old call of 'fire logs – log men!' would be heard in Sparkwell every Saturday afternoon. After the logging had finished the woods would be replanted with young trees for the next crop. Meanwhile however, Ellis had a dream which he had entertained since

19

childhood – a dream of having his own zoo, and not only this but one where the animals would live in fields, roaming over grass and under trees. With the help and support of his family, and under the watchful and critical eye of his unconvinced father, he opened the Dartmoor Wildlife Park on 27 June 1968. On the first day 45 people visited the attraction; almost all were Sparkwell residents who came up to encourage and wish the family well.

During the early years of the Park, Ellis and his family would supplement their income by planting the thorn bushes, under contract, that now form the green hedges lining the A38. The Park exhibited mainly British and European animals when it opened, but this collection was added to with the arrival of the first pair of tigers in 1980. Since then it has expanded to house the largest big cat collection in the West Country, and has bred many tigers and jaguars which have been sent all over the world to make up breeding pairs to try to boost numbers of these increasingly endangered species.

At first Goodamoor House itself was used as a café and shop, then in 1988 the Jaguar Restaurant was built and the house was left to the family once more. As the Park expanded, so too did the family. Ellis had three children by his first wife, and two children by his second wife; all of whom attended Sparkwell All Saints Church of England Primary School. They followed in the footsteps of his sister Maureen who had also attended. The school roll has been swollen since by the attendance of his seven grandchildren through the years, and last year he became a great-grandfather with the addition of Tern Jade Wingett who was christened in All Saints Church in 1998 by Father Freddy Denman.

The Daw family have been a part of Sparkwell's community for the last 50 years, during which time Ellis has helped to raise funds for the Sparkwell Parish Hall by holding rodeos and ram roasts, and his children and grandchildren have participated in the sponsored walks. Ellis has supported Sparkwell's many causes, helped to hold off Amax's expansion plans, and designed and built the Sparkwell village sign which won the Devon County Village Sign Contest in 1986.

The resounding roars of the lion at dawn and the calls of peacocks during the day can be heard throughout Sparkwell and give the village a certain element of uniqueness.

Main: *Ellis Daw with some of the many young people who come to the park for work experience each year.*

Left: *Ellis Daw with Dice, still one of the residents at the Wildlife Park.*

BIRCHLAND FARM

Birchland Farm was owned and farmed in the late 1920s by the Sandovers, including the two daughters (one of whom became Clara Honey of Battisford) and sons Sid (who remained at Birchland), Stan (who delivered milk and lived at No.1 Newton's Row with his wife Ellen), Bert (who with his wife Annie farmed Beechwood Farm until the late 1950s), and Charlie (better known as Char, who owned the Lyneham Inn and whose only son Peter was killed during the Second World War).

Bill Sandover owned the Cornwood Inn and Jim Sandover owned the George Hotel at Plympton, later buying the Elfordleigh Hotel and improving the golf course. Leslie (Les) Sandover became Clerk to the Plympton Rural District Council and served that body for many years. George Sandover was a butcher in Ivybridge.

Since the death of Mr Sid Sandover on 16 January 1978 (whose wife, Isobel, died on 25 June 1962), the farmhouse and buildings have been sold. Some of the land was sold to Ellis Daw of Goodamoor and some to AMAX, who owned the mineral rights of the farm and who would have worked the proposed Wolfram Mine at Hemerdon Ball had it re-opened. Mr May now owns the farmhouse.

HOUNDALL FARM/HOUNDALL HOUSE

For many years a Mr Rowe lived here, followed by Derick and Enid Hext. The farm has now been split up and the barns converted to residential use.

HOLLAND FARM

Holland Farm belonged to Plympton Grammar School and the rent from the farm was used to fund scholarships for Hele School. It was sold in 1958 when the Education Authorities took over Hele School. The buyer was Mr Joe Hendy who in turn sold it to Plymouth City Council for development. During the Second World War a wireless station was erected, run by civilian RAF workers. From here it was possible to track planes half way round the world. With the installation of water mains in the area, coverage was somehow drastically reduced at the radio station, although why this was still remains unexplained!

This was also the site of a searchlight and lorry-mounted anti-aircraft gun. The station lights would have to be switched off during blackout. All the telephone wires were taken to it as part of the war effort and nobody else could have a phone as a result. All told 12 lines were installed at the station and the nearest telephone for public use was at Voss Farm. As technology moved on no

*Clockwise from top:
Holland Farm –
demolished to make
way for Langage
Industrial Estate;
Previous inhabitants
of Houndall Farm,
Enid and Derick Hext,
celebrating their golden
wedding anniversary, 12
October 2000; Houndall Farm in 1993. The barns
have now all been converted into homes and the
farm is no longer worked.*

use was found for the station after the war and it is now the site of Langage Industrial Estate.

CHADDLEWOOD FARM COTTAGES

These properties have now all been demolished and replaced by industrial estates.

BATTISFORD LODGE

This building was demolished for the Plympton bypass. It was originally part of Battisford Farm, owned by the Honey family (Richard Honey still farms there).

COLLAFORD FARM

Dr Slee (the vet) moved to Collaford from Applethorn Slade. Mr George (a headmaster at Ridgeway School) took over and it was he who instructed the Young Farmers in public speaking.

CHOAKFORD FARM

At one time this farm was run as a lairage for animals en-route for France. Many years ago it was a much larger farm but over the years it has been split up. The Sparkwell Parish Hall and Playground Trust, when raising money to build the parish hall, held several successful barn dances in the lairage building.

TUXTON FARM

Over the past years Tuxton Farm has been owned by Mr Wenmouth, Norman Dingle, Mr Arthur West (farmed by his son Norman) and The Plymouth Co-operative Society. It is now owned by W.A. Daniells.

SMITHALEIGH

When Smithaleigh was a farm it was lived in by Charlie Roose, a butcher who had a business in Alexandra Road, Plymouth. Another resident was Mr Turpin, a Sunday School teacher at Venton Chapel (whose neighbour at the time was Mrs Nelder). The farm has now disappeared and in its place is the 'New Country Inn and Caravan Park.' Surplus land was sold off to neighbouring farmers. When Arthur Roose (the son of Charlie Roose) died, his wife applied for planning permission to convert the farmhouse and buildings into a motel, and despite several applications, permission was always refused. The house and buildings were then sold privately and eventually planning permission was obtained to convert it to a motel and caravan park. The land was then sold to adjoining farms in the reorganisation of the farms in that area affected by the A38 trunk road.

CHALLONSLEIGH FARM

The old farmhouse at Challonsleigh caught fire and was destroyed, to be replaced by a new house built by Mr Hall. It is said that the blaze was started by a corn drier.

HIGHER CHALLONSLEIGH FARM

Mr Hall had the house built and he had a son and a daughter. For many years this was the home of Mr ans Mrs Pursley who sold the property to Mr Lapthorne in 1971.

COOMBE FARM

Coombe Farm was owned and farmed for many years by the Pellow family. Mr and Mrs Pellow senr lived in the old farmhouse and farmed Coombe Farm until retirement, building up a well-known Friesian herd. The farmhouse itself, in which Mr Charles Marshall used to live (and from where he bred shire horses), became derelict but is now owned by Mr Len Harvey who runs a milking parlour from the site and uses the milk in his ice cream.

FORD FARM

Ford Farm has changed considerably over the years; around 1970 the A38 split the property up and landlocked ground north of the road. Mr Jack Stephens now owns the farm.

HINCHCOMBE

For many years Hinchcombe was the home of the Cane family. It is now home to the Harris family, whilst the land and outbuildings are farmed by Mr John Cane of Cadleigh, Ivybridge.

VENTON
WOODCOCKS EYE

This was originally two cottages and was used as the farmhouse belonging to a farm known as Yollands. The Cane family of Hitchcombe purchased the farmhouse and buildings, added the land to Hitchcombe and tried to sell the house. The property was advertised for two or three months in the name of Yollands Farmhouse, but there were no replies to the advertisements. On looking at an old OS map, the agents discovered that the farmhouse was originally known as Woodcocks Eye (where cock fighting took place) and then re-advertised the property accordingly. They had soon received over 150 replies from interested purchasers and the property was finally sold to Wing Commander and Mrs Van der Kiste.

VENTON
FOLLY COTTAGES, MARDEN HOUSE, STERT COTTAGE, WAYSIDE & SUNNYSIDE

The Wingett family lived at Marden House (which was built by Mr Phillips of Lee Mill). The family also owned Folly Cottages, and arrived in the village (from Plymouth) after their doctor advised the parents of Amy Gent to get away from the city and take their daughter to live in the country where she could benefit from plenty of fresh air. Reg Wingett (Station Master at Cornwood) married Miss Ford from Grazealders who suffered ill health and was advised by doctors to move out of the valley. Her solution to this problem was to move to a considerably higher altitude where she lodged herself for 12 months in a tent pitched in one of her father's fields facing the moor! Extreme the move might have been but the fresh air cured her! Goodness knows what the doctors of that age would think of the pollution today what with the A38 and the proposed new gas fired station!

There was a wood at Graze Alders and a path leading to Sparkwell, which is still there today. Folly Cottages remained in the Wingett family for some years until they were sold to Phyllis and Len Long, Ken and Sheila Hill and Albert and Jean Netherton. Later the Longs and Nethertons had bungalows built across the road.

Across the way was also Stert Cottage where the contractor Ike Goss lived with his thrashing machine. Further up the road next to Half-a-Coffins (next to the present garage) were three cottages. Gladys James and her mother lived in one. The occupant of another of these cottages was well known for cider making and the local men used to call in to imbibe the odd pint. Many a man, having given a few coppers for the cider, would wobble on home. These were strictly 'men only' evenings; women attending such a gathering would certainly have been frowned upon.

Further along the road is a pretty picturesque thatched cottage known as Wayside where a Miss Rowe lived, to be followed later by Mr Sandy Peacock the dentist.

Lord Seaton originally owned the piece of land on which Sunnyside (now Barnuts) stands.

Top two: *Folly Cottages* and *Mardon House.*

Above: *Ethel Collier's (née Wingett) Gran and Grandad Gent, Auntie Amy Wingett and Reg and Ida as babies at the beach.*

Left: *Ethel's grandmother.*

Far left: *Ida Hopper (née Wingett, far right) on a camping trip.*

HILLSIDE COTTAGES

On past Wayside on the right there are two cottages, formerly a row of five. Recently a fireplace here was exposed. Among former tenants were the Pengellys. Col Cody, who lived 'on the steps' (this being the last cottage in the row), would give the children 3d. to fetch him a bucket of water from the tap. Apparently he lived like a hermit. In another of the cottages lived Mr and Mrs Fred Bennett and their son Roger. They moved from Plymouth when the threat of the Second World War loomed. Mr Bennett anticipated conscription and in order to keep his electrical business in Plymouth going he volunteered as a fireman. At that time Venton had no electricity and he toured the area collecting signatures on an electrical supply form, which led to the supply of electricity in Venton. This did his business no harm whatsoever as after the installation of the supply he gleefully towed around again taking orders for wirelesses (radios) and electric kettles. Most people were more than pleased to take up the offer of a radio because formerly the old wirelesses were powered by an accumulator (a battery type glass case which had to be taken to the local garage or shop to be charged). Very often this lead to acid being spilt and clothes were sometimes ruined.

THEN AND NOW Hillside Cottages in 1940 and in 2000.

Top: *The Wingetts at Venton.*

Second from top: *An unknown gathering at Venton.*

Above: *A Wingett family picnic at Ed Weir, Lucas Wood.*

Right: *Mr Fred Bennett and his son Roger in his fireman's uniform, c.1939/40.*

HIGHER & LOWER VENTON FARMS

Lord Seaton sold Higher Venton in 1920 for £2000 and at one time the Hoskin and May families farmed here. In 1940 there was a fire which damaged many buildings and the farmhouse is now used as a private dwelling. Prior to the electrical supply farmer Tom May had a generator which supplied power via batteries to the farm and cottages. Mr Bennett also installed for Mr May a field telephone. Generators were not the easiest to handle; indeed, Mr Bennett, attempting to start the machine, suffered a bad cut to the lip when the handle slipped from his grasp. He still has the scar to this day. He reckoned it healed quickly due to the very tasty salty soup Mrs May had made that day from a recently slaughtered pig.

Having moved from Higher Venton to Lower Venton Farm, Steven Hoskin and family farmed here for many years. It is now the home of the Andrews family and is still being run as a working farm.

Fire at Venton Farm, 1940s.

VENTON METHODIST CHAPEL

The chapel was constructed in 1872 and closed over a century later in September 1996. It was a place of worship for many of those living in the outlying areas and also provided Sunday School for the children. Phyllis Long and her friend Jean used to get told off by Mrs Hopper for chattering during the service.

Donald Hill, Linda Wellington and Valerie Netherton representing the chapel for the festival of queens in 1957.

Amongst the worshippers were the Triggers, Nethertons and Chudleys to name but a few.

There was great excitement when Sunday School prizes were given out and tea was in a marquee. After the tea party people would change to go back to sing in the chapel where Mr Hopper was the organist. As there was no water supply to the chapel itself the water was supplied by Shipland Cottage not far away.

Charabanc outings to the beach took place annually and when the Elford family experienced the joys of the charabanc for the first time, they sat on the backrest and rested their feet on the seat, thinking that this was the way to travel.

Bonfire night would be great fun with many people gathering at Stert Cottage, the home of Ike Goss. Here there would be a bonfire complete with guy and fireworks, toffee apples and jacket potatoes cooked in the fire. Phyllis Long (née Hill) recalled: '... the children would blacken their faces and go around with a tin asking for a penny for the guy and the monies would be shared out.' She can also vividly remember eating a jacket potato oozing with butter and the black off the potatoes and their faces would run down over their chins and hands, a 'filthy but very happy' experience. One bonfire night a heavily pregnant Josie Dalton (née Trigger) attended the party and her labour pains started. She hurried away and her daughter Sadie was born that night.

Mrs Turpin of Folly Cottages had 21 children, but not all survived. People had large families around the 1900s and women would despair to find themselves pregnant again. There was a sad saying: if a woman lost a baby either stillborn or through miscarriage 'she had churchyard luck'.

Phyllis Hill recalled looking forward to the visit by the circus to a site near the Hunting Lodge with much excitement. The elephants and the other exotic animals were unloaded at Ivybridge Railway Station and it was with bated breath that she would enjoy the circus performance.

THE CHAPEL COMMUNITY

Far left: *The chapel.*

Far left below: *Blessing in the church-yard grounds of the chapel for Jenny and Ian Marshall, September 2000.*

Left: *John Parsons, founder of the chapel and Sunday School teacher.*

Below: *Jaqueline Vincent, Valerie Netherton, Bridget Vincent and Donald Hill representing the chapel for the carnival in 1969.*

VENTON METHODIST CHURCH
WELCOMES YOU TO ITS

CENTENARY CELEBRATIONS

ON

5th & 6th May 1973

SATURDAY 5th MAY
4.00 p.m. THANKSGIVING SERVICE Conducted by
        Rev. J. RUSSELL POPE (Chairman of the District)
5.15 p.m. TEA
6.45 p.m. CONCERT Given by:-
        SPARKWELL WOMEN'S INSTITUTE CHOIR
        WOODFORD JUNIOR SINGERS &
        VENTON SUNDAY SCHOOL
        Together with GREETINGS FROM FAR & NEAR
        CHAIRMAN:- Mr. REG. TALL of Wotter

SUNDAY 6th MAY
        SPECIAL SERVICES IN THE AFTERNOON AND EVENING
3.00 p.m. ALD. F. J. STOTT, O.B.E., J.P.
6.00 p.m. REV. R. T. G. MITCHELL

PROCEEDS £72.04

Above: *Sunday School, 1960s. The children are dressed for the festival of queens. They include the Simms children, Paul Dalton, Donald Hill, Val Netherton, Bridget and Jaqueline Vincent, and Mrs Trigger is also present.*

Right: *Notice for the Centenary Celebrations in 1973.*

Above right: *Preparations for the last Harvest Supper at the chapel in 1996. Phyllis Long is the auctioneer helped by Mary Chudleigh.*

Bottom right: *Lawrence and Margaret Baskerville and Frances and Ray Pearse, c.1980s.*

CHAPEL OUTINGS OF THE 1930s—'40s

Ted Hext at Plympton ready for the off for the first of the chapel's trips to Penzance.

Above centre left: *Len Gulley, Tilly Gulley, Emily Wingett, Hilda Gulley, Brian Gulley, c.late 1940s.*

MOUNT PLEASANT COMMUNITY

Clockwise from top: *Left to right:*
Nancy Bristow (née Hill),
Pamela Old (née Lardeaux) and Phylis
Luckett (née Reed);
Nancy and Mike Hill with Spot the dog;
Charlie Hopper and Mr Perryman;
left to right: Ida and Amy
Wingett, ?, Charles Wingett;
Clara and Laurence Hooper,
August 1953;
Michael and Mavis Hill
with Tiddles.

Top: *Research has failed to turn up the answer to this picture – perhaps readers can help?;*
inset: *Charles and Ida Hopper with Reg and Sylvia Wingett and an Austin 7.*

Above: *The Sanders family, c.1900. The mother is Carrie and the children include Florrie, Ernie and Richie.*

MOUNT PLEASANT

A few hundred yards up the road from Venton Chapel lies a cluster of cottages known as Mount Pleasant. For many years the Gulley and Hill families lived there and at one time the Hearns and Turpins were also residents. The Gulley family ran a taxi and haulage business.

Water was obtained via a pump some yards away on the other side of the road. On two separate occasions planes were forced to crash land in the field opposite the cottages due to lack of fuel and at one time there was talk of an air strip being put there because of the suitability of the length of the field.

Nancy Bristow (née Hill, aunt of the darts player Eric Bristow) would buy milk off Mr Hooper, who had fields and farmed at Mount Pleasant, and they would drink it straight from the cow – delicious!

GRAZEALDERS, LUCAS WOOD

The Ford family farmed at Grazealders for many years before the property was taken over by the Simms family. It is no longer used as a farm and all the fields have been sold off to horse owners for grazing. There were a number of allotments here.

A substantial number of wooden bungalows were built in the area of Lucas Wood during the Second World War, many of them to house people who came out from Plymouth and several were burnt down by accident.

PARISH HALL FUNDS

Although land was given generously by the parish by the late Lord Seaton on 24 December 1946 for a hall and playground, it was not until 1979 that a steering committee was formed to actually consider building a hall. The formation of the Sparkwell Parish Community Council with an Activities Committee and a Fair Committee, together with grants obtained, provided the funding for the Sparkwell Parish Hall. This facility was opened on 3 November 1984 and a time capsule is buried deep at the entrance.

A ceremony for digging the first sod was held on 20 September 1983 and a topping-out ceremony took place with the pegasus weathervane donated by Jack Harvey, Chairman of the Hall Management Committee, being placed on the roof. And the hall was not without publicity when completed – differences with the builder resulted in Mr Conybeare sitting on the hall roof as a protest!

An enormous thermometer displayed the fund-raising success outside the Sparkwell Stores. A monthly newsletter was delivered to every house in the paris – with a great deal of information about past and forthcoming events. The Royal British Legion organised an annual sponsored walk and sponsored pony rides were also popular, a caravan stall was parked each weekend at the back entrance to Fursdon, a good site opposite the Wildlife Park, and ram roasts and rodeos were held at the Park. A regular barn dance was organised in the lairage at Choakeford Farm. From 1981 the Sparkwell Fair was the main fund-raising event, held at Beechwood, which included a gymkhana, excemption dog show, baby show, majorettes, tug-o-war, a carnival procession and many stalls and amusements. There was also the Fursdon Cup for the

VILLAGE'S UNIQUE SPIRIT LEADS TO TOP HONOURS

Major David Ruttledge, one of the money raisers for the Sparkwell Parish Hall Fund.

SPARKWELL'S community spirit has amazed community council officials and landed the parish first prize and a place in a national competition.

And successful efforts to raise the staggering sum of £20,000 have now qualified Sparkwell for a county council grant towards the building of a parish hall.

The deadline for qualifying for the county council grant was last Friday and only hours before time ran out community council chairman Major David Ruttledge proudly announced that the target had been met.

Having already received a promise from South Hams District Council that they too would match the £20,000 it means that work on the parish hall, which is estimated at £60,000, can start as soon as the grants are made in hard cash.

The euphoria at raising the money was still obvious and there was a reason for double celebration when the results of the community council's competition was announced.

To mark the venture's success the community council have made a video film of the project which monitors the progress of the scheme since it was first considered four years ago.

Interviewer Mr James Derounian and cameraman Mr Alan Tibbits of the community council of Devon visited Sparkwell and the site on which the parish hall will be built.

The ground is at present occupied by the village playing field and used by the local school. Originally the site was bequeathed to the parish by Lord Seaton, who requested that it be used for a playground and parish hall.

The hall is a little late in coming but that should not detract from the outstanding efforts made to raise the £20,000 since 1978.

Every conceivable type of money raising event has been arranged in that time and a last minute attempt to boost the total by £2,000 to the £20,000 mark was successful. Four

Cameraman Alan Tibbits (left) and James Derounian of the Devon Community Council interviewing the Rev Frank Heasman, Vicar of Sparkwell, Major David Ruttledge, Mrs Enid Hext, Mrs Betty Ruttledge and Mrs Lesley Masey

events were held in the final two weeks and really tested the locals' generosity.

Planned for the hall is a building which young and old throughout the Sparkwell parish will be able to use. Outside will be a concrete kick-about area and tennis court and the present children's playground equipment will remain.

The community's 14 organisations have been involved in the fund raising and Major Ruttledge had words of praise for everyone who has helped.

"It has been truly amazing, the efforts which everyone has made have proved what a marvellous feeling of community spirit exists in the area," he said.

Mr Derounian said the film would be used to show other villages what was possible to achieve through hard work and imagination. Sparkwell's success also qualified the parish for a national competition involving other counties and which would be judged in the near future.

Present at the filming were Major Ruttledge; Mrs Enid Hext, president of Sparkwell WI and a committee member of the Sparkwell branch of the Mothers' Union; Mrs Betty Ruttledge, leader of Sparkwell Over 60s Club; Mrs Lesley Masey, leader of the 1st Sparkwell Guides and leader of the Young Wives' Club; Rev Frank Heasman, the Vicar of Sparkwell; Mr Reg Anderson, a Sparkwell parish councillor; and Mr Tom Weatherby, joint owner of Sparkwell Stores where a target 'thermometer' has been kept since the fund raising began.

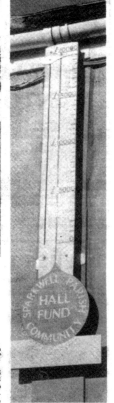

The £2,000 target on display outside the general stores, Sparkwell

Left: Fund-raising efforts for Sparkwell Village Hall were pursued with passion in the village, as testified by this local newspaper report.

best-kept garden in the parish. Philip Munro organised the first vintage rally in 1988, which greatly added to the popularity of the event. The Fair was held in Newnham Park for a few years, but is now held in the village again.

The inter-parish quiz, organised by the Ivybridge Community Association, was won on more than one occasion by the Sparkwell Team and the Best Run Village Hall competition, organised by the Community Council of Devon, was won on three occasions, the plaques being displayed over the main entrance.

NOTES ON LEY FARM
by Mr Treneman

The following information is gleaned chiefly from various articles in the volumes of the Devonshire Association Transactions:

'Leye', 'Ley' or 'Leigh' is an Anglo-Saxon word meaning 'the clearing in the wood'. In the Domesday Book, Leye is recorded as a manor of 227½ acres. This acreage refers to cultivated land only and does not include rough pasture and woodland. (Dvn Assn, Vol. XIX: 'Beginning of Plympton History' by R.N. North). Who held Leye and who subsequently held it can be discovered in the Association's Transactions dealing with the history of Plympton Hundred. In the 13th century it belonged to a Lady Florence de Leigh who, I believe, bequeathed Leye to Plympton Priory.

At the time of the dissolution of the Augustinian Priory at Plympton, 1538/9, Nicholas Slanning was one of its annuitants. As early as 1520 he lived at Leye and possessed certain rights of maintenance from the Priory – it is thought that it supplied and fed a horse for him. It has not been discovered what rights he enjoyed over Leye. However, in Volume XIX of the Devon Association Transactions mention is made by Winslow Jones of the Slannings of Leye. I gathered that either the above Nicholas obtained Leye from the Priory at its dissolution, or his son John obtained it in 1545/6 when he purchased various lands in Shaugh, Bickleigh and Newton Ferrers.

In an inquisition post mortem taken after the death of a Slanning in a duel with a Fitz of Tavistock in 1599, Leye is described as a messuage and 20 acres of land. If this acreage refers to the total extent of the holding, acquisitions must have been made since. However, the document refers to other lands in Plympton and the 20 acres may have referred to arable land only, so that more than 20 acres of actual land may have surrounded the Slanning house. It may be possible that either before, or at the dissolution, the Domesday manor of Leye was broken up and that its acreage has changed little since.

Slannings resided at Leye until 1653 at least. At about that time the family became fewer in number and probably there was need for one household only so that although they owned Leye, they resided only at their larger house at Bickleigh. The last of the Slannings died in 1700 (as a result of a wound received in a brawl) intestate. His aunt, Dame Elizabeth Modyford, was granted administration of his effects. At her death in 1724, the Slanning estates (including Leye presumably) devolved to her two daughters. Only the younger of the two married and the estates passed to her son James Heywood. When he died in 1798, all the estates were sold (and with them Leye presumably) to Manassah

Lopes from whom are descended from the lords Roborough.

Prince, in his 1810 volume, Worthies of Devon, claims that Leye became the residence of the younger branch of the Slannings. It devolved from the Slannings to the Parkers and was 'lately sold by John Lord Boringdon to Mr Snell'. Obviously, Prince and Jones disagreed unless Parker and Lopes are the same man, or unless, due to a quick sale or a bequest, Leye passed from one Lopes to Parker or vice versa.

From a glance at a document owned by the father, we gather that George Snell leased Leye to George Sander for a period of 14 years. In the 1858 Directory of Devon, George Sanders and Richard Wotton are listed as farming Leye together. Presumably before, or soon after the expiration of the lease, Richard Wotton purchased Leye from Mr Snell. He died in 1914 bequeathing Leye to the father.

FOR SALE BY AUCTION   TO CLOSE AN ESTATE

PLYMPTON   S. DEVON

IN THE PARISH OF PLYMPTON ST. MARY, ¼-MILE FROM THE EASTERN OUTSKIRTS OF THE CITY OF PLYMOUTH AND 6 MILES FROM THE CITY CENTRE.

THE VALUABLE FREEHOLD
AGRICULTURAL PROPERTY
known as
"Ley Farm"
comprising
Attractive Character RESIDENCE
with about
81 ACRES of extremely PRODUCTIVE, FERTILE and LEVEL LAND
with VACANT POSSESSION

LUSCOMBE, MAYE & CO.

have received instructions from the Executors of the late MR. H. E. TRENEMAN to offer the above for SALE BY AUCTION (subject to Conditions as will be read), at

THE MARKET HALL, Market Road, PLYMPTON (Nr. St. Mary's Church)

On MONDAY, 3rd DECEMBER, 1973, at 3 p.m.

Auctioneers :
LUSCOMBE, MAYE & CO.
114 RIDGEWAY, PLYMPTON
PLYMOUTH.
'Phone 36547
also at SOUTH BRENT AND KINGSBRIDGE

Solicitors :
WOOLLCOMBE & YONGE,
22 QUEEN ANNE TERRACE,
NORTH HILL, PLYMOUTH
'Phone 65335

Sale Notice for Ley Farm, the auction for which was held on Monday 3 December 1973 at 3p.m. at 114 Ridgeway, Plymouth by the auctioneers Luscombe, Maye & Co.

Dick Honey's sale at Higher Langage Farm in 1959.

The Dartmoor sheep are inspected.

VOSS FARM

John Cockram and family live at Voss Farm, which is thought to have had links with the Priory.

LYNEHAM INN

Charlie Sandover ran this public house for many years and it has long been a very busy pub, having a popular outside play area for children.

APPLETHORN SLADE

This property belonged originally to the Priory and was used by Sabbatical monks. A family called Rossiters lived there in the late-13th century and Mrs Rossiter had no less than 20 children, although only six or seven survived.

At one time (1946), the farm belonged to Mr Clarence Mumford whose family business was the car and tractor sales firm. He purchased Applethorn Slade for the princely sum of £4000, to promote and sell from there the Ferguson T20 tractor. It is now home to Alan and Jean Jones.

HIGHER & LOWER LANGAGE FARMS

Higher Langage, mentioned in the Domesday Book, was sold to Len Harvey in 1959 and is currently a thriving ice-cream company which keeps a Jersey herd for the creamy milk used in their delicious ice cream.

The Kingwell family lived at Lower Langage for many years renting the property until 1888 when it was purchased for £4500 – a substantial sum back then. John Kingwell had bought a Ferguson T20 tractor and remembers driving it into St Andrews Cross, Plymouth (the Mumford garage), to have it serviced. On reaching the garage he expressed his surprise at the then high-tec procedure of putting the tractor into a lift to be taken to an upper floor for the servicing.

John's father would take his morning milk to Stephens Dairies, Plympton, and had to be there by 8a.m. The evening milk would be separated and in the afternoon separated milk would be given to calves and the rest made into cream and butter. His father had a few private customers but Stephens Dairies took the bulk of the milk. The Land Army girls and sailors from Beechwood Camp would help with thrashing the wheat in the winter. Several straw ricks went up in smoke and some thought that a group of Irish people were responsible, as cigarettes and matches with paper wrapped around them were found in several ricks. The fires had to be put out very quickly because of wartime blackout. Dredge corn would be fed to the cattle.

The two dwellings known as Moor View Cottages belonged respectively to Higher and Lower Langage Farms as tied cottages. Eric Exworthy's parents and family lived there at one time.

Applethorn Slade.
Main: *Lower Langage.*

Some of the Perry family at Sherwell Farm with their families, early 1900s. Included are Sam, William Tickle (3rd from left, back), his wife Hannah Elizabeth (known as Annie, née Perry) (3rd from left, centre row) and their son Reginald (3rd from left, front). Hannah Elizabeth died in childbirth aged 35 and is buried in Sparkwell churchyard with her daughter who lived only eight days. Also in the photograph are Edith, Lillian, Dick (who was the survivor of the twins) and Ernest (who took over the farm when Samuel Richard died). Edwin is not in the picture and it is thought that there are two others missing.

Sherwell Farm estate manager Mr Perry.

Parkside was originally called Moor Farm and was sold by Lord Seaton to the Sanders family. At one time it belonged to Beechwood and later it was the home of Mr and Mrs Collings, the latter an ex-professional ballerina who, with her husband, had many famous people to stay including Margot Fontayne, Moira Shearer, Beryl Gray and Anton Dolan. Mr Blatchford (a chef) would cook for Mrs Collings' famous dinner guests. Mr Smythe, a vet, was also resident at the property. The ground, however, was sold off.

Bickfordtown Farm, tenanted by Jack Stancombe and before that farmed by Harry and Muriel Roberts. When Jack Stancombe took over, Maurice Stancombe married (in April 1957). Jack remained there until 1960. When he moved to Sparkwell Farm he took over the tenancy from Bill Roberts (Harry's son).

Charity dress parade for Save the Children at Beechwood, June 1966.

The 4th Lord Seaton in the late 1940s with his wife Mabel Vivian at Beechwood.

BEECHWOOD

These memories come from the Earl of Morley of Sparkwell 1941–46:

Because our home was requisitioned during the war our whole family plus an uncle and three cousins, who were based with us, transferred ourselves en-bloc to Beechwood and we have many happy memories of Sparkwell.

When we first arrived I (with one cousin) was still at school, but six months later we joined the Army; my memories are therefore based on two school holidays plus periodic leaves. Of the other cousins one was in the Navy and one in the Army in India and my two brothers were still at school although one joined the Army later.

There were many personalities in the village. The vicar was the Revd Walter Knight-Adkin, formerly Chaplain of the Fleet and Dean of Gibraltar. Col Conran lived at Blacklands, Col Anstice at Goodamoor and old Mrs Coryton at Fursdon. The postmistress was Mrs Yabsley with the Post Office in the front room of her cottage, next to the Treby Arms with the village hall immediately behind it. The Home Guard platoon was commanded by Mr Tallamy, a former regular soldier who looked after the roads. My cousin and I served in the Home Guard during our school holidays and used to spend nights in the cricket pavilion on Headon Down. The china clay pit spoil dumps were all camouflaged and I can remember them starting to dig Wolfram Mine near Hemerdon Ball.

The village was dominated by the Naval camp in the wood immediately south of the village and their loudspeaker system was going all day and night and echoed through the wood and the village. Lying in bed at night one heard the trains; nearly always the two engines struggling up Hemerdon Bank and stopping to leave the second engine at the Hemerdon siding.

One night in April 1941 I was woken by a policeman throwing stones at my window. The telephones were all out and he wanted to contact my father who was running the Great Western Railway.

They wanted him to go to the Hemerdon signal box, whose telephone was still working to make a decision about train operations, because one of the major blitzes on Plymouth was in progress. Because there was a chance that he might have to go into Plymouth on an engine he took me with him, wearing my father's 1914 steel helmet as we walked across the fields. In the event we did not go to Plymouth, but I spent several of the small hours of the morning in the signal box watching how the signals worked and with trains backed up all along the line waiting to go into Plymouth. Another memory is driving into Plymouth to help rescue a cousin of mine whose home had been bombed and bringing some of her possessions back to Beechwood to be stored. My mother kept chickens at Beechwood and once begged some corn for them, presumably from Mr Sandover, and when told that this was against the law she said 'that is not dishonest it is merely illegal.'

I should also mention Mr and Mrs Knott who came with us to Beechwood. Before the war he was our chauffeur/handyman and she was our cook. On the 3rd Sept. 1939 he joined the balloon barrage and by 1941 was a corporal in charge of one of the balloons based on fishing boats anchored in the Sound. On his periodic days ashore he hitched back to Beechwood.

Sparkwell then was much smaller than it is now and with only the wireless for news (no TV) life was much simpler. Shopping had to be done in Plympton (but with petrol rationed, only once per week) and many people like us kept chickens and grew their own vegetables. In one case we had an old man called Mr Mathews to help us with the vegetables.

Mrs Enid Hamlyn would go to Beechwood to play Lord Seaton's piano before she purchased her own.

(Phyllis Hill, born in Crownhill Cottage, recalled how Beechwood girls had to curtsy and boys raise their caps when Lord Seaton went by. If they did not, they would be reprimanded in school the next day. Going out of Sparkwell towards Hemerdon, she related, the remains of a bridge can be seen which was built for the hunt to go over to reach the moors. The Seatons sometimes used it as a route to church.)

Top: *Beechwood House from the air.*

Right: *A suit of armour at the house.*

A 1926 Humber at Beechwood.

BEECHWOOD HOUSE

by J.Q.C. Mackrell

Were the Augustinian friars Beechwood's first historic settlers? Although many will doubt it, the visual evidence is intriguing. The photograph on page 41 shows a rounded arch in the early Norman style, at a height that suggests an earlier ground level of at least six feet lower. The arch, topped by a narrow lintel, just visible in the photograph, is flanked by two recessed crosses and surmounted by a third.

The building could, of course, have been a barn. Yet, the configuration of three crosses around the doorway posits a degree of piety, rare even in a medieval peasant. Where crosses appear in secular buildings, it is usually to admit daylight but these crosses seem poorly sited if intended to illuminate the interior. The fine lintel, the dignified archway beneath, the elegant crosses themselves, as also the east-west orientation of the building, are all consistent with it having once been a chapel.

To left and right of this small stretch of wall are two deep vertical cracks which separate it from the wall on either side. Why did the architect of the stables, which probably date from the 1850s, incorporate the earlier façade? Parsimony here would hardly be in keeping with the rest of the stable block, where a large coach, a team of six horses and a groom were housed in splendour that the poor of the time might have envied.

The remnants of the earlier building served no decorative purpose, indeed hardly match the massive battlements above, which bear emphatic witness to Victorian romanticism. The most probable explanation for the preservation of the earlier building is surely that the stable's architect respected its antiquity. If it was in fact a chapel, is there any possibility that it was linked to Plympton Priory? This daring surmise is inspired by a remark in James Hine's *Plympton in the Olden Time* (1867, p.10). He writes there:

... in Plympton St Mary there are several chapels subject to the Priory – one at Newnham, another at Hemerdon and a chapter house attached to a Lazar house of which there are now no remains.

Sparkwell with so many other claims to fame, surely deserves at least one medieval ruin. Yet, whether a professional archaeologist, whom we hope to lure here in the summer, will underwrite this tentative claim, even after being plied with a good deal of wine, remains to be seen.

Beechwood itself is thought to date from 1797 and to have been completed in its original form by 1802. The first owner, Richard Rosdew (1757–1837), a banker and the City Coroner, gradually amassed a patchwork of fields around the old farm of Moor, the present Parkside. It was Rosdew's achievement to landscape the grounds and ponds in practically their present form around a simple Georgian country house. Rosdew was succeeded at Beechwood from 1837–54 by Captain Richard Zacariah Mudge, his wife's nephew.

Lord Seaton (1778–1863), a connection of Mudge through his wife, Elizabeth Yonge, purchased Beechwood in 1856 for a sum probably below £20000. He appears to have planted many of the beeches and Austrian pines. His architectural influence was less fortunate, as he Victorianised Rosdew's Georgian building by adding a rather stolid porch and neo-classical bays to both drawing-room and dining-room, all three of which have required, or still require, expensive remedial work. Seaton also built a servants' wing, which was fortunately demolished, after becoming unstable, in 1985. As a result, the house's appearance has come closer to its original Georgian form, with the gain of an attractive courtyard where the wing used to stand.

Lord Seaton was far from fitting popular conceptions of a stuffy Victorian worthy. After playing a daring part in the school rebellion at Winchester, which was suppressed by troops in 1793, John Colborne, after this early apprenticeship, was commissioned as ensign at the age of 16. Thereafter he rose steadily up the ranks to Field Marshal on merit alone, at a time when many commissions were bought. It was while he was Military Secretary to Sir John Moore in the Peninsular War from the age of 29, that Colborne obtained his grounding in warfare. He reinforced it by the study of Frederick the Great, Guibert and Jomini, whose works, then neglected, provided the best introductions to Napoleonic strategy. Colborne, who spoke Spanish, Portuguese, French, Italian, German, Latin and even Swedish (learnt when he accompanied Moore on his ill-fated embassy to Gustavus III), with tastes for literature and painting, was an atypical soldier of the time. That may well have helped him to transcend the blinkered mind-set of so many around him – most dramatically at Waterloo. Colborne's intervention came at the fateful moment when neither side held the advantage and the outcome of the battle lay in the balance.

Napoleon, true to form, threw his strategic reserve, the Imperial Guard, into the scales, to tip the balance in his favour. Colborne, as if he had read Napoleon's mind, seized the initiative from him and launched his regiment against the flank of the advancing Guard. The resulting panic among the Imperial Guard gave the British guardsmen their opportunity to press home the attack, and so turn a setback into a rout. While there are many other reasons for Napoleon's defeat, ranging from the advent of Blücher with his Prussian force, to Wellington's intuitive generalship, Colborne's initiative was uniquely fitting in turning Napoleon's tactics against the master himself.

The 1st Lord Seaton

The man who lived all his life as a soldier and died a Field Marshal, in later life was at heart a peaceable and enlightened statesman. Not for Colborne after Waterloo, like so many brother officers, embittered retirement on half pay on the final abdication of Napoleon, whose ambitions had done so much to further their careers. Instead, Colborne took a lengthy leave of absence from the Army to tour Europe with his family. It was fully in keeping with his wide interests that he spent at least as much time in art galleries and looking at historic buildings, as in visiting the battlefields of Frederick the Great.

In 1821 Colborne's civil career began with his appointment as Lieutenant-Governor of Guernsey, where he showed his life-long interest in education by reforming Elizabeth College. From 1828 Colborne served in Canada, first as Lieutenant-Governor of Upper Canada, later as Commander of the Armed Forces when he suppressed the Canadian Rebellion of 1837, to become, briefly, Governor General. He clearly relished the opportunities to develop the country's resources, promote education and protect the Indians from exploitation. By the time Colborne became High Commissioner of the Jonian Islands from 1843–49, he had become exceptionally advanced politically for his day. His experience in Canada had shown him the value of making concessions well before they were demanded. As a result, he proved astute in maintaining amicable relations

with the liberal nobles, who through attending Italian universities had become imbued with the ideals of the Risorgimento. Colborne's extension of the franchise was so radical for its day, that a critic in *The Times* asked sourly why his lordship had failed to launch a bill in the House of Lords to bring a similar 'benefit' to his own countrymen. Back in England in 1849, Colborne reverted to his career as a soldier, first as Commander of the camp at Chobham, which provided at least some of the preparation, which was needed so badly for Britain's role in the Crimean War. Afterwards Colborne served as Commander-in-Chief of the troops in Ireland at the Curragh. Following a brief retirement at Beechwood, he died at Torquay in 1863.

Beechwood continued largely unchanged under the Field Marshal's eldest son, James, the second Baron (1815–88). James' son, John Reginald, the third Baron (1854–1933), created 'Reggie's Garden', a small romantic park with bamboos and exotic shrubs, while his wife, Elizabeth Beatrice, created her own flower garden and was also instrumental in building a small Catholic chapel adjacent to the house.

During the First World War Beechwood had visitors, who set new records of eccentricity for the neighbourhood. They were a team of refugee Belgian acrobats. They appear to have cooked their meals over a fireplace in a corner of the garden, which may earn them a claim to be pioneers of the barbecue. They remained serious professionals, however, who kept in practice by exercising their arm muscles on a pull-up bar, still extant at the entrance to the chapel. The acrobats' devotion to their art was such that they are said to have swung from the chandeliers to the consternation of their hosts.

Ulick (James Ulysses), Reggie's youngest brother, was the fourth and last Baron Seaton (1933–54). As a soldier in Egypt (1884–86) he fought at Omdurman, one of the last battles, at which the British Army donned their traditional red uniforms.

During the Second World War the wood at Beechwood served as a much-needed rest camp for sailors to recuperate from heavy bombardment in Plymouth. For Sparkwell's children the camp offered the spice of adventure, sweets and cigarettes. The sailors numbered among them several professional footballers; including Frank Squires from Swansea, Frank Tweedsdale from Grimsby –

sporting heroes of legendary fame, at least in the parish of Sparkwell. The redoubtable Woodpeckers left the reputation of the football teams from neighbouring villages in ribbons. Players from the Woodpeckers would on occasion kick the odd ball around with Sparkwell's lads, so laying the foundations of their renowned sporting skills. The sailors, some of whom were housed appropriately in Smugglers' Wood, brought that ancient art up to date with the help of their young disciples. The sailors would throw over the steel fences tins of cigarette tobacco called 'ticklers', bought at NAAFI prices and destined to be resold for a profit to civilians. Once the sailors had checked out innocently at the guard room, they would retrieve their tobacco and reward the children with coppers and sweets. Many in the village still recall the lively Christmas parties in the wood. Yet, when a desperate need was felt for

chocolates, cookies or cigarettes, it was to the American troops at Hemerdon with their greater resources that the children turned.

Suddenly, early in June 1944, there were no vehicles and no troops – an uncanny silence. It was 'D' Day, herald of victory and the much-lamented end of free goodies for children. The demolition firm of L.J. Stephenson came to remove the Nissen huts. All that remained were their concrete bases, still visible beneath the brambles, and the low, dark morgue with its sinister slab for the laying out of corpses. There the children would play at ghosts, sorrowful at the loss of sweets. Almost before victory was celebrated, the lead salvaged from the camp was stolen. It was a sign that life was back to normal. The golden era of the post-war years had begun.

Main: *Charlie Taylor and Gerald Tucker in the garden.* Above: *Gerald Tucker, William, Kathryn and John Mackrell, 1987.* Above right: *Mrs Nancy Little with her pets at Beechwood.*

In 1954 John Edmund Colborne-Mackrell (1906–78), the son of Edith Cordelia Mackrell, granddaughter of the Field Marshal, inherited Beechwood. He had been the last Governor of the Sudan's Bahr-El-Ghazal Province, where he had introduced the growing of cotton, which could have been the mainstay of the country's prosperity on achieving independence in 1954 had the country not been overtaken by prolonged civil war. A keen gardener in the Sudan, he made Beechwood's market garden a going concern before his death in 1978. His wife Katherine (1909–87) fenced for England (and also against Sir Oswald Mosley, whom unfortunately she failed to dispatch to a hell worthier of him, than the one he and his Black Shirts had in mind for others). She graduated in fine art from the Slade and produced some delightful clay figurines. The example below, based on close personal observation, shows a jockey the worse for drink – often the case – outside the Dublin races.

Since 1987 their daughter, Mrs Susan Rosemary Colborne-Foster, and to a lesser extent their son, Dr John Quentin Colborne-Mackrell, have cared for the estate. A happy improvement, brought about through the negotiating skills of Mr Paul Wiseman and the generous help, both in money and advice, of South Hams District Council, the Countryside Commission, and the Devon Bird Watching and Preservation Society, has initiated the return of the two ponds to their original state. Bird-watchers should soon be able to observe the waterfowl, notably the herons, in what is reputedly the third largest heronry in Devon.

Finally, the house has one inmate who always remains while others come and go. The 'Man in Armour' stands on guard in the outer hall. His suit is hardly fashionable, even for the 17th century, as it is a motley collection of items, though all are genuine. The 'Man in Armour' (*see page 37*) still strikes terror into the hearts of the imaginative. On one occasion when his visor suddenly snapped to, an electrician working in the area was reduced to a nervous wreck. A young visitor froze in terror during a nightmare, as he observed the 'Man in Armour' scale the outside of the house to reach his bedroom. Normally, however, the 'Man in Armour' just casts a bemused eye on those strange people around him, who bustle about never ready for combat.

Top: *Mr Jack Colborne-Mackrell with his wife and daughter Susan, 1955/6.*

Above: *The Norman arch in the grounds.*

Right: *A figurine made by Katherine Mackrell.*

PRINCIPAL SOURCES

David Lambert, Beechwood House, 1993, typescript.
G.C. Moore Smith, *The Life of John Colborne*, 1903.
The Colborne Papers;
Recollections of Mr Gerald Tucker.

Left: *Roy (Oxo) Exworthy at the farm in 1982. (Monica Exworthy tells us that Oxo was given his nickname by his brother Eric. During the 1940s/'50s, in the heyday of the Oxo adverts, Roy always wore a red jumper similar to that worn by the 'Oxo kids').*

Below: *Farrier Mr Westaway shoeing Clyde at Beechwood in 1976. Standing by is Oxo.*

Below left: *Keith Clague, Maurice Stancombe, Edgar Clague and Jack Stancombe at the farm in the 1960s.*

Bottom: *Steve and Phyllis Hoskin with their children John, Philip, Mary and Margaret.*

❧ BEECHWOOD FARM ❧

Mr and Mrs Bert Sandover moved into the farm in 1921 and farmed there until 1957 when they had Santon built. Mr Sandover was always affectionately known as 'Uncle Bert' to all. In 1957 Jack Stancombe took on the tenancy having farmed Bickfordtown Farm for 14 years before. He remained there until his death in 1964, when Beechwood Farm was taken over by his daughter Monica and Ray (Oxo) Exworthy, who are still there. Although no longer being farmed – it has been a mainly dairy and beef farm for much of its history – they run a DIY livery yard for horses.

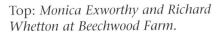

Top: *Monica Exworthy and Richard Whetton at Beechwood Farm.*

Above: *Beechwood Orchard and the horses Clyde, Henry and Ted. This site is now the Seaton Orchard housing estate.*

Right: *Richard Whetton, Steve Scully and Roy (Oxo) Exworthy, 1985.*

Above: *A similar scene with Blackie and her twins in 1992.*

Left: *Richard in 1986.*

Above: *Maurice Stancombe baling.*

Right: *Heather Stancombe in 1963.*

Below: *Harry Roberts and Heather Stancombe, 1960.*

Below: *Len Cobb, Harry Roberts, Norman Blackler, Jack Netherton and Bert Finch.*

❧ SPARKWELL FARM ❧

ORIGINALLY KNOWN AS ROOPES AND ROGERS FARM, SPARKWELL FARM WAS BUILT IN 1790 AND BOUGHT BY THE WOOLLCOMBE FAMILY IN 1793. THIS FARM WAS HOME TO THE COACHMAN'S WIFE IN THE EARLY 1900S. LATER, MAURICE STANCOMBE FARMED IT – MAINLY AS DAIRY AND BEEF UNTIL HIS DEATH IN NOVEMBER 1991.

THE HOUSE AND PART OF THE GROUND WAS SOLD TO CHARLES AND SYLVIA SERPELL, THE PRESENT OCCUPIERS. SYLVIA SAID THAT 'MR ROBERTS MOVED TO VICARAGE COTTAGE AND WHEN HE DIED HIS PERSONAL EFFECTS WERE DISPOSED OF.' SOME ITEMS WERE PUT ONTO A TIP AND OUT OF THIS 'RUBBISH' SHE SPOTTED A LOVELY OLD WASHBASIN AND JUG, AND DULY PICKED IT UP AND KEPT IT. 'IT WAS AS IF IT WAS MEANT TO BE' SAYS SYLVIA, 'BECAUSE SEVERAL YEARS LATER IT IS BACK IN SPARKWELL FARM, ITS ORIGINAL HOME.'

Top left: *Maurice Stancombe and David Anstey with Boots in 1960.*

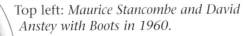

Left: *Maurice with Roy Lapthorne in 1991.*

Below: *View over the farm.*

NEWNHAM (Old Newnham)

The house is interesting because it has seven different roof levels and if seen from the air is of an irregular crucifix pattern. It is also of interest because of its early attempts at indoor sanitation; the overhang of the fifth roof level contains down pipes believed to have been for this purpose and dating from around the 1520s. Renovations continued throughout the 16th and 17th centuries during which time the porch was added and the main hall and entrance hall rebuilt. The house has always been in private hands and remains so to this day.

It can be seen behind the trees whilst driving along Newnham Road and the bell tower is clearly visible. There is still speculation over what happened to the original bell which hung there, which was dated about 1580, and would now be worth several million pounds! The bell was said to have been of Russian design and this fits in well with the general form of the house which is particularly unusual.

NEWNHAM PARK (New Newnham)

This house was built on the site of Loughtor Manor in 1703. The basement still remains dated from the 16th century, although it is believed that the original Loughtor Manor was standing in 1160. The house is of a standard two-storey rectangular design with rear extension added in 1826 and a porch added in 1907. The park passed to the Strode family in 1525 when Elizabeth Strode (aged 10) married Philip de Courtenay of Mollard, Lord Loughtor (aged 12). The Cobbold family resides there now.

REPORT ON OLD NEWNHAM AND PLYMPTON

Visited on Wednesday 9th May 1962

Historic Note

At the request of Mrs Grigg-Strode, whose family has owned and occupied this house since the fifteenth century, I made a careful inspection on Wednesday 9th May 1962.

The accompanying memorandum gives an outline of the history of this most beautiful building which has undergone many alterations in its long life. Each period has left its stamp upon the structure but escaped detrimental restoration.

I am of the opinion that the building dated back to the thirteenth or early fourteenth century. It would appear that it was originally constructed for defence. The remains of arrow slot loop-holes with deeply splayed internal reveals may be discerned at the points marked 'A' on the accompanying plan.

These suggest that the entrance was then through the archway No 3 and that the wall forming the southern boundary along which the stream runs was originally ramparted.

A blocked up door which may have lead onto the top of the wall shows on the first floor level in the south-east corner of room No 2.

The inner arch of the gateway appears to have been replaced in the fifteenth century and the outer arch in the seventeenth century.

The great hall (17) may well date from the early fourteenth century. The two pointed arches recently uncovered in the west wall, the main roof truss timbers and some of the wall masonry are all that now remain of the original structure. The screen's passage was probably then at the west. The bay and adjacent windows, and the present entrance

Old Newnham Farm, Plympton. The property was built before 1285, although the majority of its construction dates from the 1540s. It was originally built for Simon de Plympton whose son John took the name Newnham (from the farm at the hill's bottom) in 1358. In the early 1400s the estate passed via marriage to the Strode family whereupon the chapel was built in 1423, although it was only granted a Matins licence.

door were probably inserted later in the fourteenth century and the porch added in the fifteenth century.

The great kitchen with its great hearth and six light east windows probably date from this period.

A chapel is recorded to have been built in 1432. This, I think, was probably room No 22, now used as a kitchen on the ground floor and the bathroom above. The roof over this portion has three arched and collar trusses, the central one being richly moulded both sides in typical fifteenth-century section and the other two trusses moulded one side only.

The chapel would then have been full height, entered from the end of the contemporary screen's passage. (21)

The solar room No 9 with its finely covered transversed beams, bearing a Tudor rose, and the great bedroom above with its ceiling divided into square panels by heavily moulded beams are probably also Tudor construction. Jacobean panelling was later fixed along the north wall of the latter room and a semi-octagonal Queen Anne cupboard (B) inserted beneath the staircase.

At the extreme south end of the west range is a most interesting orial guard robe (C) on the first floor which used to discharge over the stream which still runs along the south boundary below.

Some time, perhaps in the eighteenth century, a floor was inserted in the great hall and chapel and the sash windows inserted in the rooms (23 and 24) in the west side of the present screens passage. I believe that at one time there was an eastern Elizabethan wing beyond these rooms.

Additions were also made in lean-tos (18 and 19) to the north of the hall.

The date of the western projection No 14 is obscure but I am inclined to put it fairly late. The floor of this room is the living rock.

It would seem that the shallow layer of soil above the rock precluded the possibility of sinking cesspools and that the projection No 6, in the middle of the west wall, which has no opening at ground level and is now used as a bathroom on the first floor, was built and used for this purpose, constructed entirely above ground. The now roofless free standing structure, again without ground floor opening but step leading up outside may well have been a similar structure, perhaps eighteenth century.

Structural Condition
As most of the masonry dressings are of granite there is comparatively little surface deterioration except of the tracery of the orial windows. However since the seventeenth century progressively less of the building has been occupied. The old guard room No 2, and the kitchen and adjoining building (14 and 15) have been disused for many years.

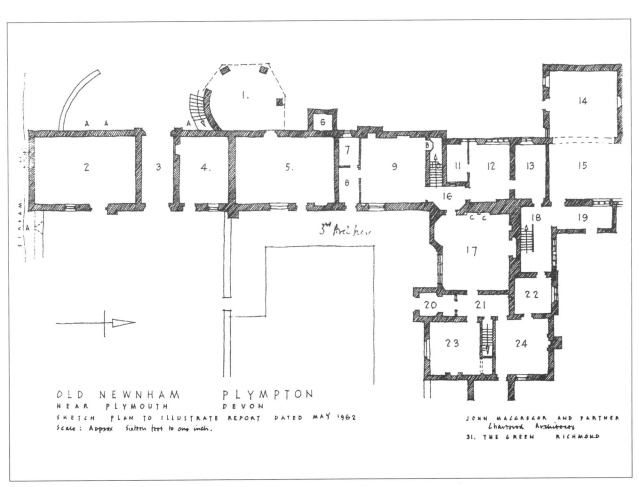

1 and 2 Blacklands Cottages in the early 1900s and (inset) *in the 1940s with Nora Reglar and Mrs Bennett with Roger Bennett outside.*

Arnold Olver (with horse) oustside the Treby Inn (before the pumps were installed).

CHAPTER 3: AGRICULTURE

Farming in Sparkwell Parish in the early-19th century was certainly a very primitive affair when compared with the methods of today. With most of the agricultural activity taking place on small, owner-occupied farms and a few small gentleman estates, farming was made prosperous mainly due to the First World War. During the 1930s farming went through something of a hard time but the outbreak of the war saw increased food production and the modernisation of farming methods and technology. In 1851 the parish of Sparkwell was split in two by the railway which also divided some farms. Modern grants and aided land for farmers who had to move uphill to higher land (which was harder to farm) ensured, however, that the coming of the railway did not herald a downturn in the fortunes of the local farmer.

Elsie and Margaret Wotton and Edward Colgate at Great Stert, 1937.

The south side of the line became known as the lowland and the north side the upland, which attracted more grants. The trend during the 20th century was a move away from mixed farms towards specialising either in milk, beef or grain, with the small farms being sold out to neighbours to make bigger units. The north of the line is also associated with Dartmoor and some farmers had a right to stock the moor with cattle, sheep and horses. The south of the area carried on in a more general way, the farms being of a small acreage where general farming with a living made from a few cattle, sheep and hens.

There were a few small farms in and around the village which was also home to both a blacksmith and a wheelwright. Produce was sold in the village or taken by carrier to the city markets.

Almost all of the land in the parish is given over to farming and the three small estates within the parish each contain farmland. The Domesday Book reveals an estate south of Sparkwell known as Langehywys (which in Old English means 'long piece of land', later – c.1785 – to be called Langage). Plympton Priory owned Langage, Applethorn Slade and Voss Farm. The Priory is still recalled in some of the field names at Langage

such as Great and Little Priors. In 1238 Plympton Court hanged D.E. Langehewis for stealing sheep.

In the 20th century, farming was mixed, small farms keeping a few sheep, pigs, poultry and cattle. The sheep were kept to clean up after the cattle, with the cows for milk, which was then sold raw in the village or made into cream or butter to be sold around the villages. Around the 1930s ploughing was carried out with horses and this continued until the late 1940s when tractors came into wider use. John Kingwell, for example, worked three horses on his farm.

During the Great Depression sheep sold for just 10 shillings (50p in today's money) but during the Second World War the farming industry once again enjoyed a return to prosperity. During the war just about anything was sold, including cider apples.

The introduction of grants in the 1950s also helped improve the farmer's lot and the British Isles became more and more self-sufficient with the increased use of manure and better land management improving yields. By the 1950s and '60s production levels had improved still further with the introduction of sprayed artificial fertilisers and with still better management, but the public became more aware of the possible pitfalls of using sprays and other modern practices and a decline in production began to develop.

During the 1970s–'80s the parish reacted to another physical division within its boundaries after the A38 cut across the south of the region. At Ford Farm the ground to the north side of the new road became landlocked. This was sold off to neighbouring farmers. The downward trend in the fortunes of the farmer continued and by the end of the 1990s farming was in a recession which was compounded by the BSE crisis.

On 29 March 2001 the foot and mouth epidemic hit Lower Challonsleigh Farm resulting in the culling of hundreds of animals on this and nearby farms. Farmers within the parish went through an extremely worrying period, hoping all the time that no further outbreaks would occur.

❧ HARVEST HOME ❧

Above: *Getting the harvest home at Venton.*

Top right: *Harvesting at Venton.*

Right: *Harvesting using a scythe.*

Above: *Perratons owned the steam-driven traction engine for thrashing corn.*

Below: *The steam thrasher at Baccamore (see also page 16). Included are Reg Short (2nd from left), Reg Serpell (next), Stan Tall (next, sitting), Miss King (holding basket), Polly Tall (next), Stan Sandover (in front of Polly), Harry Masters (next), Ken Collings (hands on hips).*

Above: *The hayrick is finished. Pictured are members of the Wingett family at Venton.*

LEE MILL

The area of the parish at the River Erme in Lee Mill and the ground to the west is chiefly given over to mixed farming. In the early 1800s the Abbot family had a big holding in the Lee Mill area with a pub and a cider press and a farm with land on both sides of the river.

HEMERDON

Farming west of Sparkwell and north of the railway line is dominated by Dartmoor. These farms lie against the Plymouth boundary. Here there are a number of small holdings.

At the time of writing, the area around Langage is set to become an industrial estate as, on 15 November 2000, permission was granted for Wainstones Gas Powered Station, which will produce electricity.

ELFORDLEIGH: R. PALMER & SONS, AGRICULTURAL MERCHANTS AND MILK HAULIERS

Adrian Palmer started the business at Treen in 1935, at which time he was living at Sterts Farm, which was farmed by his uncle Joe Rowe. As he only had one lorry, he collected the milk in churns from the farms and delivered them to Radnor Dairy. On returning to Stert he unloaded the empty churns and replaced them with the animal feed. He delivered that and then reloaded the empty churns ready for the early morning start –

no 40-hour week in those days! During the war he had a store in the old chapel in Longbrook Street, St Maurice. Many people kept chickens in their back gardens and would go to the store on Saturday mornings to collect the feed which was on ration. In 1948 Adrian and his mother Rhoda Palmer moved to Elfordleigh despite the fact there was no water supply or mains electricity. A churn of water was brought home each day and a generator supplied electricity. Adrian married Sheila Hutt in 1959, who having lived in Kent 12 miles outside of London all her life, soon had to get used to using flat irons and cooking with calor gas. Fortunately the water supply had been installed in 1949. Their daughters Carol and Elaine were born in 1960 and 1962 respectively. Sheila worked in the office, but it was a real eye opener to discover that 'cake' was something consumed by cattle.

In 1961 electricity arrived which meant that Adrian was able to make barley meal and crushed barley. The store had been expanded and included two silos enabling him to buy the corn from the field as it was harvested. The milk rounds had expanded and three lorries collected the milk. However, this stopped in July 1979 when the Milk Marketing Board insisted that farm collections had to be made by tankers, thus putting dozens of local farmers 'out of milk' because it was not worth their while buying a tanker for 15–20 gallons of milk per day. Fortunately the agricultural feed side of the business continued to thrive until Adrian finally retired in September 1990. Since that time the business has been continued by John Serpell.

NFU dinner in the heyday of farming, c.1940s.

Above: *Lesley Willis with the horses at Holland Farm.*

Left: *Reg Serpell ploughing with his horse.*

Top right: *An old seed drill for planting mangolds and turnips.*

Right: *Harry Masters and Stan Tall cutting hay at Baccamore Farm.*

Left: *Bill Tapp and Bill Downing working with a double-horse hay sweep.*

Below: *Of course, horses were also used for transport. This is an old photograph of Grandad Wotton.*

❧ ... TO THE ❧ MODERN MACHINE

Right: *The corn mill at Elfordleigh.*

Far right: *Reg Serpell ploughing with a Fordson T20 tractor.*

Below: *Peter Tremain and Dick Trigger silaging.*

Bottom left: *John and Eric Kingwell at Langage Cross.*

THE ROUND BALE

IN 1964 A HUGE PLASTIC BAG MADE TO HOLD 800 TONS OF SILAGE WAS INTRODUCED TO BLACKLANDS FARM. IT WAS THE LARGEST OF ITS KIND AT THE TIME, MEASURING 80FT BY 65FT BY 7FT HIGH – AT A COST OF £120. IT WAS TO CONTAIN ENOUGH SILAGE TO FEED 100 FRIESIAN COWS AND THE IDEA WAS BROUGHT OVER FROM NEW ZEALAND. ONCE SEALED GRASS BECOMES 'PICKLED' AND IF THE WEATHER IS WARM IT IS READY FOR USE IN ABOUT TEN DAYS.

This is thought to be a group of Sparkwell schoolchildren in the early 1900s.

Lee Mill School, 1915. This is now a private house.
The photograph includes: Aileen Elliott, Ron Elliott, Derek Elliott, Dennis Willis, Esme Basset, Bernard Brown, Betty Downs, Ken Downs, Roy Pearse, Terence Willis, Margaret Thomson, Freddy Harper, Sylvia Pulley, Jill Wright, Peggy Willis, Bunty Cummins, Clarrie Downing, Edward Willis, Gordon Elliott, Betty Willia, Terry Wright.

CHAPTER 4: EDUCATION

The present, and apparently first, school was built at the crossroads between Beechwood House and Sparkwell Farm in 1850 to serve also as a chapel of ease. It was built at the expense of Colonel Mudge of Beechwood who sadly died before the land for the school was given over, an event which lead to some acrimonious correspondence between lawyers for the Mudge family and Lord Seaton. Lady Seaton believed that the piece of land promised for the erection of a school was part of the Beechwood estate and should not be handed over, because the sale would detract from the estate's value. Letters of witness to Colonel Mudge's intention were delivered to lawyers for the family who pointed out to Lord Seaton's solicitors, that if the case went to High Court (which seemed highly likely) then the value of the piece of land in question would devalue that of the estate itself by a sum far less significant than the cost of High Court proceedings. It was at this point that they conceded.

A church was built adjoining in 1859 and from then on it was used entirely as a school. Despite its private ownership, being essentially a church school it was generally known as a National school from its establishment and was conveyed to trustees in 1868. The school continued and under the LEA after the 1902 Act remained a voluntary Church school. It became a junior school in 1929 and in 1952 was given controlled status. Hundreds of children have passed through the little school at Sparkwell all with fond memories of their time there. Below are just a few of those reminiscences.

Sparkwell School, 14 May 1909.

✣ DOWN THROUGH ✣ THE YEARS

SCHOOL HEADS
MRS HEATH
MRS PADDON
MR FARNHAM
MR MCCARTHY
MR SOLOMAN
MRS MITCHELL

Above: *The children in 1914.*

Right: *1925. Left to right, back: Maude Williams, Dick Honey, Boysey Glitton, Stanley Reed, William Nelder, George Downing; in front of back row standing: Lily Reed, Arthur Rowe, Eileen Hoskin, Joy Downing, Nora Macbean, Muriel Macbean, Kathleen Downing, May Honey, Edith Lee, Peggy Yabsley, ? Rossiter, Teresa Exworthy, Annie Mearns; sitting: Barbara Rowe, Doreen Collings, Elsie Hambly, Gladys Lee, Olive Williams, Molly Harris; front: Gordon Downing, Stan Downing, Reg Reed, Eddie Rossiter, Fred Reed, Leslie Macbean, Donald Hoskin.*

The school, 1930s. Left to right, back: Fred Reed, Leonard Elford, Norman Bowden, Reg Reed, Eddie Rossiter, ? Rossiter, Donald Hoskin, Les Hurn, Stan Downing, Gordon, Downing; middle: Ernest Roberts, Dolly Elford, Olive Williams, Gladys Lee, Gwen Clemo, Doreen Collings, Kathleen Mumford, Eileen Hoskin, Teresa Exworthy, Peggy and Joyce Yabsley, Lily Reed, Pauline Turpin, Harold Reed; front: Denis Hurn, Charlie Collins, Edith Penwill, ? Hoskin, Ivy Downing, Joyce Collins, Molly Harris, Vera Exworthy, Norman Nelder, ? Rossiter, Ken Hurn, Raymond Hill.

Left and above: *Mrs Drake's class, c.1950, and Jean Wingett, 1951.*

Above: *Sparkwell School, 1973. Left to right, back: David Hanna, Paul Dalton, Graham Mattacott, Julian Chudley, Paul Collier, Tracy Exworthy, Andrew Needham, Heather Denny, Martin Vincent, Linda Mattacott, Jonathan Chudley, Caroline Vincent, Robert Newton, Steve Hunt, Ian Denny, Jeanette Collier, Craig Needham;*

middle: Neil Elford, David Small, Tina Tremain, Ann Evans, Marina Howard, Sadie Dalton, Shirley Hunt, David Warley, Christine Vincent, Julie Elford, Lynne Denny, Andrew Newton, Hilary Hanna, Sarah Allen, Brian Mattacott, Donald Hanna;

front: Karen James, Julie Evans, Bernard Chudley, Paul Hanna, Julie Clague, Bryan Taylor, Nigel Denny, Sally Cooper, Peter Watts, Nicola Bailey, Ian Exworthy, Brad Needham, Paul Andrews, Neil Collings, Richard Mumford, Louise Tremain.

Left: *Allison James, 1977.*

I remember when...

ROSE COUCH
(NÉE KINGDON, 1901–1995)

I started school when I was five years old in 1906 [and stayed until] 1915. I think I must have started school with May Tucker, Eddie Perry [and] Francis Mumford. My brother Bill was already at school in 1904 and my sister Eva, who was two years younger, started in 1908.

We lived at Hemerdon and walked to and from school in groups. There were as many as 60 children living in Hemerdon and Bottle Hill. It was safe to walk then as we only saw a few cars a week; it was pony and traps [although] we hardly ever got a lift on one (and never in a car). May Tucker and I used to walk home on the hedge which we were not allowed to do, but we thought it was quicker. We were always getting told off from Mr Glover, the coachman at Woollcombes (Hemerdon House) when he saw us there. We would wait until he was out of sight then get on the hedge again.

There were very few houses in Sparkwell and the council houses at Birchland Road were not even built.

The outside of the school hasn't changed except that the yard was flatter, and there used to be a tree by the side gate which we used to call a penny tree. There was also a beech tree by the church. On the inside were two classrooms the same as now. The windows all had bars on them (these were iron ones), the screen was the same between the two classrooms. The toilets were not flush ones as now, but with big wooden seats with one long channel. Running water would go through the channel. The toilets were in the same position as they are today.

We used to have three groups – infants used the top classroom and we had two groups in the bottom room with the older children near the door. Our lessons were maths, English and history which were done on slates; we were allowed to use pen and paper when we were in the eldest group. I remember an inspector coming to take us for our history exam. We also went on nature walkabout every three weeks. We had drill (PE) – these were games in the school yard. Games played were 'in and out the dusty windows', 'Gathering nuts in May' and others. We also did a lot of plays; these were for anyone to come to see in our school. Our desks were wooden and the seat attached with ink wells in the top of the desk and lids lifting up.

TEACHERS
Mr and Mrs Cornal were our teachers. Mrs Cornal taught the infants and Mr Cornal taught the older children. They had a son and a daughter and lived in Beechwood Cottage. There was also another teacher called Mrs Furnix who lived at Hemerdon.

UNIFORM
There was no school uniform but girls wore a long white apron over their dresses and the boys wore a collar and tie as can be seen in the photographs taken in 1909.

SCHOOL BELL
This was rung every morning by one of the older boys and they used to take it in turns. Everyone lined up then we used to march into school. If anyone was late we were given the cane or ruler (wooden ones).

PLAYGROUND
We all had separate playgrounds; boys in one yard and the girls in another. We were not allowed to mix to play but the boys used to get into the girls' playground anyway.

MITCHING (PLAYING TRUANT)
If we stayed away from school without good reason we were given the cane the next day, but this hardly ever happened – no one ever mitched school. I cannot remember getting homework to do – our lessons were all done

Rosina Couch (née Kingdon) is far right at the front and her sister Eva is fourth from the left at the front. Bill Kingdon is fifth from the left in the third row up.

Sparkwell School, 1936. Left to right, back: Ken Hill, Dolcie Lee, Winnie Collings, Eileen Exworthy, ?, Jean Weston, Richard Hurn; 3rd row: Ernie Reed, Ron Barker, Reg Lee, Phyllis Hill, Pam Ewings, Phyllis Taylor, Blanche Lee, Joyce Anstey, Kathleen Collins, ?, George Pengelly, Sidney Reed; 2nd row: Vera Maddock, Barbara Anstey, Betty Lee, Helen Mudge, Jean Balsdon, Barbara Roberts, Dorothy Barker, Nancy Pengelly, Nancy Hill, Maureen Maddock, Beryl Cairns; front: Ken Collings, Roy Exworthy, John Mitchell, Norman Barker, Dennis Tucker, Normon Lee, Gerald Clague, Peter Mudge, Ron Goss, ?, Brian Cairns, Cyril Downing.

at school. The doctor and dentist used to call once a year, sometimes twice.

SCHOOL DINNERS (LUNCH HOUR)
There were no school dinners and we all brought a packed lunch with us which we ate in the playground if dry and in the classroom if wet. Twice a week we would get a hot dinner. Our mother used to walk to the gateway, just before Lawns Cottage, with a pasty or meat and potato pudding. This was wrapped in a cabbage leaf to keep it moist. We ate our dinner and walked back to school, making sure we were not late or we would get the cane. If we were meeting our mother with the dinner we had to get permission to leave school. We never had anyone to look after us at playtime or lunchtime – we were trusted (or the thought of the cane stopped us going out). I remember my cousin at school, who was a little backward [having the following conversation]:

Teacher: 'How old are you?'
Boy: 'Don't know Sir.'

Teacher: 'Well go home and ask your father.'

NEXT DAY
Teacher: 'Did you ask your father?'
Boy: 'Yes Sir.'
Teacher: 'How old are you?'
Boy: 'About 80 Sir.'
Teacher: 'Don't tell lies.'

My cousin got the cane because he told lies, but being slow he did not realise that his dad was joking.

CHURCH
We went to church once every week, and the vicar Pender Hodge Cudlip came to us twice a week. We had prayers and hymns in school every morning and someone played the piano for us to sing. I can remember the extension being built on the church – this is where the altar is now. I have a photo of my brother Bill and myself in the extension.

Pender Hodge Cudlip was our parish vicar and when coming to the school he would come through a gate in the

vicarage by the tennis courts, and come down beside the church. This was called the hunting gate. I remember when he died – it must have been about April because we older children all attended the service and then marched up to the cemetery where he was buried, and all dropped a posy of primroses into the ground on top of the coffin.

There was a Sunday School at Hemerdon Mission Hall (still there now), not Sparkwell Church. We went three times a Sunday; it was always full. I have a Bible that was presented to me in 1911 for good attendance. I didn't really like school very much, especially sums – although I could do them (but not long division). I left school when I was 14 and there have been four generations [of my family] at the school: my mother was Alice Louise Bawden, there was myself and my brother and sister Bill and Eva Kingdon, my daughters Rosemary and Muriel Couch, and my granddaughters Jacqueline, Beverly and Joanne Stevens.

Mrs Enid Taylor (née Matthews)

I and my sister Dorothy started at Sparkwell School in 1922. I was 10 years old and my sister 12. There were only a few houses in Sparkwell then, the council houses had not been built, and only a few children in the village. About 40 attended school, most of these coming from Venton, Hemerdon and the farms around. The head teacher was Mrs Heath and [the] infants' [teacher] Miss James. The old teacher's house was Beechwood Cottage, before the new one was built where it now stands.

The school bell would ring for a quarter of an hour each morning – children would take it in turns to ring it. We would then line up in the playground where the head teacher would come out and welcome us. The girls led in first and the boys after. Each one would salute the headmistress as he passed her. We all assembled in the big room and had morning prayers and a hymn, usually 'New Every Morning is Our Love' and evenings we finished with 'Now the Day is Over'. The infants then went to their room and we took our seats at the desks, and had Bible readings. Following this there would be arithmetic and learning tables, then our playtime. When we returned it would be a different subject – English dictation, spelling, history, etc. The village children went home to lunch, but for the children who stayed there would be a large urn on the old-fashioned large stoves filled with coke and a large heavy fireguard around. They would be able to get hot water to make a cup of cocoa or whatever they brought. Some parents would bring a hot dinner so far and the children would walk so far to meet them and eat it by the wayside.

Afternoons were mostly [spent] painting, drawing and map drawing. Mr Heath was a good artist and he would take us for lessons. The girls would also have sewing lessons and knitting. I remember making an apron, summer shirt, night-dress and pillowcases. Mrs Heath would take us for this, also embroidery and learning to patch and darn. [In] music lessons – or should I say singing – we learnt some lovely songs and the school would ring with the sound of music. The boys would do different classes and would make things from wood, etc. One of their jobs was to fill the ink wells and wash them before refilling them from brown stone jars. We all used pens with nibs and when the nibs were crossed or worn down we would put a new one in, and we used a pencil quite a lot.

The only ones I know living in the village that went to school with me are Emily May (née Luscombe) and George Lee. Mrs Couch was much older than us. I remember how we used to do exercises in the playground, or gym as it's now called winter and summer. We also used to dance the Maypole on May Day, making a spider's web with ribbons and wearing white dresses with flowers in our hair, the boys wearing shorts and shirts. On Empire Day we took money to school and received a certificate.

Sparkwell School in the 1920s. Left to right, back: Maud Williams, Daisy Elford, Phyllis Dodd, Dora Perry, Dorothy Lee, Enid Matthews, ?, Fiz Warren, Kath Downing; front: May Honey, Jessie Reed, Peggy Yabsley, ? Hoskin, Jeanette Lavers, Mollie Blackler, Maria Macbean, ?.

DOREEN THORRINGTON (NÉE COLLINGS)

I remember going to school at the age of five in 1926. The school consisted of just two rooms, as well as the cloakroom area. The older boys even did woodwork lessons, whilst the girls were taught to knit and sew. It was indeed very crowded; I remember the heavy wood and iron desks we sat in to do our lessons, and the very dusty wood floors, and the old tortoise coke fires.

It was not until after the Second World War that school dinners were introduced. Pupils that came from outlying areas walked to school, as there weren't many that had any form of transport. They ate their sandwiches in the porch at lunchtime. The school yard was on a slope, which rose to meet the steps leading into the church grounds. There was a path marked out with stones as this was the right of way to the church of All Saints.

The children from Lee Mill joined us on May Day to dance around the maypole and we had a sports day on St George's Day. During the time I was at Sparkwell I was taught by Mrs Heath, the headmistress, and Miss James in the infants class. When I reached 11 I was transferred to the Plympton Senior School with all the pupils over that age.

Dr W.L. HOOPER

I was born and brought up at Bank Cottage and was a pupil from 1936 to 1942 going on to Plympton Grammar School and then Cardiff University. When I first attended school the headmistress Mrs Heath still kept – and used – a thin flexible cane which was stored above the blackboard. Mrs Paddon however dispensed with that form of punishment.

My father was the dairyman who supplied the school with wide-necked one-third-pint bottles of milk for many years. The bottle tops were of cardboard which could be perforated in the middle and the straws were pieces of real straw. Miss Drake the infants teacher would warm the bottles in a tin oven over the coke-fired combustion stove which invariably filled the classroom with smoke until it got going.

The school bell was still in use when I was a pupil and during the [Second World] War we all carried our gas masks in cardboard boxes. When the air-raid warning sirens sounded everyone from the school took shelter under the trees in Venton Lane.

The school first had electricity in 1937. It was oil lamps before that.

The school, 1933. Left to right, back: Eileen Hoskin, Muriel Macbean, Kath Downing, Jessie Reed, Jessie Simpson, Doreen Collings; middle: Doris Taylor, Olive Williams, Gladys Lee, Nora Macbean, Peggy Yabsley, Ivy Downing, Gwen Taylor, Elsie Macbean, Pauline Turpin; front: Audrey Downing, Lily Reed, Doris Turpin, Teresa Exworthy, Joyce Yabsley, Dolly Elford, Molly Harris.

A class of 1952. Left to right, back: Miss Drake, George Bone, Ivor Sowden, Brian Gulley, Michael Hill, John Jenkins, Mrs Paddon; middle: Rodney Willcocks, Margaret Hurn, Elizabeth Collings, Mavis Hill, Jean Wingett, Adrienne Kelly, Victor Pearse; seated: Alan Warley, Lorraine Blatchford, Stella Collings, Yvonne Quest, Judith Couch, Christine Lee, Elizabeth Elford, Dennis Warley; front: Brian Hill, Kathleen Mumford, John Small.

Sparkwell School, 1950. Left to right, back: Miss Drake, Ken Goss, Roger Osborne, John Sowden, Brian Gulley, George Small, Barry Commons, Brian Rendle, Michael Jenkins, Ralph Tippett, Roger Bennett, Mrs Paddon; 3rd row: Margaret Hurn, Joyce Tippett, Mavis Hill, Cynthia Serpell, Rita Tyrrell, Joan Osborne, Maureen Daw, Jean Wingett, Alan Scott, Rodney Squires; seated: Dennis Warley, Naomi Lavers, Adrienne Kelly, Judith Couch, Yvonne Quest, Stella Collings, Wendy Parsons, Lorraine Blatchford, Alan Warley; front: George Bone, Tony Squires, Ivor Sowden, Rodney Willcocks, John Jenkins, Michael Hill, Brian Hill, Tony Collier, John Small.

LORRAINE DENNY
(NÉE BLATCHFORD)

Although I was looking forward to starting school I was very nervous on my first day. Miss Drake was the infants teacher. She wore thick pleated skirts and a jumper or twin-set, thick stockings and flat tie-up shoes. Whenever she was outside she always wore a 'beret' on her head (I think it was called a 'tam-o-shanter'). She rode to school from Wembury on a scooter-type motorbike and later drove a three-wheeler car.

I remember learning to count by using coloured counters, large ones were the tens, small ones units. Mine were yellow ones because I was in the yellow team. Other teams were red, blue and green. We stayed in those teams right through to the age of 11. My first reading books were 'Janet and John'; later I progressed to Ladybird books. Writing was done in an exercise book using a pencil. I well remember doing lots of copying of the alphabet, big A (capital), little a, etc. I also did lots of drawings and colouring in pictures using big coloured wax crayons. When I moved down to the juniors all our written work was done with a pen, the nib of which was dipped in ink.

Mrs Paddon was the junior teacher and headmistress. She wore thick costumes and whenever any visitor came to the door she always got up and put on her hat before greeting whoever it was. The day started at 9 o'clock. The bell was rung. We had to line up in the playground in our teams. Sometimes because some of us were learning to play a marching tune on the piano, we all had to march in supposedly in time to the music. Most of the time Mrs Paddon would play. Assembly followed – two hymns, two prayers and a Bible reading. After that we had hygiene inspection. Everyone had to hold up their handkerchiefs, anyone forgetting to bring one would have to do 'lines' at play time. I remember some children cheating by holding up crushed white paper in the palm of their hands. Fingernail inspection followed; something was put on your finger nails if you bit them. A scripture lesson sometimes followed, then arithmetic.

Charts of tables were always hung on the wall and when we thought we knew each one off by heart we could recite it to Mrs Paddon. If we got it right we could move on to the next one. As I moved along I remember chanting capacity and weight tables such as '2 pints = 1 quart', etc. The money table was also learnt parrot fashion, e.g. '12 pence = 1 shilling', etc.

After morning play time it was usually English which included handwriting, composition (essay) and spelling. More charts were around the room with pictures of an object and the word written beside it. Frequently we had spelling tests. Some mornings we had music and movement from a radio programme, jumping around pretending to be a frog or standing still being a tree. PE lessons were made up of walking around balancing a bean bag on your head, skipping, bouncing a ball and occasionally playing a ball game. Running around in navy-blue knickers (which had a pocket in them for a hankie) and a white T shirt – ugh!

Geography was a subject I enjoyed. We did lots of map drawing, filling in capital cities, etc. A radio programme called 'Travellers Tales' was also used. Another programme was called 'Singing Together'.

Sometimes we had needlework lessons in the afternoon and at Christmas time we always made calendars from cardboard squares covered with wallpaper, a pretty picture cut from old cards stuck on the front with a small calendar placed underneath the picture. Paper decorations were made. We always had a large Christmas tree and a lovely party.

When we were in the top class we were made 'monitors' [and] the boys were put in charge of filling the ink wells. If you happened to be sitting in front of some of the boys, they would dip your pigtails into an ink well and you would get ink dripping down your back. I don't remember the girls getting the cane, but the boys very often did. At the end of the day two monitors would carry Mrs Paddon's case up to her front door. The year 1953 was Coronation year; lots of celebrations took place and we all had a day off school.

Mrs Collings and Mrs Taylor served the school meals. The school building is exactly the same as now, even the same cupboards. The girls' toilets have slightly improved... with pull flushes.

A photograph taken at school of Lorraine Denny (née Blatchford) in 1950.

LESLEY MASEY (NÉE MUDGE)

I started school in September 1952. I think there were four of us – myself, my cousin Dinah (Kit) Mudge, Edwin Little and I think Barry Hambly. David and James Mudge and James Underwood were also at the school but they were a little older. Mrs Paddon was still the headteacher. One game we played involved running around a rope. I did this and promptly fell and cut my head open. I was taken into school, made a cup of hot sweet tea and made to lie on a long blue table. My mother was sent for and our new vicar, Michael Mann, who was passing, was summoned in. I think he had knowledge of first aid. I had to lie there for what seemed ages.

All that seemed to go through my mind was that this table was one we ate our dinner from. Sports day seemed a grand affair with a party and four cakes – one for each team. These were decorated in red, green, blue and yellow, the colours of the teams. There was a separate table for teachers and local gentry. I think about 50–60 children attended coming from Lutton Square to Sparkwell. The other half of Lutton went to Cornwood. Girls and boys played in separate playgrounds. If there was a funeral we had an early playtime and had to play quietly.

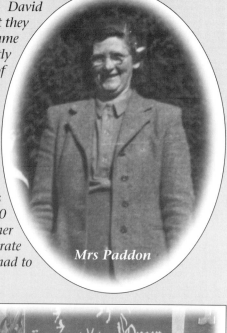

Mrs Paddon

Above: *Mrs Paddon's class of 1953.*
Left to right, back row: Margaret Hurn, Elizabeth Collings, Mavis Hill, Adrienne Kelly; middle: Christine Lee, Stella Collings (peeping), George Bone, Judith Couch, Ivor Sowden, Brian Gulley, Jean Wingett; front (standing): Yvonne Quest, Victor Pearse, Brian Hill, John Small, Lorraine Blatchford, Jacqueline Trigger, Deirdre Jenkins, Jean Tucker, Kathleen Mumford, Dennis Warley, Alan Warley; seated (back): John Jenkins, Michael Hill; seated (front): Elizabeth Elford, Beryl Downing.

ADRIENNE GORDON
(NÉE KELLY)

I was a pupil of Sparkwell School from Jan 1947 to July 1953. On my first day I remember a lady sitting at a desk with lots of bottles of milk on it. A boy came in and opened a desk and put something inside. I cautiously looked inside and it had lots of books in it – my first encounter with a school desk. Mrs Paddon, as the lady turned out to be, spoke to me and I went to another room where I met another lady Miss Drake. There was another girl starting that day; her name was Yvonne Quest, and we sat together threading yellow and blue beads. At school dinner we sat down at long tables, and I said very loudly 'lovely grub' which was a radio catch-phrase of the day. That became my nickname for a while. I soon settled into a routine of going to school, but after a couple of weeks this was shattered when blizzards came and we were snowbound for about three weeks.

Mrs Paddon was my idol and inspired me to my first ambition to be a teacher. She had a brown felt hat. I was fascinated by her hat, which reminded me of a rabbit. Miss Drake was a real character. I remember her as very stern. We would line up in the school yard in teams and march into school. Rodney Sowden and Roger Bennett had piano lessons and one of them would play the march for us to go in to. The boys would salute to the teachers. In the summer we would go to Mrs Paddon's for PT on her lawn. The lawn smelt of chamomile. Our sports days were held in the field up the hill from school. Mr Sandover 'Uncle Bert', would remove the cows from the field and white lines would be painted on the grass. We sat on a big tarpaulin.

School dinners came from Plympton in containers. One day we had hot-pot which was inedible because it was extremely salty, and another time we had milk jelly and nearly everyone was sick afterwards – including me. We had to order our dinners every day, and when I was in the top class it was my responsibility to go to the phone box and ring in the order. Mrs Paddon gave me 2d. to make the call. In those days the phone box would take pennies (old money) and one would have to press A if connected or B if not connected and [to have] your money returned.

One day when I was in the juniors there was a major innovation – the wireless arrived. From then on we had several radio (wireless) lessons a day and it was a great honour to be allowed to switch it on. The church was a strong influence on the life of school. Every term started and finished with a service in the church and the vicar was a frequent visitor. The first vicar I knew was Mr James. Mrs Paddon announced that he was moving to a new parish, she said the vicar will give his 'address' – but he never did. Holy days were very popular, as after church we had the rest of the day off. One thing we found very puzzling was that certain children went home before church. We knew that they were Catholics and naturally assumed Catholics did not go to church.

As a Church school we were expected to learn the catechism. Christmas celebrations always followed the same pattern. We [made] calendars, paper chains interwoven crêpe paper and Chinese lanterns. Father Christmas visited and I remember when I was six Father Christmas leapt out from behind a screen with a loud 'HO HO HO' and terrified the life out of me. I wouldn't go near him for at least two years and I certainly did not want him coming down my chimney!

From Hemerdon to school we would occasionally get a lift from Brenda Sowden's uncle in his post van, then later on Adrian Palmer's milk lorry. He carried as many as seven children in the cab of his lorry. However, we had to walk home. Later our parents clubbed together for Mr Locke's taxi to fetch us. On one such occasion I remember it was teeming down, and when we got to Hemerdon the water was pouring over a field hedge and running in torrents down through the village. Mr Locke had to carry me over the stream. That was the day of the Lynton and Lynmouth floods.

On the whole our days at Sparkwell School were very happy and carefree, but we were all saddened by the death of Ralph Tippett and worried by Eric Exworthy's polio. His brother 'Oxo' had to stop delivering milk and Jean McIndoe, his next-door neighbour, had to stay away from school for several weeks. Another event that saddened us was the death of the King. The wall of the classroom was covered with pictures of the Flying Enterprise, the shipwreck which gripped the nation for about two weeks. There must also have been a picture of the King, because when Mrs Collings came in to tell us that he had died, Rodney Willcocks spontaneously left his seat and kissed his picture. The following year we celebrated the Queen's coronation. The school was patriotically decorated and 2 June was a national holiday.

Miss Drake

Sparkwell School, 1997. Left to right, back: Rebecca Griffiths, Claire Jones, Simon Parsons, Caroline Serpell, Edward Hext, Glenn Taylor, Kadie Hunt, Kyle Rickman, Natalie Dobbs, Katie Greenough;

4th row: William Balsdon, Darryl Cummings, Andrea Smith, Sophie Sherriff, Kieran Ravenscroft, Kirsty Ireland, Amy Ellis, Elizabeth Kelway, Adam Van-Landewyke, Sandie Dobbs, Douglas Brown;

3rd row: Ashley Wilkinson, Naomi Powell, Jamie Swift, Hannah Tucker, Daniel Moore, Abigail Sidebotham, Kurtis Seccombe, Nadine Corrick, Hannah Dunn, Robert Wotton, Toby Mattacott, Adam Chrimes;

2nd row: Phillip Cummings, Hayleigh Walker, Nadine Wilkinson, Victoria Serpell, Sharon Sherriff (secretary), Matthew Rich, Heather Newall (classroom assistant), Sam Kelway, Dee Godfrey (teacher), Mitchell Walker, Peter Soloman (headteacher), Joshua McCammick, Freddy Denman (Chairman of Governors), Donald Brown, Jeannie Lambert (teacher), James Ghillyer, Fiona Murray (teacher), Emma Uren, Norma Skelley (dining helper), Tim Grimes, Lorraine Denny (mealtime assistant), Sam Hearn, Christine Wilton (mealtime assistant), James Reid, Christopher Uren, Sasha Aneer-Ali;

front: Tom West, Zoe Spinks, Duncan Molesworth, James Eddy, Joe Dunn, Michael Chrimes, Evan Grewall, Hannah Tucker, Christopher Jones, Laura Glinn, Alistair Brown.

VE Day Celebrations at the school, 1995. Left to right, back: Simon Parsons, Edward Hext, Kieran Ravenscroft, Tom Wotton, Natalie Dobbs, Rebecca Griffiths, Kirsty Ireland, Claire Jones, Kyle Rickman, Jeannie Lambert (teacher); front: Kurtis Seccombe, Adam Van-Landewyke, Matthew Beaver, Ashley Wilkinson, Darryl Cummings, James Wroe, Douglas Brown, Sandy Dobbs, Sophie Sherriff.

Sparkwell School, millennium photograph.
Left to right, back: Emma Uren, Tim Grimes, James Ghillyer, Toby Mattacott, Josh McCammick, Nadine Corrick, Robert Wotton, Naomi Tucker, Megan Fellows, Donald Brown, Sam Hearn;
4th row: James Wotton, Matthew Ghillyer, Nathaniel Coggins, Nadine Wilkinson, Victoria Serpell, Christopher Uren, Jade West, Kelly Pearce, Tom West, Leah Daniels;
3rd row: Holly Molesworth, Kane Hunt, Alastair Brown, Jake Wood, Jacob Bryans, Laura Glynn, Ewan Grewal, Phillip Cummings, Duncan Molesworth, Ian Keenan, Hannah Tucker, Katie Uren, Cary Gorman, Liam Wills;
2nd row: Kira Coggins, Gemma Parsons, Karen Goshawk, Heather Newall, Christine Wilton, Sue Murdin, Ann Mitchell, Kate Imm, Sarah Mattacott, Norma Skelley, Lorraine Denny, Aaron Hammond;
front: Harry Cobbold, Gabrielle Hardwick, Aidan Corrick, Gemma Gorman, Dean Hammond, Robert Welsh, Hannah Sims, Keanu Coggins, Lucy Matthews, Victoria May, Claire Ghillyer.

In May 1883 application was made for the chapel to become a parish church in its own right and by order in Council in August 1884 it became the Church of All Saints, Sparkwell, and was licensed for 'marriages, baptisms, christenings and burials'.

CHAPTER 5: RELIGIOUS AFFAIRS

ALL SAINTS CHURCH

Divine Service on Sundays was first established in Sparkwell in the village school in 1840 and services were conducted by the Vicar of Plympton St Mary, The Reverend William Coppard. The parish at that time covered a large area of some 10000 acres and included seven villages besides several outlying farmhouses. By 1857 the schoolroom was deemed totally unfit for divine service. It was noted at the time that: 'it is frequently crowded to excess and several persons refrain from attending in consequence of the want of accommodation.'

An appeal was launched in July 1857 to raise funds for building a chapel in Sparkwell and land for this was given by Field Marshal Lord Seaton of Beechwood. There was a long list of subscribers, most of whom were local but there were others from as far afield as London, Oxford, Wells and Windsor. Individual sums varied from £50 to 1 shilling and among the smaller ones was a subaltern's day's pay, 6s.10d. Specific gifts, in addition to the site, included: the granite given by Mrs Praed of Delamore, plate for Holy Communion given by George Sidney Strode of Newnham, the font donated by Baldwin Bastard of Kitley, and the bell given by Henry Hele Treby, who was also treasurer to the appeal.

The chapel building was designed by Mr Roger Elliott, architect of Plymouth, and was built of local stone with granite dressings at a cost of £1169. It was completed in 1859 and consisted of the nave, chancel and south transept. The style was described as 'geometrical or early decorated'. The seats then were open, moveable benches with total accommodation for 240 persons. One of the original chancel windows was in memory of William Braddon of Blacklands (sic) who, it is recorded, 'survived the savage attack of a former domestic for twelve months, but sank under it in 1858.'

The chapel was consecrated on 3l May 1859 when the morning sermon was preached by the Venerable Archdeacon Downall and the offertory amounted to £41.9s.5d. – equivalent to some thousands of pounds today. The Reverend Graham Colborne, Rector of Dittisham, preached in the evening. He was a son of Field Marshal

Lord Seaton and was Rector of Dittisham for no less than 60 years. An early record states that 'ever since the Church has been opened, it has been fully occupied and sometimes to overflowing.'

Services in the new chapel continued to be conducted by the vicars and curates of the mother church. William Coppard died in 1865 and later vicars included the Reverends Merton Smith and Mercer Con.

When the chapel became a parish church in its own right in 1883 (see caption opposite), the parish had a population of 1000 and the church had accommodation for 217 of which 25 were rented seats and 192 free seats. The patrons were the Dean and Canons of Windsor who had acquired both Plympton St Mary and St Maurice together with numerous other West-Country livings under the will of King Henry VIII on 7 October 1547.

The Revd Pender Hodge Cudlip, MA, of Hertford College, Oxford, was installed as the first vicar on 6 November 1884 when the church was consecrated as a parish church by Bishop Temple of Exeter. Pender Cudlip is to this day the longest serving vicar and remained in office until his death in 1911. During his ministry, especially the early part, a number of furnishings and additions were provided. A 'heating apparatus' had already been installed in 1881 and the organ was built by William Tucker of Plymouth in 1885. Three new stops were added the following year. Then came the font, lectern and pulpit, the last donated by the Reverend William Bastard. The private chalice and paten of the now late Revd Merton Smith were given in his memory by his brother specifically for use in the church and a carved oak screen in his memory was dedicated on 30 June 1886.

Much of the work was designed by the Revd Ernest Geldart, a well-known amateur architect and decorator, who devoted much of the latter part of his life to Church art. His major work in Sparkwell was as architect for the vicarage (built 1886) but in the church it included the drawings for the All Saints banner. This was beautifully worked by Mrs Robert Woollcombe and first used in June 1887. Revd Geldart designed the brass cover for the font and also produced drawings for a carved oak litany box and for the carvings on the

❧ CHOIR ❧

Above right: *Joe Collings, a choirboy for 75 years at All Saints, who began singing in the days when choirboys had to serve an apprenticeship.*

Above: *The choir in 1960. Women were not allowed to join the choir until 1960. Left to right, back: Raymond Cooper, Richard Bradford, David Thorrington, John Jones, David Jones, Jennifer Thorrington, Gillian Bradford, Fred Cooper, Joe Collings; 3rd row: Shirley Downing, Yvonne Nelder, Rosemary Reynolds, Kay Phillips; 2nd row: Michael Knight, ?, Michael Jones; front: ? Reynolds, ?, Beverley Stevens, ?, ?.*

Left: *Procession led by the choir at Sparkwell in 1945.*

Sparkwell Choir, 1944. Left to right, back: Fred Cooper, Joe Collings, William Collings, Mr Knott, Revd Knight Adkin, Mrs Hooper, ? Mashers, Arthur Lee, Albert Tracy, George Lee; middle: Denis Tucker, Albert Rendle, Norman Lee, Gerald Tucker, Norman Collins; front: William Hooper, ?, Gordon Steele, David Anstey, John Rendle, William Miller, Michael Anstey, Jim Lardeaux, William Gulley.

pulpit, both of which were erected by E.L. Luscombe & Son of Exeter.

Half an acre of land was donated and laid out as a burial ground by the Woollcombe family of Hemerdon. This was duly consecrated on 23 November 1888 and the first burial took place on 9 February 1889. The granite pillars and iron gate of the cemetery were again designed by Revd Geldart. In 1895, authorisation was obtained for a new choir vestry to replace the use of the south transept. It was built at the north-west corner, where 'a piece of the wall was giving out', at a cost of £86, which was taken from church funds.

In May 1895, Mr E. Sedding (architect) made the following observations:

... the chancel is in a bad condition structurally, apart from its arrangement which is extremely bad... owing to the mean arrangement of the chancel, it is not possible to plan correct seating accommodation. The organ arrangement speaks for itself. The chancel shall be rebuilt for it will inevitably collapse some day.

Bill Thorrington, churchwarden, verger and sacristan 1988–96.

A fund was started but only £177 had been collected by October 1902. The vicar then published a wider appeal for funds and further appeals were made in November 1903, February 1905, May 1906 and finally in April 1907.

Under Mr Sedding's plans the chancel, in addition to being restored, was to be extended by 4 feet in width and 12 feet in length. The plans were duly approved by the Incorporated Church Building Society and by April 1907 a tender for the work from Mr Sam Phillips of Lee Mill (Steve Hoskin's grandfather) for £623.15s.0d. had been accepted. Additional funds were needed for widening the screen, to pay the architect's fees, to take down and re-erect the organ, etc., and the total cost amounted to just under £769. The new chancel, organ chamber, memorial choir stalls, altar rails and credence table were dedicated by the Lord Bishop of Exeter at Harvest Festival on Wednesday 23 September 1908. Offertories at the service amounted to £18.6s.5d. and a profit of £3.17s.6d. was made on harvest teas, bringing the total subscriptions over the sum required. The card advertising the services included the footnote: 'N.B. carriage will meet 10.30 up and 10.50 down train to Plympton, 2/- double journey.'

The windows on the south side of the church are all of clear glass and give the church a bright,

light look, with one exception; the stained-glass windows have Victorian glass. They are fine examples of the period and were all given in memory of past generations of worshippers. Those in the east end of the church all had to be taken down and replaced when the chancel was restored and extended in 1908.

The oldest windows are those in the sanctuary: the one in the north wall in memory of William Braddon and that on the south side in memory of Barbara Treby of Goodamoor who died on All Saints Day 1858. The two long, narrow windows at the west end of the church are in memory of Thomas Were Fox (1860) and Elizabeth his wife (1862) of Fursdon and were given by their children. The window in the Lady Chapel was given by a Mr Hewlett as a memorial to his wife Anne Frances Hewlett who died in 1864 and the window near the pulpit is in memory of Henry Hele Treby (1867) and his wife Blanche (1876) of Goodamoor.

The fine east window behind the altar portraying the Resurrection and Our Lord appearing to Mary Magdalene in the garden was dedicated in 1898 to the glory of God and in memory of John, Lord Seaton (who had given the land for the church), his wife Elizabeth, and James, Lord Seaton, and his wife Charlotte by their descendants.

The victory window in the centre of the north wall was given in 1945 by Lieut Colonel and Mrs Conran of Blacklands to the glory of God and in thanksgiving for victory in the Second World War. The inscription is from the introduction to 'The Desert' by Louise Haskins and the concluding part of the speech quoted by King George VI at the end of his Christmas broadcast in 1939: 'Put your hand into the hand of God. That shall be to you better than light and safer than a known way.'

Besides the screen, reredos and windows there are memorial tablets commemorating the following:

Vice Admiral George Woollcombe of Hemerdon who died in 1865 and his wife Mary Elizabeth (1887).

The Revd George Ley Woollcombe, sometime Rector of Sennen and of St Mewan in Cornwall, who died at Hemerdon in 1902.

William Adam Conran of Blacklands who died in 1893 and his beloved wife Robinan Augusta (1882).

Clockwise
from top:
*Amy and Ernest
Wingett, 1892;
Mr and Mrs Joe Collings (back)
on their wedding day in 1918;
Mr and Mrs Frederick
Tucker, c.1928;
Ida and Charlie Hopper with Ernest
Wingett to their right (bride's father)
and Ethel Collier (sitting), 1920s;
Phyllis Long (née Hill) on her wedding
day to Len Long, December 1948;
Reg and Marjorie Serpell, 1943;
Jane Conran and Captain F.
Woodward, July 1948.*

❧ Parish Weddings, 1898–1986 ❧

Left: *John and Lorraine Denny (née Blatchford) with the Revd Derek Reynolds – this was the first wedding ceremony which he performed at the church. Before the service John had to be quickly baptised as they discovered that he had never been christened and that the wedding would not otherwise be able to go ahead.*

Below left: *Eric and Veronica Exworthy's wedding, June 1958, at Sparkwell Parish Church. Left to right: Roy Exworthy, Sidney Exworthy, Kate Exworthy, Eric Exworthy, Veronica Exworthy (née Trigger), Doris Trigger, Henry Trigger, Josie Trigger; front: Pat Bone, Jacqueline Trigger.*

Below right: *Frank and Lynne Cummings (née Denny), 5 April 1986. Included to the left of the bride and groom are Frank Arthur, John Jones, John Arthur, Tony Knight (organist), Paul Verran, Denise Bevan, Sarah Masey and Andrew Wilton. To the right of the couple are Edith Luckraft, Enid Hext, Lisa Wilton, Claire Verran and Revd Leslie Howarth (at this time the church was in interregnum).*

Bottom left: *William and Doreen Thorrington (née Collings) with Mr and Mrs Joe Collings to their right and Gwen Taylor (Clemo), bridesmaid, 1941.*

Bottom right: *The wedding of Ernie and Gladys Sanders.*

❧ PARISH ANNIVERSARIES ❧

Left: Mr Bill and Doreen Thorrington (née Collings) celebrate their golden wedding anniversary in 1991.

Below: Silver wedding celebrations in 1989 for Pam and Tony James with 'Jethro' at his entertainment venue at Lewdown.

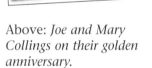

Above: *Joe and Mary Collings on their golden anniversary.*

Right: *Mabel and Harry Roberts on their diamond wedding, 1974, taken when they lived in No.1 Church Hill.*

Left: *Golden wedding anniversary of Ernest and Emily Wingett, who were married on 1 March 1898 by Revd Pender Cudlip.*

Above: *Mr and Mrs Ernest Wingett on their Diamond anniversary remember their wedding day at the Parish Church.*

The central sanctuary lamp was given by Douglas Conran and his family in loving memory of their Aunt Geraldine Conran while the north and south sanctuary lamps bear the inscription: 'Given by many old scholars, 1936, in remembrance of Geraldine Conran, the children's friend 'To the Glory of God'. On the south wall there is a memorial tablet to the nine men from Sparkwell who died in the First World War 1914–18. To this has been added the names of those who fell in the Second World War 1939–45 and most unusually this is a larger number, 11.

The present incumbent, the Revd Freddy Denman, is the 13th vicar since 1884. The complete list, which is reproduced below, is on a board near the font. Among the vicars, Walter Knight Adkin (1942–45) was a Naval chaplain and later Archdeacon to the Navy; Norman Henry Clark (1945–49) was Bishop of Plymouth and Archdeacon; Michael Mann was later Bishop of Dudley and Dean of St George's Chapel, Windsor; Frank Heasman officiated at the special service to commemorate the centenary of the consecration as a parish church in 1984 when Bishop Michael Mann preached the sermon. In the early 1960s fine new oak pews were installed. Many were paid for by parishioners and dedicated to the memory of members of their families. At this time Bill Collings rang the church bell and Eadie Collings was caretaker.

Sparkwell Vicarage

VICARS OF ALL SAINTS, SPARKWELL

1884–1911   PENDER HODGE CUDLIP
1911–17   THOMAS WOODMAN
1917–24   ERNEST ARTHUR MILNE
1924–31   EDWARD HAROLD SMITH
1931–42   FRANK PHILIPS SHORTO
1942–45   WALTER KENNETH KNIGHT ADKIN
1945–49   NORMAN HENRY CLARK
(BISHOP OF PLYMOUTH AND ARCHDEACON)
1955–60   ROYCE WYNDHAM STEVENSON
1960–62   MICHAEL ASHLEY MANN
1962–73   DERRICK WILFRED REYNOLDS
1973–85   FRANK RICHARD HEASMAN
(DIED IN 1985 AT BOVEY TRACY)
1985–87   REVEREND KENNETH NEWING CONDUCTED SERVICE
AT SPARKWELL UNTIL A NEW VICAR WAS IN PLACE.
1987–   FREDDY DENMAN

❧ CHRISTENING ❧ & CONFIRMATION

Below: *Double christening of Sheila Long (left) and Robert Stonehouse (right), 1950s.*

Above: *Confirmation candidates Lynne Denny, Paula Serpell, Nigel Philp, Nigel Denny, October 1981, with Bishop Mann at Cornwood.*

The grandfather and great-grandfather of Yvonne Pinder (née Nelder) outside the wheelwright shop behind the Treby Arms

Mr Jim Nelder and Mrs Ada Nelder with son William (in front of car) outside the Treby Arms before the petrol pumps were installed and (inset) complete with pumps.

CHAPTER 6: SHOPPING

From about 1937 until the 1950s, Mr Newman of Cornwood carried passengers to Plymouth with their goods or to do shopping and would bring them back with their shopping together with any parcels for people in Sparkwell and Cornwood. Before him Mr Short had provided the same service in the 1920s. Mr Short's van was pulled by two horses, although he later took on a motor van and he also took parcels to Plymouth and brought back shopping.

In about 1939 a man used to come around and take orders for the Co-op at Lutton, which would be delivered at the same time as the bread. Between 1943 and 1947 Mr Foster came from Underwoods the grocers at Plympton to take orders, which were delivered later in the week. There was a Co-op shop at Hemerdon and one at Lutton which also sold wellington boots and items of hardware. From 1925 onwards Mr Hooper delivered milk in Lee Mill and Sparkwell (he kept his milk churns down in the well at Sparkwell to keep them cool) and Mrs Taylor and Mrs Dorothy Lee would collect the milk from Conran's at Blacklands. From 1943 until 1949 Mr Spurr the gardener at Fursdon collected the milk from Miss King at Baccamore for the Corytons who lived at Parkside. Eric Exworthy delivered milk from the 1960s to about 1989.

From 1943 Mrs Townsend ran a shop next to the pub and Mr Townsend was the Plympton postman who spent his spare time in Mr Serpell's market garden. Mrs Townsend was a big lady and used to sit in the shop wearing a white apron that was always immaculate. She had cheeses on the counter, from which you could choose the piece you liked and she would cut it to size. The children would buy a halfpenny worth of sweets, which she would put in a paper bag shaped like a cone, and biscuits would be chosen from large tins. Gobstoppers, sherbet dabs and various other delights filled the display in the window (gobstoppers were about the size of a golf ball, and one could easily get stuck in your mouth). If anyone needed a doctor, she would hang a little plaque on her gate with 'doctor' on it. When travelling through the village he would see the sign and therefore knew someone needed his medical attention. After Mrs Townsend, Mr Norman and Vi Nelder ran the shop. Sadly Norman died and later Vi married 'Bubbles' Clague. The shop was sold again in 1979 to Tom and Jean Weatherby.

In 1939 the Post Office was run by Mrs Yabsley with Miss Taylor and was where the post box is now with the public telephone inside the shop; Mrs Mudge, meanwhile, was delivering the telegrams. The Post Office then moved to Churchway and was run by Mrs Tucker who opened for three days per week. It then moved just across the road and Mrs Smith became the postmistress. The Post Office closed in 1999 due to Mrs Smith's illness. Unfortunately, today there is no Post Office in the village and although attempts have been made by the Parish Council to obtain the services of a mobile service to visit, it had proved that this would be too much of a security risk because of the lonely roads and location.

There have been two undertakers in the village: Mr Charlie Nelder and Mr Pillage (who took over from Mr Nelder and who was also the blacksmith and, it is thought, the wheelwright). Mr Charlie Nelder lived opposite the school; his workshop was where 'The Bungalow' is now. The children used to watch him make the coffins. Mr Pillage's workshop was behind the pub (and next door to the pub was his cottage). Some of the older residents of Sparkwell can still remember to this day the smell of the horses being shod and the clang of the hammer as he made or repaired items required by local residents.

From 1943 Mr Bill Nelder took over the Treby Arms after his parents died and he also had a shed next to the Treby Arms, in which he sold hardware items – china, paraffin, methylated spirits, bowls, buckets, cloths and all sorts of other items. At Christmas Bill Nelder would have a display of sweets, chocolates and presents in the Treby Hall (where films were also shown) for people to see and buy. The site of his shed (later the car park for the pub) was once a small copse where the children would play. One game involved

kicking a tin around and one would have to run away and hide in the trees then run out kick the tin and hide away again.

In the 1930s there was a wooden hut in the lane by the Treby Arms where a Mr Dick Lee cut hair. The Corona man delivered soft drinks in Sparkwell and other surrounding villages.

Between 1943 and 1967 Mr Keast the butcher from St Maurice delivered meat, as did Mr Damerel from Colebrook. Fruit and vegetables were delivered in Sparkwell, Hemerdon and Venton by Ken Collings, on behalf of Reg Serpell, and later John Serpell took over this service. Before 1946 Miss King reared and sold Christmas turkeys, geese and chicken and Mrs Kingwell and Mrs Serpell also sold poultry for the festive season.

During 1923 a Frenchman travelled around selling onions, which were strung around the handles of his bicycle. Around 1935 before the Second World War a man used to come with a basket of fish and sell door to door as did another man selling bananas. It is said they walked up from the Plympton station. There was also a man who used to come around selling drapery at each house.

From 1943 until 1950 Mr Shepherd would come from Ivybridge selling oil and all sorts of hardware. Mr Bunker from Houndle Wood sold fish and all sorts of fruit, vegetables and grocery items, Mrs Bowden sold newspapers at Wayside, Sparkwell, and also delivered some. Harry Arthur came from Lee Mill delivering Sunday papers.

Before 1943 and again, after the war, the Co-op coalman used to deliver the coal which was marked at 2s.6d. per cwt bag. From 1939 onwards there was a NAAFI shop in the woods at Beechwood. At the time sailors were billeted there whilst waiting to go overseas and there was also a cinema, hospital and mortuary.

In 1944 Miss King and Marjorie Serpell would walk to Cornwood Station to collect day-old chicks, which were put on the train at Brent from Trotts Hatchers. Around 1948 Lord Seaton gave the ground where the village hall now stands, Reg Serpell ripped it over and removed all the gorse bushes (which were then burnt) and the vicar Revd Stevenson mustered the boys of the village to pick up all the stones. Steven Hoskin from Venton Farm put in the seeds and rolled them down. Later the site became a speedway cycle track.

During the Second World War many of the village people were employed in the clay industry, some worked on the railway and others in farming and agriculture. In the 1940s there was one man (name unknown) who used to ride on horseback from Lee Mill to work at the clayworks at Stockers Pit and another who would ride a bicycle from Lee Mill, leave it at Beechwood Cottage and walk the rest of the way to the clay pits.

During the war there were also numerous jobs to be had at the Wolfram works at Hemerdon. In their spare time, many people worked on the land helping with the harvesting of the hay and corn at farms such as Baccamore. Reg Serpell used to fetch the Land Army girls from Lynham House to help on the farm. Miss King from Baccamore had a stall in the Plymouth market and after the blitz in the Tin Pan Alley where she sold cream and eggs and other dairy produce.

Lewis Locks, who lived at Hemerdon, used to run a taxi business in the village and the surrounding area. People living in the village drew their water from various places; including one site opposite Beechwood Cottage, one in the wall opposite the Men's Club, one on the corner by the entrance to Back Row and another by the Treby Arms.

In the early-20th century, deliveries were common and today mobile shops still go around the villages – including the fish man Mr Sutton (Sea Fresh) and grocery man Mr Phil Smith who visit regularly with their wares. For some half a century ago, however, shopping involved far greater distances than today; Mrs Collings, for example, would push her daughter (later Mrs Thorrington) in the pram from Sparkwell to Plympton and back to obtain fresh bread.

View of the Post Office sited next to the shop in Newtons Row.

CHAPTER 7: IN TIMES OF WAR

THE ROYAL BRITISH LEGION & THE ARMED SERVICES AT SPARKWELL
by Gordon Chudley

At a meeting of ex-servicemen held in the school building on Monday 11 July 1932, Sparkwell branch of the British Legion came into being. (This organisation did not become 'Royal' until the 1970s.) The founder members included Lord Seaton of Beechwood House, Lt Col Conran of Blacklands, and others who will be remembered today by the older residents of the parish, those with names such as Sandover, Collings, Silverlock, Nelder, together with a lady – Miss Yabsley, and the vicar Revd Shorto, from All Saints Church.

Memories of the 'Great War' were still fresh in the mind and frighteningly vivid for some. The casualty list engraved on the war memorial in the village of Sparkwell reflects the private tragedies endured by ordinary people in ordinary families. In this small parish no less than three households mourned the loss of more than one son in the carnage: there were Herbert and Thomas Bawden, Fernley and William James, and George and James Ryder.

In those days there was no Department of Social Security and financial relief for the inevitable victims of war was most inadequate. These men of Sparkwell were well aware that they were the 'lucky' ones who had returned from war physically unscathed and they would have felt themselves duty bound to help those who were still suffering from their ordeal. This was the principal reason for forming a British Legion branch in the locality.

At that inaugural meeting the annual subscription for all members was fixed at 2s.6d., a not inconsiderable sum when a man's earnings averaged between £2 and £3 each week. Meetings were held very frequently in those early and enthusiastic days, and very successful dances, whist drives, socials and coach trips were organ-ised for branch members and villagers. In the days before television there was little else to break the tedium of work-a-day life in the parish; conse-quently any village function was well attended. The branch members held their meetings at a number of different venues in Sparkwell village;

the school, Beechwood House, Treby Hall, Blacklands (Welbeck Manor) and the Men's Club.

Throughout the 1930s the branch prospered and continued its work of raising money to further the charitable aims of the British Legion. But the dark clouds of war were gathering yet again, final-ly to burst over Europe in September 1939. In December of that year, the branch committee debated whether or not to hold the usual Christmas party. The scarcity of food was worsen-ing and there would be few luxuries to place before the children. Finally it was decided that the party ought to go ahead but in a modified form. The event was held in Treby Hall and the headache of organising the refreshments was given to Mrs Conran, the wife of the Chairman. She was not, of course, present at the meeting. She was only a woman after all!

Bill Thorrington.
Main: *Dr Glanville, Chairman of Devon Royal British Legion.*

Sparkwell Home Guard, outside the Treby Arms, 1940. Left to right, back: Ken Hurn, G. Muttram, Bill Collings, Bill Collings senr, Basil Stephens, C. Taylor, C. Collings, Tom Williams, H. Steele, A. Palmers, W. Kitts, Risdon Rowe, G. Mumford, Ned Honey, Tim Collings, Stan Bowden, G. Townsend; front: Dolphus Tallamy, Fred Pengelly, 'Keysie' Collings, Watty May, Alf Collings, N. Nelder (on motorbike), Stan Sandover.

Sparkwell Home Guard. Back row includes: ? Kingwell, ? Oxenham, ? Westlake, George Lee, Alfred Lee, Stan Tall, ?, Bill Collings, Charlie Serpell, Leonard Gulley, Steve Hoskin, Joe Collings, Alf Collings, Harry Masters; left to right, middle: S. Clemo, Harold Reed, Ned Honey, Bill Chapman, Tim Collings, Adrian Palmer, Stan Sandover, Bill Nicholson, Reg Short, Tom Matthews, Bob Phillips, George Townsend, Reg Serpell; seated: Col Conran, Lt Wheeler, Major Bull; front: Charlie Miller, Archie Phillips, ? Wilks, Les Mutton, ? Hunt, ? Reed, Ron Barker, Reg Lee, Ted Lardeaux.

Top: *Royal British Legion, Sparkwell branch at the dedication of the new branch standard, 11 July 1982.*
Above: *Left to right: Gordon Chudley, Bill Thorrington, Jack Harvey and speaker at a Remembrance Day lunch, 2001.*

During 1940 and 1941 committee meetings became few and far between. The parishioners of Sparkwell had other more pressing matters on their minds. After the shock of Dunkirk, the enemy invasion of these islands became a very real possibility. One of the measures devised by Sir Winston Churchill to combat what was seen then as a most immediate peril was the introduction of the LDV (Local Defence Volunteers), later known as the Home Guard.

The LDV might best be described as a citizen army of men who were able bodied, of any age and of all walks of life, usually led by a retired Army officer. At first they had no uniforms apart from an arm band proudly embroidered with the letters LDV, and they were given no firearms. These men armed themselves with anything they could find that might pass as a weapon – pitchforks, clubs, staves, the occasional private shotgun – anything in fact that an ingenious mind might devise. Eventually they were issued with the familiar Army uniform of the period, and were equipped with the standard 0.303 Lee Enfield rifle and bayonet.

Sparkwell Company of the Home Guard was part of the 15th Devon (Plympton) Battalion commanded by Col W.D. Conran who lived at Blacklands (now Welbeck Manor). The Battalion comprised six companies; Sparkwell, Wotter, Cornwood, Ivybridge, Elfordleigh and one other. The region for which the Battalion was responsible included urban areas, villages, hamlets and open moorland.

Sparkwell Company was made up of about 40 men commanded by Major W. Ball assisted by Lieutenant F. Wheeler. (The picture of the unit was taken in 1945 outside the Parish Church in Sparkwell, shortly after they had attended a Church parade.)

The War Office was aware that there were numerous enemy espionage agents, known as 'The 5th Column,' operating in cells throughout the country. In the event of an invasion their job was to disrupt communications, cut the railways, damage the public services and to cause general mayhem in the British war effort. The Home Guard was deployed to counter this threat.

The wolfram Mine at Hemerdon was considered to be at risk from sabotage, so a contingent of men from the Sparkwell Company was always on duty to protect it. The ore from the wolfram mine contains the rare metal tungsten used to harden steel, a characteristic which made it essential to the manufacture of wartime munitions. Another obvious target for saboteurs was the railway viaduct at Slade, the protection of which was the duty of the Cornwood Company (see *The Book of Cornwood and Lutton*, p.133).

The vastness of Dartmoor presented a particular problem for the Home Guard. The enemy might consider the moor to be an ideal place on which to drop paratroopers, espionage agents, or others engaged in the general disruption of the war effort. To frustrate this threat a mounted platoon was set up, based at Elfordleigh, also a part of Major Ball's command. The horses were provided by Arther (Dibby) Halling and were stabled in Plympton near the George Hotel. The moor patrol, fully provisioned for a six-hour tour of duty, would set off before dawn. Apart from its personal firearms, the patrol also carried explosives. In the event of an invasion the men might be required to blow bridges, block roads and generally impede an invading force. On occasion the patrol was sent to locate and pick up the crews of enemy bombers shot down by the anti-aircraft defences of Plymouth. The moorland patrol eventually became known affectionately as 'Dibby's Lancers'.

In October 1942 Sparkwell Village attended the funeral of one of its own – Leading

Left: *John King (far left), who lived at Baccamore, during the First World War.*

Below: *Robert Clague during the First World War.*

Aircraftsman Frederick Reed. At that occasion the Chairman of the Sparkwell British Legion branch read the eulogy. In April 1944 a parcel of food and some cigarettes were sent to Private Reginald Reed, a prisoner of war in Germany and brother of Frederick. At least Reginald's family had the consolation of knowing that this son was alive. Before the war had run its course yet another family grieved for two of its sons – Earnest and Harold Cox.

In 1942 a rest camp for Naval personnel was set up in the wooded area immediately south of Sparkwell Village. The camp, commanded by Lieut Whitworth, was primarily intended to provide a period of rest and recuperation for the survivors from ships that had been sunk by enemy action. When this period of rest was over, the men would be sent back to sea in other vessels to continue the fight. The camp consisted of about 20 Nissen-type huts for the living quarters, a NAAFI canteen which also served as a cinema, or on occasion a dance hall, and a brick-built sick bay.

The cinema was open to the villagers at no cost and would have provided a welcome diversion for them. The influx of scores of young men into the community was certain to have an impact on the residents living in the immediate vicinity of the camp, in particular on the eligible young female population. Also, no doubt, the takings behind the bar of the Treby Arms would have shown a substantial increase. At a branch meeting of the British Legion in June 1942 it was decided to supply the Naval camp with two copies of every issue of the organisation's bi-monthly journal.

In 1943 the Americans arrived and were billeted in tents on the lawns of Hemerdon House. In that year Sparkwell branch suddenly seems to have become fired with a new enthusiasm after almost three years of relative inactivity. At about the same time a musical quartet calling itself 'The Sparklets' was formed by four young people of the parish: John (Jumper) Collins (banjo), Harold Reed (drums), Percy Bickham (violin) and Miss May Blatchford (piano). Once again Sparkwell branch began organising dances and socials at which The Sparklets eagerly gave of their musical talents. At these events American soldiers were much in evidence, often outnumbering the sailors from Beechwood Camp. As an indication of the success of these functions, the 1943 St Valentine dance made a profit of £7.15s.0d, whilst the Easter dance made £4.9s.0d. When one considers that the entry tickets cost 1s.6d. these profits were quite substantial.

The year 1943 ended with the now customary Christmas party held in the school on 29 December. Again poor Mrs Conran was 'shanghiad' into organising the catering, this time for 150 guests! One is forced to wonder whether she exercised some hold over the local purveyors of rationed food, or whether she wielded some quasi-legal influence upon the catering departments of the various military establishments set up in the area! The Americans were always a soft touch as the local children soon discovered, for they did not go short of chocolates and sweets as did their confederates in other parts of the parish who were forced to make the best of their meagre 2oz per week ration. During the war years, the Americans and the Canadians apart, many other nationalities of military personnel came to these shores: men from Poland, France, Australia and New Zealand to name only a few. Near Chaddlewood House, now surrounded by a housing estate, a camp for the turbanned soldiers of the Indian sub-continent was established. Although these men, accompanied by their mules, were frequently encountered on the roads of Sparkwell Parish, they were rarely, if ever, seen at any of the local social functions. A half century ago it was understandably difficult for the local population, many of whom had never before seen a coloured face, to accept a culture so very different from their own. Indeed many of the local womenfolk were unreasonably afraid even to meet these soldiers along the road.

As the year 1944 dawned, the tide of war was beginning to turn in favour of the Allies. Wartime life in Sparkwell continued in reasonable harmony with the thousands of British and foreign troops billeted in and around the village. Dances, socials and cinema shows continued to be popular. But rumours of the '2nd Front' were being whispered abroad. In late May and early June, large numbers

Above: *The last dance to be held in the Naval camp at Beechwood. Those present include: Barbara Cooke, Eileen Exworthy, Vera Exworthy, Joe Bull, Mr Hirons, Nancy Hill, Pam Lardeaux, Barbara Roberts, Rose Couch, Ted Lardeaux, Cmdr Whitworth (in charge of camp), Revd Alan James, Suzanne James, Mrs James, Jane Conran, Col Conran, Jack Couch, Muriel Couch, Marjorie Lee (?), Gordon Steele, Mr Steele senr, Mrs Roberts, Harold Reed, Grandpa Collins, Mr Mudge.*

Right and below right: *A plane crash lands in a field at Mount Pleasant, 1940s.*

Bottom: *National Registration Card of Frederick E. Tucker, dated 2 August 1940.*

of American military vehicles began moving into the parish. The build-up continued until many roads and lanes were packed with a multitude of war vehicles. It became ever more difficult for the local population to move about. Abruptly, during the night of 5–6 June, the military presence disappeared! The invasion of Europe had begun. The residents of Sparkwell had the place to themselves once more.

With the departure of the invasion troops the parish's active part in the war effort came to an end. Sparkwell branch of the British Legion continued to organise social events for the parish and in January 1945, Treby Hall, an old wooden-framed corrugated-iron structure situated behind the village pub, was permanently rented from Mrs Nelder and used as the branch headquarters. A piano was bought for £30 and duly placed in the hall. Obviously the members of Sparkwell British Legion had great plans in mind for future social occasions. (Treby Hall was demolished in the late 1970s.)

PEACE

In May 1945 the German war ended. A dance was held to celebrate the event and to welcome Private Reginald Reed on his return home from a prisoner-of-war camp in Germany. Hostilities having ceased, the country as a whole began the long process of returning to peacetime routine. The thousands of conscript soldiers came home to be de-mobilised and to take up civilian life once more. Rationing would remain in force for another six years before food and clothing could be bought without one having to surrender precious coupons. Church bells could ring out their message once again without causing panic.

At a branch Committee meeting in March 1946, it was decided to pursue the idea of building a community hall in Sparkwell. By fortuitous circumstance the Beechwood Naval rest camp was shut down later that summer, and in consequence the hospital building it contained became of no further use to the Navy. In March 1948 the building was offered at no cost to the British Legion in Sparkwell. The offer was, of course, eagerly accepted.

Whilst the remainder of the camp had been constructed of temporary Nissen huts, easily built and easily dismantled, the hospital was conventionally built in brick with all the domestic facilities installed. After survey the building was valued at £7000, a very substantial sum at the time, and in order to make it suitable for the use of the local populace as a community hall, a number of alterations were planned, to be carried out at a cost of £300.

POST-WAR BRITISH LEGION

At the time, Sparkwell branch Committee included Capt. L. Silverlock (Vice President), Maj. J. Silverlock (Vice Chairman), and Mr H.W. Hirons (Secretary). To raise the sum of £300, lengthy and long-winded negotiations were conducted between these gentlemen, British Legion Headquarters and a number of financial institutions. Sadly, despite all their efforts, these discussions came to nothing and in March 1950 the branch Committee were forced to admit defeat and the project was dropped. The building was left to fall into dereliction. It became a playground for village children and the haunt of erstwhile young lovers. It was finally demolished for safety reasons, in the early 1980s.

Throughout the 1950s and '60s the branch continued to flourish under the leadership first of Lord Seaton and then of Mr Humphrey Woollcombe, both serving in the office of branch President. On the death of Mr Woollcombe in 1969, the office of President was discontinued. Mr William Thorrington was elected branch Chairman in 1961 and continued in that post till 1989. In those years the branch boasted some 50 to 60 members. There was always a party at Christmas time and a coach trip in the summer.

It is interesting to note that in almost every one of his annual reports during the branch AGMs, Mr Woollcombe emphasised the need to recruit young people. At the time of writing the Royal British Legion is desperate for young members to join its ranks. In the foreseeable future, as the years take their inevitable toll, the Legion must fade into history. Mr Woollcombe was ahead of his time.

EXTRACT FROM THE DIARY OF LIEUT ROBERT WOOLLCOMBE, ROYAL MARINE ARTILLERY, 12 MARCH 1859

Robert's ship, the Paddle Frigate HMS *Retribution*, was in harbour at Plymouth under orders for the Far East and Robert had taken a few days leave at Hemerdon. His father was a Plympton magistrate and his meeting would presumably have taken place there. If so, he would have been coming in from the west by the main drive, and Robert must have been leaving by the lower drive on his way to the Beechwood siding to catch his train:

Received orders for the Pacific, went home and at 6 o'clock while at dinner, William rushed into the room to say I was sent for as the ship was ordered to sea that night. My father was away at the Magistrates meeting so I waited until the last moment. At last drove off to catch a train. When halfway out the lawn saw him come in the other way, hailed him and he galloped up and with a hearty shake of the hand and a "GOD BLESS YOU MY DEAR SON" which I well remember (although this is written May 31st) I drove off with a cigar in my mouth as a consoler. I suppose until the ship does not quit the station for the best part of four years. The wise ones say we shall not be out two years. Time will show. Got into Plymouth, did a little shopping in an awful hurry met my servant at Aunt Sarah's, Princess Square, had a cup of tea and went off finding of course the ship would not sail that night and the next day it blew hard and foul.

LETTER FROM GEORGE WOOLLCOMBE TO HIS UNCLE HENRY AT PLYMOUTH

H.B.M.S. TONNANT JANUARY 26TH 1815
OFF CHANDELEUR ISLAND.

My Dear Uncle,

As my letter to my father may probably miscarry, by writing to you I have a double chance of one coming to hand, it is merely to tell you not to be alarmed at seeing my name returned among the wounded, for tho' I shall be reported slightly, I know it would cause considerable alarm if you did not hear from me at the same time. General Lambert's despatches will no doubt give you a full account of our unfortunate and unsuccessful attack of the enemies' lines before New Orleans. I was wounded on the opposite side of the river, by means of a Canal which had been cut from Blind Lake where our boats were into the Mississippi the Barges and Cutters of the fleet were brought into the river and took over 85 Regt. under Col. Thornton, the Marines and two divisions of Seamen.

I was attached to the 1st division, tho' there were but six men belonging to the Tonnant, all the rest belonged to the [diary illegible here] ... were sent over to take some batteries which the Yankees had thrown up and which considerably annoyed our camp and it was also intended to divert their attention whilst the principal [?] attack was made on the other side. We easily succeeded in taking the 1st battery but at the 2nd we met with a good deal of opposition. 85th and Marines went round by a wood, and 1st division of Seamen (2nd were not up in time) were brought up a road in face of the battery where there were two carronades pointed towards us firing round and grape beside a number of men with rifles... we were in a pretty hot fire. I was standing close to Captain Money when he was wounded, and very soon afterwards I received a shot across my left toes, which hurt me so little that I was going on when about a minute afterwards I received another just above the ankle of the same foot: I walked about half a minute afterwards and then was obliged to sit down. I am happy to say that both are very slight and that the bone is not at all touched. I had another ball through my trousers of the same foot a little above the other, which did not touch the skin, so that I think myself a very lucky fellow not to lose my leg. I am now getting on famously and hope in a short time to be able to walk about, as I have now been talking a long time about myself I dare (say) you think it time I should change the subject. I will begin by desiring you will remember me to my grandfather and tell him that tho' at a distance I remember that it is his birthday and that I hope it was passed in the same manner it used to be, as I have not heard from home since the beginning of September I do not know whether you have yet? William with you or not, but I hope he is... I received a very kind letter from Admiral Bedford, if you see (him) I will thank you to thank him for me. All the army are now re-embarking and it is said that we are going to attack Mobile but I believe no one but the Admiral and General know, an [?] exchange of Prisoners has been agreed on which [?] I think does not look like another attack. Some even think that the troops will be landed at another Place and another attack made on New

Orleans, I hope it is true and that it will be taken, as the people of England will not like it at all, so many men being killed and wounded and nothing taken, after so many splendid victories on the Continent of Europe. I do not hear anything as to my being made a Lieutenant, but I hope I soon shall be and that very soon afterwards I shall return to Plymouth which I suppose I shall hardly know as there have been so many improvements.

With kind remembrances to all friends at Plymouth I remain My Dear Uncle your affect. Nephew
George Woollcoombe

P.S. If Edward Jago is still with you do not forget to remember me to him. Should you write to me (which I hope you will) direct to flag [?] ship as a three decker is coming out and Tonnant is going home.

WAR COMES TO SPARKWELL
THE FORMATION OF 'SPECIAL OPERATIONS UNIT 203'

The following article was edited by Josh Dalton with the kind permission of Mr Andrew Wotton senior and Mr Richard Wotton.

Shortly after the outbreak of war, Mr Richard Wotton of Great Stert Sparkwell was seconded to a special unit known as '203 G.H.Q. Auxiliary Unit' formed by the then War Minister Winston Churchill under the local command of Captain Falcon of 'Slade'.

He was given the initial rank of Corporal which was then confirmed to Sergeant at an early stage. His younger brother Andrew Wotton volunteered at the same time and they were enlisted on 14th August 1940. It was to be clearly understood that this was not a Home Guard unit and that they would not receive any public recognition as this was to be known as 'Churchill's Secret Army.' They were specially trained in the art of sabotage, guerrilla warfare and concealment, then armed with sophisticated weapons and explosives and in the event of invasion could expect a very short life expectancy.

Indeed as a secret force they would would have received no mercy from the enemy in event of capture. Their existence was unknown even to the Police and on more than one occasion members of this unit were mysteriously released from arrest following a phonecall to a special number in Whitehall. A secret bunker was dug on Hanger Down which was crammed full of weapons, explosives and provisions. The existence of this unit of brave men comprising the officer and seven men remained a closely guarded secret until the '50 year secrecy act' revealed all and tribute was paid to their bravery by the award of a medal.

WI members celebrating the coronation in 1953.
Left to right, back: Elsie Small, Hilda Muttram, Enid Taylor, Emily May, Vi Collings, Mrs Goss;
middle: Mrs Parry, Mrs Bray, Muriel Jeffery, Chrissie Collings, Norah Reglar, Rose Couch, Lily Steel,
Olwen Beable, Mrs Trout; sitting: Olwen Gibson, Gladys Olver, Maud Bennett, Ada Hooper, Dorothy
Lee; front: Heather Olver, Rosemary Taylor.

Sparkwell Youth Club's 1976 entry for Yealmpton Carnival.

CHAPTER 8: GROUPS & SOCIETIES

PARISH COUNCIL

Plympton St Mary Rural District Council registered as a parish in 1884 which included the villages of Sparkwell, Hemerdon and Lee Mill, and the hamlets of Venton, Bottle Hill and Elfordleigh. When the church was built the parish of Sparkwell was duly represented on the Plympton St Mary Rural District Council by two parish councillors. In 1965 Plympton St Mary became part of Plymouth City Council and the village of Sparkwell and its surroundings became a parish in its own right known as Sparkwell Parish Council, part of the South Hams District Council. The first Chairman was Mr Hooper, a local farmer and dairyman supplying the village with milk.

The Parish Council consists of a maximum of 11 elected members and a parish clerk who is usually well versed in council procedure. The main function of the council is to advise the people of the parish about their problems and liaise with the South Hams District Council, particularly regarding planning matters. It has a very important local quality in as much as all parts of the parish (in an area which is quite large) are represented on the Parish Council.

At the time of writing, the present members are: Rosemary Giblett, Chairman; Mrs Sally Fairman, Vice Chairman; Leo Harris; Tony James; Stuart Mitchell, Dennis Root, George Small, Tom Weatherby; David Crawford; Alan Jones. The clerk is Mrs Elizabeth Groom.

Parish Councillors, 2001. Left to right, back: Tom Weatherby, Tony James, Leo Harris, George Small, Alan Jones; sitting: Elizabeth Groom, Sally Fairman, Rosemary Giblett, Dennis Root.

MEN'S CLUB
Leo Harris

The Men's Club was founded on 14 April 1897 by the Second Lord Seaton. It began as a reading room to allow copies of the London papers to be accessible to the villagers, among them the *Gazette* and the *Illustrated London News*. This was a very valuable source of information at the turn of the century, as it was a time of so many changes in society and the facility enabled the community to be aware of the tremendous changes that were taking place beyond the tranquil boundaries of the village. Later, other lighter periodicals were added like *Punch* and *The Field*. The club soon became the centre of sporting activities, including snooker, billiards, darts and table tennis. Cricket appears to have been foremost of the sports enjoyed. Among other activities associated with the club were archery and rifle shooting as well as football. One of the most famous was cycle racing, the well named Sparkwell Spitfires in their black and white insignia showing themselves to be worthy half brothers of Hells Angels!

Whist drives and dances were held, positive proof that the club has always welcomed ladies and indeed could not have survived without their support. From 1939–46 the club was utilised by the Home Guard and more lately the annual horticultural show has taken pride of place as a village get together there, encouraging young and old to share their skills. Handicrafts, cookery and children's miniature gardens are always an attractive feature.

The Men's Club sponsors a different charity each year. Recent benefactors include Guide Dogs for the Blind, Diabetic Society, Talking Newspapers and Pockington Home for the Blind. The club has been linked to many groups in the village and has always been a part of village life. It is unique in that it mirrors the changing social life through the years. At our centenary dinner we had two members who had attended our jubilee celebration dinner, Ken Collings and Sydney Tucker, two long-serving members. The club owes a great debt to certain families in the village, e.g. Collings, Nelders, Sydney Sandover (who was treasurer for over 50 years), Leo Harris (Chairman for 17 years),

MOTHERS' UNION

Left: *Mothers' Union outing to Cotehele, c.1952.*

Below: *Mothers' Union 'knit in', 1985. Left to right: Joan Knight, Joan Arthur, Margaret Serpell, Enid Hext, Lesley Masey, Doreen Thorrington, Marjorie Serpell, Hilda Wotton, Lorraine Denny, Norma and Clair Skelly, Pat Philp, Vanessa Philp.*

Right: *Sparkwell Mothers' Union, 1940s. Back row includes: Nora Reglar, Mrs Muriel Jeffrey, Gwen Elford, Phyllis Hoskin, Enid Taylor, Gladys James, Mrs Steel, Clara Hooper, Christine Collings, Mrs Muttram; middle, left to right: ?, Mrs Harris, Mrs Perry, Mrs Tucker, Mrs Cundy; front: ?, Mrs Hender, Mrs James (vicar's wife), Mrs Trout.*

Below: *Sparkwell Mothers' Union, 1950s, outside Fursdon House.*

Top: *Men's Club, 1986.*
Left to right: Norman Toomer, George Small, John
Small, Leo Harris, David Small.
Above: *The Men's Club Darts Team, 1992.*

John and George Small. John Mackrell maintained the link with the Seaton family and was our guest of honour. Apart from the centenary dinner we had a coffee morning at Hemerdon House, wine and cheese at Beechwood and a summer 'splash' at Fursdon. We ended the year with a dance at the Jaguar Restaurant (the Wildlife Park).

In 1986 it was decided to build new houses near the club and South Hams Council informed us that the clubhouse would have to be demolished to make way for a new road; they also said it

would not last another two years! We fought them on both counts and the building still stands – just! The road was diverted.

This determination to survive has kept the club going up to the new millennium and hopefully will remain so for future generations to come. The club entered the year 2000 continuing to act as catalyst promoting open tournaments in darts and snooker and a good Christian family way of life. A cross-country run was a great success.

SPARKWELL YOUNG WIVES GROUP
by Lorraine Denny

The group gathers at the vicarage on the last Tuesday of each month. Many people have given time to come and talk or demonstrate on a whole range of interesting subjects, some local and some further afield. Each year an event such as a small fête or cream tea on the vicarage lawn takes place with any money raised going to a chosen charity. We combine with the Mothers Union in attending the 'Women's World Day of Prayer' held each March, and help at events such as coffee mornings. We recently joined in a sponsored knit which had to be done by candlelight because of a power cut in the village.

In 1996, a cheese and wine reunion evening was held to celebrate our 21st anniversary, an event which proved very successful. It was lovely seeing some old friends again. Some time ago it was decided to drop the 'young' from our title and we are no longer affiliated to the Church. Although we are now a very small group we still continue as Sparkwell Wives Group, meeting regularly in the church room. We keep a charity box for the Church of England Children's Society which is donated to them each year. On VE Day we provided a party for all the parish children.

MOTHERS' UNION

The Mothers' Union was founded in 1876 by Mary Sumner in the village of Old Alresford, Hampshire, where her husband, George, was rector. The movement spread quickly, but it wasn't until just after the First World War that a branch was formed in All Saints Church, Sparkwell. The year 1976 was the centenary of the founding of the Mothers' Union and Sparkwell branch members worked kneelers for the church. An altar cloth was made to commemorate the 100 years. The carpet at the high altar was given by members and the silver cross and candlesticks in the Lady Chapel were given when the branch went into abeyance for 12 years. In later years it was formed again, but like many organisations numbers fell (to only ten) and, not being able to make up the members, it disbanded in 2000.

Sparkwell WI
'Today's women working for tomorrow's world'

The WI aims to:
* Improve and develop the quality of life, particularly in rural areas, for women and their families.
* Advance the education of women in citizenship and in public issues, national and international.
* Enable women to work together to put into practice the ideals for which the organisation stands.

The WI was started in 1897 in Canada by Adelaide Hoodless in Stoney Creek, Ontario, because one of her children died as a cause of what she believed to be her own ignorance of hygiene; so she started classes for local women on domestic science. The first WI in the UK met in 1915 at Llanfairpwll, Anglesey. Sparkwell WI was founded in 1937 and by December 57 members had enrolled (subscriptions were 2 shillings). The inaugural meeting was held in the Treby Hall and the founder President was Miss Isobel Anstice (later to become Mrs Sandover) of Goodamoor. Meetings continued to be held at the Treby Hall for a short time, then at the Men's Club and the barn at Goodamoor until 1948 when they met in the new Birchland Hall (an ex-Army Nissen hut).

Members collected foxglove leaves, foxglove seeds and rosehips for medical purposes. Thousands of blackberries were harvested and 123lbs of jam was made in 1942 to raise funds for the war effort.

In 1945 a choir was formed with Mrs Olver and Mrs Hooper conducting and acting as pianist respectively. During the war invitations were issued to Beechwood camp for ten Americans and ten sailors to join members for social occasions.

In 1947 a concert was organised to raise funds for WI Denman College for which the entry was one shilling. Mrs Hooper played the piano, Mr Collins was on banjo and Harold Reed played drums. The first WI harvest supper was held on 23 October 1956 when members paid 1d. towards the cost of the meat (cooked by Mrs Jeffery and Mrs Pummell). At the time of writing the President is Mrs Heather Harvey.

Sparkwell Women's Institute
Millennium Service
6th September 2000 All Saints, Sparkwell
Rev. Fr. F.G. Denman

Hymn

And did those feet in ancient times
Walk upon England's mountains green?
And was the Holy Lamb of God
On England's pleasant pastures seen?
And did the countenance divine
Shine forth upon our clouded hills?
And was Jerusalem builded here
Among those dark satanic mills?

Bring me my bowl of burning gold!
Bring me my arrows of desire!
Bring me my spear! O clouds unfold!
Bring me my chariots of fire!
I will not cease from mental fight,
Nor shall my sword sleep in my hand,
Till we have built Jerusalem
In England's green and pleasant land.

Top: *The WI in 1994.*

Second from top: *WI at the opening of the Birchland Hall, 1948.*

Above: *Clearing out the hall before it was sold, September 1981. Left to right: Heather Harvey, Enid Taylor, Gwen Roberts, Florrie Mudge.*

Left: *programme for the millennium service.*

Far left: *At Anthony House, Torpoint, 1965.*

Halloween party, c.1983. Left to right: Sarah Massey, Jane Verran, Lisa Wilton, Denise Bevan (sitting), Samantha Case, ?, David Wills, Claire Verran, ?, Adam Webb, Andrew Wilton, Andrew Gregory, Leighton Randle, Sarah Wills, Christopher Ashworth (bending), Richard Wilton.

YOUTH CLUB 1959–62

Vicar Michael Mann arrived in Sparkwell in 1959 and one of the first things which he did was to start a youth club for the young people of Sparkwell, Hemerdon and Lee Mill. The club met once a month and alternated during winter between the three villages. It attracted youngsters from Plympton, Shaugh Prior and Cornwood with a fairly regular attendance of 20–30 young people.

It was during the summer months that the club took off; once a month a family service in Sparkwell Church was held at the close of which a coach would be waiting outside to take the youngsters down to the private beach at Mothercombe which Mrs Milday-White kindly allowed them to use. The youngsters would take a packed lunch and around 4p.m. they all piled back into the coach and returned to Sparkwell for evensong. After evensong the youngsters went down to Sparkwell School where they danced and jived until 10p.m. before returning home. This was a very popular event and there used to be between 30 and 40 youngsters involved during the day.

Revd Mann was greatly helped in the venture of the club by a number of people from the villages, especially the Thorringtons of Sparkwell,

the Harveys of Langage and the Knights of Plympton plus others.

Although no pressure was put on the youngsters, making attendance at church before and after the summer outings was a condition for a seat on the coach. It was the Church youngsters that formed the backbone of the club and it was they who brought in a number of their friends, some of whom became confirmation candidates, choristers and servers. At that time the facilities of the youth club were extremely limited. In Sparkwell itself there was only the aged British Legion wooden hut as the use of local schools was bound up with regulation and caretaker's hours.

Mr Mann was only the vicar for three years, as in 1962 he was prevailed upon to return to Nigeria where he served as District Officer for nine years prior to his ordination. In those days vicars were not paid a great deal and his wife took in overseas students to assist with the family budget. Two students came from Kuwait and after a few days at the vicarage they sent home a telegram asking to be sent elsewhere, giving their reason for this request: 'there is no funning in Sparkwell'! Mr Mann on the other hand, recalled: 'I always thought there was plenty of 'funning'.'

Babes in the Wood, *1999. The picture includes: Ann Tremain, Caroline Serpell, Sarah Harris, Sylvia Serpell, Margaret Harris, Wendy Matthews, Paula Serpell, Tony James, Vanessa Philp, Peter Tremain, Martin Vincent, Peter Sullivan, Cheyanne Daniels, Laura Glinn, Leah Daniels, Naomi Tucker, Hannah Tucker, John Halloran, Ellie Glynn (sitting on lap), Freddy Denman, Sarah Wills.*

An early village play or May Day celebration at Birchland Road. The picture includes: B. and Maureen Hewins, Kath Downing (née Mortimore), Rosemary Taylor, Jean Western, Brenda Sowden, Pam Lardeaux, Phyllis Read, Norman Nelder, Derek Reglar and Charlie (?) Collings.

PLAYGROUP

Playgroup's Christmas party, c.1972. Left to right: Nicholas Allen, Nigel Philp, Karen James, Peter Watts.

In the mid 1960s Mrs Jean Farnham, following a consultation with Miss Logan, a health visitor, decided that there was a great need for a pre-school playgroup in Sparkwell, both for children to develop social skills and prepare them for Primary School and for the mothers to have a morning off to shop or do other jobs knowing that their children were being looked after. There was an enormous amount of red tape; so many square feet were required per child, there needed to be toilet facilities, etc. With a lovely group of mums, including assistants Glenda Denny and Sheila Tapper, the playgroup had many planning meetings in the schoolhouse and with grants from the village trust and the county, together with help from the school, the group eventually opened for two mornings per week in the Men's Club with children aged between two and four upwards. The milk would be warmed for the children on the old stove which was kept going by Joe Collings (who also used to iron the snooker table flat for the Men's Club!). There was a rota of mums to help at each session, arriving early to sweep the floor of cigarette stubs, put away the table-tennis tables, then set up the activities, including sand and water.

One of the highlights of the four years during which Mrs Farnham ran the playgroup was a project with the Ivybridge School woodwork department to design and make a climbing frame which would cost no more than the price of the wood itself. In the event it was given as a gift, presented to a small group who travelled in a mini to be presented with it. The return journey from Ivybridge with four in the car and the climbing frame on the roof rack was hilarious and it was a godsend there were no police cars around.

Before Mrs Farnham left she ran a course for future playgroup leaders in Yealmpton School. This was a ten-week course, one evening per week. Mothers also had to have chest x-rays and medicals. Some Sparkwell mothers (Ann Tremain and Lorraine Denny) attended and passed with flying colours. The playgroup ran two mornings per week and later Pam James took over as leader with Pat Philp as assistant and May Howard as treasurer. When Pam left Pat Philp took over and Kay Wills and Rosemary Lowry kept it going after that. Mrs McCarthy and Mrs Hamlyn acted as Chairpersons for meetings, etc.

OVER 60s' CLUB

The Sparkwell Over 60s' Club first met on 25 November 1953 in the Birchland Hall, a meeting arranged by the Sparkwell group of the Red Cross. The Over 60s' Luncheon Club (as it became known) now meets once per month.

SPARKWELL AMATEUR THEATRE CO.

Father Freddy Denman, together with a group of keen parishioners, decided in 1996 to draw the community together for a pantomime which would be put on in the village hall. *Goody Two Shoes* was the first show and after casting for parts there were various tasks to be undertaken. The show date was approached with great trepidation but the worries and fears were unfounded and the pantomime was a great success.

The next show, *Aladdin*, as with all productions saw some of the original members replaced by new ones – as well as a new and experienced producer. Exotic scenery also helped to set the ball rolling and the result was another good panto. In 1999 *Babes in the Wood* was selected as the chosen piece which was particularly interesting as several members of the cast, known for years locally, were watched as they blossomed dramatically into their respective stage characters. It is hard to believe that all could without embarrassment take to these roles and appear in front of an audience – again the panto another success.

In 2000, *Dick Whittington* was staged, again with new faces among the cast and, sadly, with some of the old ones missing. The show was cast and rehearsed as usual and there were fears that it would never be ready, but it went down very well with the audience. Special acknowledgement must go to Gordon and Bernard Chudley – tireless workers and prop makers, to Ann Tremain for the scenery and to John Halloran the producer. Also to Freddy Denman for being Freddy, Lorraine Denny for ticket sales, Kay Wills for the costumes, Heather Harvey for the music, Carole Wood for the choreography, and of course everyone else who lent a hand, including those back stage.

Babes in the Wood, *1999.*

Above: Fancy dress, May 1973. Children include, in the back row: Jonathan Chudley, Ian Denny, Caroline Vincent; 3rd row: Julian Chudley, Paul Collier, Martin Vincent, Graham Mattacott, Ann Evans; 2nd row: Tina Tremain, Marina Howard, Jeanette Collier, Christine Vincent, Lynne Denny, Brian Mattacott, Julie Clague, Nichola Bailey, Linda Mattacott, Sarah Allen, Nicholas Allen, Craig Needham, Brad Needham, Peter Watts; front: Nicola and Joanne Burns (twins), Bernard Chudley, Louise Tremain, Nigel Denny, Julie Evans, Neil Collings, Sally Cooper, Heather Cooper, Peter Watts.

Top right: Don Laid and Phyllis Long on VE Day.

Above: *Brownies at Blacklands, 1936. Left to right, back: Jean Weston, Phyllis Taylor, Rosina Couch, Joyce Anstey, Phyllis Reed; front: Barbara Anstey, Deirdree Shorr, Muriel Couch, Kath Collins.*

Above left: *Silver Jubilee celebrations. On the float are Paul Dalton, Tracy Exworthy, Jonathan Chudley, Paul Andrews, Andrea Exworthy, Allison James, Karen James, Joanna Lanphee.*

Above: *May King and Queen, 1993, Thomas Denny and Jayne Morris, with attendants Naomi Collier and Stephanie Carlyon. Garth Beer is driving the lorry.*

Left: *Fête at Blacklands, 1975. The children include: Karen James, Tina Tremain, Paula Serpell (behind doll) and, at the front, Sarah Wills, Clare Serpell, Allison James, Clair Skelly, David Wills.*

ALL THINGS FANCY ⚘ DRESS ⚘

In 1981 there were 11 entries from young hopefuls keen to be Carnival Queen. These came from: Heather Denny, Della Munro, Christine Vincent, Hilary Hanna, Ann Luckraft, Helen Smith, Linda Mattacott, Lisa Ridd, Shirley Hunt, Angela Chamberlain and Ruth Denny. The winner was Helen Smith of Keepers Cottage, a shepherdess at Newnham Home Farm. In 1982 Mrs Olwen Gibson organised the event and entries came from Christine Hare (first place), Donna Bray (second place) and Tina Tremain (third place). After this the event changed to Sparkwell Carnival Princesses.

Above: *Lorraine Blatchford, Elaine Tamblyn, Wendy Hillier, Romaine Broome, Jean Tucker, Carol Gibson, June Moody and Valerie Hall (now Reglar) performing* Lucy Locket.

Left: *Gerald Tucker (vicar) and the Revd Shortall standing in front of an Austin 7.*

Above right: *Silver Jubilee celebrations for King George V. Included are: Roger Bennett (vicar), Mr Downing (at the back), Delcie Lee (girl in gypsy costume) and Eileen Exworthy.*

Above: *Outside Blackland Cottages, c.late 1930s (when the railings were still in situ, before being given for the war effort). Included are Jean Baskerville, Phyllis Taylor, Pam Lardeaux, Gerald Tucker, Norman Lee, Ken Collings, Eileen Exworthy.*

Right: *Lorraine Denny (née Blatchford), aged seven, as a butterfly.*

❧ Brownies ❧ & Guides

Top left: *1st Sparkwell Guides, c.1930.*

Above: *Brownies on Parade, 1936. Miss Ann Conran and Miss Jane Conran were Guiders.*

Left: *Brownie picnic, 1930s.*

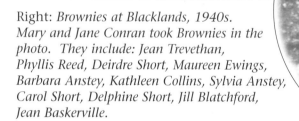

Right: *Brownies at Blacklands, 1940s. Mary and Jane Conran took Brownies in the photo. They include: Jean Trevethan, Phyllis Reed, Deirdre Short, Maureen Ewings, Barbara Anstey, Kathleen Collins, Sylvia Anstey, Carol Short, Delphine Short, Jill Blatchford, Jean Baskerville.*

Above: *Swimming in one of the pits at Lee Moor, c.1930.*

Left: *Jean Weston and Rose Couch.*

1st Sparkwell Guides

by Lesley Masey

The 1st Sparkwell Guides was formed in 1929 by Miss Isobel Anstice and Mrs Gladys Olver, both of Goodamoor, where the Company meetings were held – it is now The Dartmoor Wildlife Park). The Company remained open until the end of the Second World War when it was disbanded.

The 1st Sparkwell was reformed in 1956 by Mrs Margaret Stevenson (wife of the Revd Royston Stevenson) with Mrs Palmer as assistant. This time meetings were held in the vicarage barn and gardens during the summer and at Sparkwell School in the winter. Some of the names, together with notes of their first aid practices were still to be seen on the walls some 40 years later.

Around 1959/60 Mrs Coles took over the running of the company with Mrs McDonald as assistant. For a while meetings were held at Hemerdon Farm, the home of the Scott family (now the home of Paula and Nick West and family). Other meetings were held at Little Stert (Mrs Coles' home). One thing standing out in my mind was swimming in the river behind her house, damming up the river and using rubber tyres for those who could not swim; something that would not be allowed today as we now require a qualified life-saver to be present. Guides also used to swim in the ponds on the moor at one time. On Mrs Coles leaving, Mrs McDonald became guider, with Mrs Van der Kiste as assistant in 1963. She continued to run the company until ill health forced her to retire in 1968. The unit was disbanded as a replacement guider could not be found.

During the years 1954–65, there were times when Sparkwell Guides joined Cornwood Guides. Mrs Phyllis Channing was one of the 1st Cornwood Guiders. A Company was formed in early 1975 by Mrs Pat Burns (now Mrs Ellis) at Hemerdon. Meetings were held at her home in a barn in the summer and in Hemerdon Recreation Hall in the winter. In July of that same year Mrs Lesley Masey became assistant Guider, although this was for a very short time as Mrs Ellis left around 1975/76. As 1st Hemerdon was never a registered company this made it easy for us to move to Sparkwell and re-open the 1st Sparkwell unit on 5 March 1976 in Sparkwell School. On 4 January 1988 we became 1st Sparkwell All Saints Guides.

Over the past years Sparkwell Guides have enjoyed many activities, including crafts, giving service to others and a variety of outdoor pursuits, amongst them climbing, abseiling and a mud assault course to name but a few. A wide range of skills were covered in our programme.

Since 1975 we have had a number of meeting places; Sparkwell School, the vicarage barn and gardens, Sparkwell Men's Club and now Hemerdon Recreation Hall (which is brand new). On one occasion we also used Welbeck Manor (when Hemerdon was being built) and this was a venue that we could have got used to!

Since 1976 we have been lucky in that we have had no change of Guider and only four changes in assistants. Shirley Frame (now Lupton) gave approximately five years' service and Mrs Sue Rendle around three years. Heather Cooper (now Bullen) worked for around five years and Andrea Exworthy ten, whilst Lorna Johnson has been with us for two years so far at the time of writing.

Sparkwell Guides have had a number of Queens Guides, this being the highest award a guide can achieve. These include: Sheila Van der Kiste, Jean Cummings (now MacCormack) before 1968, from 1976–85 there were Lynne Denny (now Cummings), Marina Howard, Georgina Rendle and Heather Cooper (now Bullen), and from 1985–2000 the following achieved the award (now called the Baden Powell Award): Vanessa Philp, Marie Roberts, Clare Skelly, Sarah Wills, Andrea Exworthy, Sarah Masey, Claire Verran, Emma Davenport, Anna Quest, Catrin Blackler, Rachel Smith, Samantha Carlyon, Ceri Dobbs, Jennifer Moore, Catriona Moore, Sarah Harris, Joanne Small, Ann Eastmond, Caroline Serpell and Natalie Dobbs.

Since September 2000 the Baden Powell Award has been known as the Baden Powell Challenge, and guiding sees a whole new programme. We hope more girls will take up the challenges and learn new skills.

Sparkwell Guides, c.1957/58. Lorraine Denny is behind first on the right.

1st Sparkwell Guides reunion at Sparkwell Church, 2 March 1997. Left to right: 1. Barbara Friendship, 2. Pat Friendship, 3. Beryl Jones, 4. Shirley Bone, 5. Mrs McDonald (ex Guider), 6. Sarah Massey, 7. Lorraine Denny, 8. Lynne Cummings, 9. Lorraine James, 10. Vanessa Philp, 11. Kay Wills, 12. Sarah Wills, 13. Chanelle Sullivan, 14. Jennifer Sturdy, 15. Marina ?, 16. Ann Evans, 17. Julie Evans, 18. Heather Bullen, 19. Rose Elliott, 20. Marie Ibbottson (District Commissioner), 21. Deirdree Collings, 22. Florrie Mudge, 23. Shirley Lupton (ex Guider), 24. Marjorie Serpell, 25. Stephanie Carlyon, 26. Kathryn Smith, 27. Ceri Dobbs, 28. Doreen Thorrington, 29. Jill Phillips, 30. Georgina Rendle, 31. Lesley Masey (ex Guide and Guider), 32. Andrea Exworthy (ex Guide and Assistant Guider), 33. Claire Huxtable, 34. Jennifer Moore, 35. Catriona Moore, 36. Natalie Dobbs, 37. Lyndsay Melling.

Sparkwell Guide reunion, 24 November 1976 at Sparkwell. Left to right: 1. Mrs McDonald (ex Guider), 2. Mrs Channing (ex Cornwood Guider), 3. Mrs Roberts, 4. Mrs Gwen Clemo (Guide 1938), 5. Mrs Florrie Mudge (ex Guide 1938), 6. Kay Wills 7. Jennifer Sturdy, 8. Mary Ford, 9. Doreen Thorrington (ex Guide 1930s), 10. Lorraine Denny, 11. Dorothy Blandford (ex Guide 1930s), 12. Alex Brown, 3. Verity Phillips, 14. Hilary Hanna, 15. Jackie Ford, 16. Shirley Frame (Assistant Guider), 17. Jean Jacknall, 18. Heather Cooper, 19. Annabel Hebb, 20. Tracy Bye, 21. Georgina Rendle, 22. Marie Roberts, 23. Sharon McNeil, 24. Nicola Farnham, 25. Lesley Hasey (Guider), 26. Rebecca Legg, 27. Lynne Denny, 28. Marina Howard, 29. Sally Cooper, 30. Julie Evans, 31. Michelle Dawe, 32. Ann Evans, 33. Julie Clague.

CHAPTER 9: SPORTING LIFE

BANGER RACING

From 1985–91 Jason Hamlyn organised banger racing to raise money for Cancer Research. The events were always very well attended with a typical turnout in excess of 400 spectators and 30 entrants. The 'demolition derby' winner of 1985/86 was Mark Polly in his Volvo 'Doctor Death', on which occasion the event was held behind Birchland Road. Louise Tremain as driver and Tony James as her navigator won their heat in the 'powder puff race' and came second in the finals. Banger racing continued after this, but was held at the Newnham Estate.

Over the years the Newnham Estate (owned by the Cobbold family) have arranged many sporting activities, including national rounds of the Mountainbike World Championships, horse trials, carriage-driving trials, banger racing, four-wheel-drive off-road trials and speed events, rally car stages (as part of the S.W. Rally Club Championship) and clay-pigeon shoots to name but a few. The terrain of the estate lends itself to these and many other sports and it is also used each year by the Caravan and Camping Club for a district association meet when caravans from all over England congregate to enjoy their holiday.

SPARKWELL SPITFIRES

In the late 1940s it was decided that a cycle racing team would be formed. A band of very enthusiastic people started to make a track, approximately where the new village hall stands. Trees, bushes, weeds and debris were removed and Reg Serpell with his trusty tractor and implements dug out the basic layout of the track. The volunteers moved in and cleared the area of stones and such like. As one can imagine it took some time to reach completion to the satisfaction of all concerned. The name of Sparkwell Spitfires was adopted and tunic tops had the name and a badge emblazoned on them (these garments being made by Mrs Davies (née Taylor). Team members were Dave Anstey, Gerald Clague, Ron Stonehouse, Bill Gulley, Roy Exworthy, Eric Exworthy, the Rendle brothers, Ivan Hurn, Geoff Foot, Norman Lee, Ken Collings, Dennis Tucker, Ashley Cox and Les Reed.

Team Manager/Treasurer was George Bone and Track Manager was Harold Reed.

Just a few of their opponents included the Colebrook Tigers, Monarchs, Laira Wasps and the Kingsbridge Hammers. Transfer to away matches was provided via a lorry by a Mr Newcombe and a store for bikes was an Anderson shelter near the track.

Top and centre: *Sparkwell Spitfires. Cyclists include:*
Harold Reed, Ivan Hurn, Eric Exworthy, John Rendle,
Ashley Cox, Roy Exworthy, Bill Gulley,
Ron Stonehouse, George Bone senr, Gerald Clague,
Geoff Foot, George Bone junr (mascot), Dave Anstey.
Bottom: *Banger racing, 1986.*

Sparkwell Cricket Club, 1923. Played 21, won 13, drawn 4, lost 4.

Sparkwell Cricket Team, 1928. Left to right, back: ?, William Collings, ?, Sam James, ?, ?; middle: ?, Tim Collings, Joe Collings, Reginald Martin; seated on ground: Leslie Sandover, Mr Stanbury.

CRICKET CLUB

Originated from the Men's Club, the cricket pitch was up on the moor called Big Brake, near Stockers. There was a tin shack in which to store items and Lesley Sandover and Mrs Collings would always supply teas. Every Saturday she would go to Birchland Farm to collect a primus and urn and carry it up to the moor. Doughcake was purchased from Farleys shop in Colebrook and this would be served up with jam and cream. Mrs Thorrington claims that she has never tasted such delicious doughcake since.

Teams would come out from Plymouth. Sparkwell would also travel to the village of Maker in Cornwall. The cricket pitch remained in place until the Second World War.

The first game was played on 17 May 1902 at Sparkwell and the batsmen were:

1. J.H. Cumming (bowled by J.Y. Woollcombe)
2. P.S. Field (bowled by N. Lee)
3. W.P. Parsons (bowled by A. Woollcombe)
4. W.S. Square (bowled by H. Reinold)
5. W.S. Rayne (bowled by H. Reinold)
6. W.R. Audrie (not out)
7. L H. Byfield (not out)
8, 9 and 10 batsmen were: J.K. Fermshire, R.S. Hawker and R.C. Agneur.
E. Lugg also bowled.

Sadly the score is not known. Joe Collings was the wicket keeper and other members included Mr Blatchford and Sid Tucker.

Sparkwell Rangers, Under-13s, 1988–99 season. Left to right, back: Rob McKee, Douglas Brown, Chris McKee, Charlie Keen, Chris Hamilton, Simon Parsons, Tom Wotton, Aaron Blythe-Palk; front: Adam Hawes, Darren Opie, Darryl Cummings, Sam Boot, Peter Hillman, Luke Morley.

FOOTBALL

Earlier in the 20th century a football team was formed in the village of Sparkwell. At that stage the pitch was situated near Venton railway bridge but in later years games were played in the field behind Birchland Road. In the 1970s local youth clubs and organisations held meetings in an attempt to start a friendly inter-club league. Tony James represented Sparkwell Youth Club at these meetings and a league was formed. Alan Randall and Peter Kitts succeeded Tony James.

A very keen group of players played for Sparkwell, among them Stevie Hunt, Jonathan Chudley and Ian Denny. Games were played on the old pitch opposite Newtons Row, where the village hall now stands. Later Devon County Council levelled, enclosed and prepared a playing area where Sparkwell Rangers and the local school now play their games. Mr John Parsons runs the teams of mostly local lads. At one stage Hemerdon (see chapter 12) had both cricket and football teams.

ATHLETIC LIFE

Left: *The Swinging Indian Club's keep-fit group met at the Treby Hall and was run by Mr Day who came from Plymouth. Left to right, back: Derek Reglar, Francis Quest, John Rendle, Michael Anstey, David Anstey, David Barker; middle: Les Reed, Albert Rendle, Tony Jackson, Gordon Steele, Ashley Cox; front: Avril Short, Delphine Short, Pam Lardeaux, Deirdre Short, Amy Rendle, Jill Blatchford, Sylvia Anstey, Bennie Hewins.*

Above: *Sparkwell School Sports Day, 1969. The children include: Trevor Nelder, Graham Mattacott, Linda Mattacott, Jane Tapper, Ruth Denny, Julian Chudley, David Hanna, George Hanna, Peter Kitts, Christine Vincent, Caroline Vincent, Shirley Hunt, Terry Old, Sharon Collins, Nick Friendship.*

Above: *Presentation by Mrs Dorothy Woollcombe at Sparkwell School Sports Day.*

Right: *Sparkwell School Sports Day.*

GYMKHANA AND HORSE SHOWS

These events have taken place over a long period of time. One well-known event is in aid of Cancer Research and is organised by a committee including: John Kingwell, David Honey, Noreen Evans, Mr J. Ebsary, Mrs Christine Cane, Kathy Cane, Mrs Eames, Ms Sue Way and Miss C. Knowles. Committee members really do deserve an accolade for raising the incredible sum of £41 616 over the years for this well-deserving charity and thanks must also be given to Mr J. Colborne-Mackrell, Mrs S. Foster and Mr M. Rendle for allowing their land to be used for these events over the years – also, of course, to the riders for taking part.

TUG-O-WAR

A tug-o-war team was formed in the parish in 1982 and adopted the name Treby Tigers. The team consisted of Jeff Verran, Peter Kitts, Frank Cummings, Mark Polly, Keith Fennel, John Dryden, Malcolm Elliott, Jim (the fish) Collins and Jeff and John (surname unknown). The team shirts bore an emblem and name painted by Mrs Ann Tremain. The team competed at many events with varying results, but were very proud of the fact that they could always 'hold their own' in the celebrations after. At one stage it was decided that a ladies team in identical dress would compete against the men. After a carefully planned amount of cheating, the ladies won!

GOLF

In the late-20th century a golf course was constructed at Blacklands (Welbeck Manor). It consists of a nine-hole course, holes varying in length from approximately 100 to 500 yards. Obstacles include deep-water ditches as well as the normal bunkers and a row of trees between the 5th and 6th holes. The club has created some employment for locals and has unfortunately meant the end for yet another working farm. The course is a public facility and anyone can play after paying green fees. Elfordleigh Golf Course has recently been doubled in length from nine to eighteen holes and this club is by membership only.

OTHER

Various other sports such as badminton, snooker, billiards and darts have taken place over the years and several players have proved themselves to be of very high standard. The Men's Club and Youth Club have done much to encourage these activities. Snooker and darts still take place in the Men's Club with badminton and American line-dancing being held in the village hall. Archery was a sport reserved for the gentry, held on the lawns at Blacklands for those from neighbouring estates.

Top: *Paula Serpell (front) in the junior egg-and-spoon race at Plympton Easter Horse Show on Vealeholme Farm.*
Centre: *Men's Tug-O-War team, 1984/5, taken at Elburton Fair, where they won the event. Left to right, back: John Drydon, Peter Kitts, Malcolm Elliott, Mark Polly, Nigel Hamlyn, Duncan Hamlyn; front: Frank Cummings, Geoff Verran, Nick Wheeldon.*
Bottom: *'Women's Tug-O-War', 1984, in the garden of Galen Way. Left to right: Lynne Denny, Tina Tremain, Sadie Dalton, Angela Chamberlain – poking fun at the men's Tug-O-War for the carnival.*

Various organised shoots have taken place over the years. Villagers and guns would gather each February and spread out to various woods to shoot pigeons, covering all areas so that the birds had no trees to hide in. Clay-pigeon shooting has taken place at several venues, some locals proving excellent shots. Netting rabbits was also popular, at first as a food source and later as a sport. Indeed, an old saying asserts that 'with his vegetable patch and his rabbiting a man could support his family.' Second from left standing is Revd George Ley Woollcombe (1828–1902), fourth from left is John Nicholls (1846–?) and front right is George Arthur Ley Woollcombe (1864–1947).

The hunt used to go through Lucas Wood via a track at the back of 'The Bungalow', the home of Dorrie Cummings. It would then go on to the Treby estate down the woods through the hunting gate and on to the Beechwood and Woollcombe estates. Here the Modbury Harriers meet at Fursdon. Mrs Coryton lived at Fursdon for many years. In 1947 it was purchased by the Crowley family and Cmdr David Crowley (son) resides there today.

Claymoor and Hemerdon Ball (c.1890s) before the mining began. Arnold Olver jumps on the Smallhanger china clay works tip.

Hillside Cottages at Venton (note the five cottages), 1947, and (inset) Roger Bennett playing in the snow in the same year.

Phyllis and David Hill, Mount Pleasant, 1947.

Chapter 10: I Remember When...

Weather

The winters used to be pretty bad and most years parishioners would have to dig out the snow from their paths and the doorways to their houses. In 1947 the snow was very bad. The vicar had a burial and a track had to be cut through the road up to the churchyard. There was just enough room for the tractor to get through with the coffin. Of course after the snow was the great thaw, water cascading like waterfalls down over the hedges. Charlie Serpell's steps to his bungalow had water running down like a waterfall. Buses, lorries and cars got stuck. Another extreme winter was that of 1962/3, which is recalled by Mrs Palmer.

[I remember] coming down to breakfast to discover that during the night we had had such an horrendous snow storm with the snow so high it was impossible to see out of the windows. It was not a good idea to open the back door! The snow was level with the tops of the hedges and we spent all day answering the phone to worried farmers who, like us, were snowed in. The Council cleared one side of the road but many farmers were forced to take their milk to collection points (and a few even had to tip theirs away) as it was impossible to get to their farms.

The snow did not clear up for four or five weeks. People in the village of Sparkwell were lucky because when the men from the Co-op at Lutton managed to get through, carrying a long bath, filled with bread, their regular customers were allowed one loaf – others went without!

Drought was another extreme which caused problems. Mr Peter Tremain recalls the drought that started in May 1976 and, more recently, more extreme weather:

Blacklands Farm was milking 100 cows and the first cut of grass finished. Usually we had a second cut at the end of June, but with no rain the grass did not grow – yields dropped by 25 per cent. Corn was four to six weeks early. The first week in August the wells dried up at Birchland Farm and Smallhanger. We had no water, so had to take the cattle to the clay pits to drink, then bring them back to the farm and feed them hay. One day the cattle broke out of the field and found their own way to the pit and were drinking. It was very hot and dry everywhere.

Rain came around 20 August 1976, which resulted in the fields being white with mushrooms! The weather conditions over the years are getting wetter. Not very much snow the last few years but on 7 November 2000 floods hit southern England and parts of the North were hit badly. Around our parish roads became impassable. Just about all routes back to the village and hamlets were blocked. Ken and Deirdre Collings and Jill and Eric Phillips were stuck in water about 3 feet deep. Luckily they had a mobile phone in the car with them and Jill rang her brother-in-law, John Denny, and together with Frank Cummings he went with the tractor to pull them out, but by the time they arrived they had been rescued by the fire service and John and Frank towed them home with the tractor!

December 2000 was very cold and icy with a splattering of snow and more torrential rain.

Margaret Serpell and Nancy Hill, 1940s.

DOMESTIC LIFE

Old cooking range.

Cooking & Heating

Most people cooked on old cooking ranges, which had to be blackened with black lead. Not very many people before the 1970s could flick a switch and the heating would come on automatically as it does these days. Kindling wood had to be chopped and the fires lit and kept fuelled, which would warm one room only. Some people had fireplaces in the bedrooms and they too had to be lit and fuelled. Frost would appear on the inside of windows as well as the outside.

There were no bathrooms, no inside toilets (at least in the majority of houses) and people had buckets the contents of which would have to be buried. This was 'affectionately' known as 'bucket and chuck it'. Later people advanced to outside toilets with water. Some had streams running underneath the WCs (water closets) which would take away the effluent (including 'Bronco' toilet paper or newspaper cut up for toilet roll).

Large tin baths would be brought in from sheds, usually on a Friday or Saturday night, and placed in front of the fire when warm water would be carried from the kitchen (usually heated in kettles and saucepans). If one's hair had been washed you could not go outside as 'you might get pneumonia'.

Laundry

There were no automatic washing machines 40 years ago and people used a copper instead. In some the water was heated by electricity, but mostly around villages a fire had to be lit underneath to heat the water. The clothes would be rinsed in a tub and then put through a mangle (two wooden rollers and a handle to be turned to feed the clothes through). All of this was very hard work.

Mrs Taylor and Mrs Thorrington shared the copper and they would save up the old stumps of sprouts, dry them and use them for fuel for the machine. It was a cheap way to do the washing as it was only the cost of the soap powder, but lots of elbow grease! Mrs Thorrington also recalled when her father Joe Collings decided he was going to make some cider so he put apples into a pillowcase and put them through the mangle to mash them up. Her mother wasn't too pleased and after all that effort, the cider was no good anyway!

Waste

People were keen on re-cycling back then. Nothing was wasted. Cinders from the fire were used to make paths; paper was used for lighting the fires; greens, eggshells, etc. would make the compost; biscuits would be chosen from a large tin and wrapped up (no fancy cardboard packaging); sweets were chosen from a jar and put into a paper bag; bottles would be taken to shops and vinegar obtained; one kept one's own can for obtaining paraffin; potato peelings would be collected for pig swill and a lot of people had a cobblers 'last' and tap and heeled their own shoes (the leather would be soaked to make it easier to cut, and some people used old tyres to tap their boots). People even used orange boxes for furniture.

Clothes

In Sunday School Miss Conran ran a clothing club (the club was actually started in 1869); the children would take 1d. to Sunday School and she would add another penny to it out of her own pocket. When the money amounted to 8 shillings (40p), Miss Conran would go into John Yeos in Plymouth and get clothing tickets, bring them back and give them to the saver. Mrs Thorrington's mother would take her into Yeos and she would get a new gymslip and two blouses to go back to school with. These would last for a year. Most people before the 1950s made their own clothes with intricate embroidery which involved hours and hours of workmanship.

The caption on the back of this photograph reads: 'May 1942: pretending we're at the seaside.' This is the kind of tin bath which people took inside to wash in.

TREBY ARMS

For many years the Nelder family ran the Treby Arms situated in the middle of the village. The forecourt of the pub once contained two petrol pumps and to obtain petrol a handle on the pump had to be wound. Village youngsters were more than willing to carry out this task and Mr Nelder was always pleased to allow them to do this. He made frequent trips to the store at the rear of the pub. Unbeknown to him he had a small hole in one of his pockets and he wondered why some of the village children followed him every time he went to the store, the children gleefully picking up the odd halfpenny, penny or threepenny piece. One day out dropped half a crown whereupon an eager Dave Barker quickly scooped it up (an amused Dave said he was well worth following that day!).

To the side of the Treby Arms (now the car park) was an area known as 'Little Wood', a well-used play area for the young children. Games played included cricket, hide and seek and a game which involved kicking a tin around where one would have to run away and hide in the trees of 'Little Wood' then run out and kick the tin and hide away again. A hut on the edge of 'Little Wood' housed hardware items such as pegs, paraffin, candles matches, dusters and many more. One wonders what the Fire Safety Officer would make of it today!

To the rear of the Treby Arms, a few yards up the lane, was the Treby Hall. This hall had a great many uses over the years. All types of functions from meetings and wedding receptions to dances took place there. The dances were particularly popular, attracting people from all areas including Plymouth. Dancing was done very often to the sound of local group 'The Sparklets'. Underneath the hall was a garage where Bill Nelder and Eric Phillips parked their vehicle.

The Treby Arms has always enjoyed a good rapport with its customers and when Bill and Trudy Nelder took over this continued. Bill, a colourful character, preferred local trade to passing trade. An event leaps to mind when, one late autumn afternoon, four people called in and ordered spirits and one customer started to play the fruit machine. In the somewhat dim light it was difficult to make out people's features let alone coins taken from one's pocket. The fruit machine jammed and Bill accused the 'stranger' of putting in tokens or foreign coins, therefore causing the machine to jam, complaining: "Now

Dave Barker (aged eight), Gordon Steele and Ivan Hurn (aged seven), November 1941.

my locals who have put their money in will not be able to play, strangers should not play the machine." The 'stranger' said to Bill "You didn't tell me not to use it when I was putting my money in and that it was reserved for locals; if I have caused any problems then I apologise." Bill continued to remain upset, refusing to accept the apology. The 'stranger' then put all four used glasses on to the counter, apologised again and said "to make up for the trouble we will all have doubles". Bill filled all the glasses and asked for the money. Asked again if the apology would be accepted Bill refused and the 'stranger' retorted: "Now you haven't only got a jammed fruit machine, but eight drops of spirits that are not going to be paid for!" and with that they all about turned and walked out of the pub leaving Bill totally dumbstruck!

Bill and Trudy retired to Wayside and the pub was sold to the Gooodeneews and Sue Goodeneews' mother Barbara. In conjunction with a national brewery the Treby was altered and refurbished. They ran it for several years, certainly increasing trade and encouraging more locals. The pub was then sold on to John Dryden who again ran it successfully for a while. Keith and Marilyn Marchant later purchased part of the old village shop from the Weatherbys and made this into a restaurant and extended the kitchen. They built up a well-earned reputation for fine food and upon their retirement in the autumn of 2000 sold the pub to the new licensees Nigel and Kate King.

The interior of the pub has been altered dramatically in the last few years. It used to be as follows: on entering the front door straight in front was a stable type door, the top of which was opened to the off-sales section (Bottle & Jug), which sold sweets, beer and crisps. There was also a room with the walls covered in postage stamps! To the right was the door to the bar. Going through this door to the right was the seating and to the left was the serving counter. To the left-hand rear of the bar was the door to the exit, toilets and lounge area. The lounge consisted of a few chairs and a rather impressive old grandfather clock. This area was serviced through a hatch in the wall from the bar.

Today the pub has changed entirely and sadly the once nearby Treby Hall and the Women's Institute Hall are no longer there (having been demolished in the name of progress and replaced by houses and a bungalow).

MEMORIES: A MISCELLANY

School Christmas Party   Col Conran supplied the Christmas tree for the school. He would dress his daughter Jane up as a fairy and put her in a box at Christmas. They would visit the school where Jane would jump out of the box and kindly distribute presents to all the children in the school. There was great excitement. Gifts were not in vast supply and a simply-made present was very well received.

Loving Child   Mr Bennett's son Roger was always late home from school, because he would stop to pick flowers for his mother.

Fun and Games   The gramophone provided one of the few modes of entertainment. It was a wind-up machine with little needles to play the records, which were made of bakelite. The needles would need changing regularly. You could exercise at the same time as playing the gramophone because it would wind down and the record would become so slow that one would have to run over and wind it up again to the correct speed. Mrs Thorrington had a dog Ben who would howl as soon as the gramophone was played and, so amused was he at this, that Mr Collings would often play it just out of devilment to hear the dog!

Conkers, marbles, skipping, top and whip, hopscotch and playing cards were some of the many games played.

Taxi   Mr Lewis Lock from Hemerdon ran a taxi; it was a big car with oil lamps on the front. Of course, there were no buses then, and if fresh bread was needed, people would walk down to Plympton and back to collect it. Lorraine Denny's family (*below*) would hire Mr Lock for the day to take them to the seaside and other such places and John Denny also remembers Mr Lock taking his family to Lee Moor Pantomime in the snow. They had to walk down to Lee Moor Hill after the show to get to the taxi, but he managed to get them safely back home to Hemerdon.

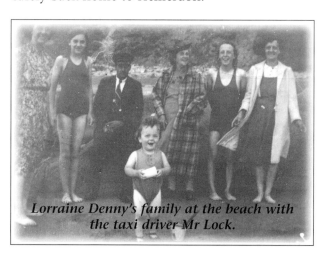

Lorraine Denny's family at the beach with the taxi driver Mr Lock.

Church   Mr Joe Collings was a choirboy for 75 years in Sparkwell Parish Church. Once a year there would be a choir outing, sometimes to Bigbury, which might be the only time people would see the sea. Mrs Collings kept the surplices laundered for 40 years, using an old flat iron to iron them (this would be heated up on an old cooking range). The church had gas cylinders for heat and Mr Joe Collings would look after these. The church had mains electricity just before the war but it was not supplied to domestic buildings until just after the war.

Old Coins   £.S.D. prior to decimalisation consisted of:

240 pennies	= £1
4 farthings	= ld.
A silver threepenny bit	= 3d.
A 12 sided threepenny bit	= 3d.
A silver sixpence	= 6d.
12 pennies	= 1/- (shilling)
24 pennies	= 2/- (florin)
30 pennies	= 2/6d. (half a crown)
60 pennies	= 5/- (a crown)
120 pennies	= 10/- (note form)
240 pennies	= £1 (note form)

A guinea was a gold coin, coined during the period 1663–1813 with a value of 20 shillings until 1717 when the value was fixed at 21 shillings. A sovereign was also an old gold coin worth 20 shillings. Now it would be worth around £80/90. Over the years some of these coins had slang names, among them 3d bit (joey); 6d (tanner); 1/- (bob); half a crown (half a dollar); 10/- note (half a quid or £1 = a knicker).

Test Your Memory   Cany anyone remember paying 6d. for a card from Joe Collings on which the name of a football team was printed? If tht team won its match, then the card holder won 2s.6d.

Men's Club   In a move to reassert its traditional decorum, the club's committee decided on 11 December 1945, to reintroduce old-fashioned dances, to be sure to keep temptation, as it were, at arm's length. The same attitude continued to triumph in the far freer 1960s. On 24 October 1966 the Chairman expressed the pious hope that the committee would fix an entry fee to discourage small girls from attending the dances.

A certain innocent mischievousness appeared among the club's rising generation. These members were nearly all choirboys, who were the despair of the vicar, the Revd James. They would engage in hassock fights, masquerade as ghosts in the church and pound out impious tunes on the harmonica. The boys were happy to be dismissed reprovingly by their long-suffering vicar, as it gave

Main: *Plympton Station (now demolished) where members of the Wingett family worked.*
Inset: *Left to right: Ida Wingett, Sydney Hill and Winnie Hill.*

them the opportunity to steal away to the club. There with lights and voices lowered they would gamble for a halfpenny a point at pontoon into the early hours of the morning.

After school the boys would feel it incumbent on them to advise Joe Collings on how to cut their hair. They would dart into the room at the back and advise a snip here and a snip there, and even help him out by surreptitiously cutting off some of their mates' hair.

Ping-pong balls would be burnt and crushed, so that the acrid smell would drive members to distraction. That was certainly the result too of the itching powder, which they sprinkled on the billiard tables. Yet, miraculously it seemed, the snooker champions continued to win their matches. That was thanks to 'the secret weapon' whereby rival sporting teams would be stuffed with pastries until they were literally immobilised and in no condition to hit a ball, let alone win a match.

A flavour of those distant, restless times is evident in the disturbances on Guy Fawkes Day, to which there was frequent mention in the committee's minutes. After Guy Fawkes night in November 1959 the club was shut on that day for several years to come. Explosions of an even more uncontrollable kind took place at the club's rifle range. 'Every young man should learn how to shoot' the fourth Lord Seaton used to insist. He would have been surprised to learn how many members of the club could blaze away without mastering even the rudiments of serious shooting. At last the members pushed an indulgent police

force too far and were disarmed, though very amicably, in the 1960s. The members presumably got a good deal of use out of their rifles, to judge by their sale price to the Plymouth Electricity Rifle club for £3.10s.0d. on 12 November 1963.

Great Western Railways The railway line runs through part of the parish. By the signal box at Venton Mr Littlejohns, a railway worker, lived in a caravan and went home at weekends. To pass away his time he would cut the grass around him with scissors!

Shaver Turpin, Dick Downing and Nobby Netherton all worked on the railway, and the men would carry wedges because the tracks would dry out, and they could then drive stones underneath to level them out. The late Mr Andrew Wotton said 'Great Western Railway Company looked after the tracks in a proper manner.' It would seem there were several occasions when men with their hand tools could do a proper job! Mr Wotton recalled:

When I was a teenager I would drive a pony and trap to visit friends at nearby Challonsleigh and Venton. We would play cards, sometimes all night. If I wanted a hair cut I went into Ivybridge. The electrical supply to the barber's shop was via a water-driven turbine from Ivybridge Mill. Occasionally the power would fail and if you were in the midst of having your hair cut, you had to wait until the fault was rectified to get the rest of your hair cut.

WAR YEARS

Deirdre Collings (née Short) remembers digging potatoes at Blacklands with the Land Army girls as Col Conran had obtained a special pass for her to stay away from school to help with the cause. Venton Lane was used for gas-mask practice and the children would have to go down there. Deirdre remembers how petrified Sheila Mumford was of the masks. Jill Phillips (née Blatchford) said:

Everyone would have to carry their gas masks wherever they went. When I attended Sparkwell School we had to have occasional 'mock air-raid parties'. Mrs Paddon, our teacher, would take us in file down the lane to Venton Bridge. There were no shelters in the school. We would put our gas masks on and lie in the hedge for a few minutes. She would give the 'all clear' and then we would file back to school again. From time to time we had to go to the room under the Treby Hall to have our gas masks tested by Mr Risdon. He was an ARP (Air Raid Precautions) person and lived at 40 Birchland Road. We had to put the gas mask on for the inspection; if he found it faulty, we would get a new one. Each Christmas I got a new case for my gas mask, sometimes it was knitted in Air Force blue (my father being in the RAF). It was the 'in' fashion to have the colour of the force which members of your family were serving in – also a brooch or a badge to the side. I had Air Force wings on mine.

The American soldiers (black and white) were stationed in the grounds of Hemerdon House. When they were preparing for D-Day, there was a convoy of lorries all through the village and our school bus, which would take us to Plympton School, could not get through so none of us went to school that day. The soldiers were giving away chewing gum and cigarettes (Camel cigs). I remember trying to smoke, they were horrible and I think that did me a favour as I never took up smoking, but I know a lot of people now smoke because of the Americans' generosity!

My friend Pam Lardeaux and I were sometimes allowed to go to the sixpenny hops (dances) at the Treby Hall run by Ted Lardeaux (Pam's father) and Mr Hirons. My Aunt May Blatchford used to play the piano in a small band with Mr Collins on banjo and Harold Reed on the drums. They were called the Sparklets.

The (black) GIs used to dance with us and taught us the 'jitterbug' dance – good fun! Before they left they gave the children a party and chocolate which was scarce in the war days.

Pam's father was in the Home Guard. One day we were asked to act as casualties at one of their mock air-raid practices at the Drill Hall, Plympton. I was bandaged up and put on a stretcher and given a drink whilst lying down and almost choked. My teacher Mr Stevens was also in the Home Guard and he asked me if I had recovered the next day in school.

Getting in the harvest, Blacklands, 1939.

Deirdree Collings' mother would not allow her daughters out when the sailors from the camp were drinking in the Treby because they would get so drunk. They would come out and try to stick each other's heads down the drain. Some of the sailors in the Naval camp would have their wives with them. Mrs Short (Deirdree's mother) had some staying with her.

There were huts in the camp on concrete plinths and around the huts would be beautifully-kept gardens. There was a cinema, hospital and mortuary. During the war searchlights were up on the 'Clump'. (Rumour has it (from some of the older people) that there is a graveyard by the 'Clump' at Goodamoor; some say it is people buried there from the plague in Plymouth and others say it is something to do with a battle.) The searchlights had to be moved to a different position because they lit up the village too much. Several incendiaries dropped in the village, one such in the hedge at 14 Birchland Road. Ken Collings' mother had one come through her roof.

A pass would be needed to go to Hemerdon (because of the American camp). Food was rationed, but people were told to use their ration tokens at certain shops. Miss Chapman ran the Co-op shop. The sirens could be heard from Plympton in the village.

The Indians were camped at Chaddlewood and would exercise their mules by walking them up to Sparkwell and back. One day Deirdree saw a plane on fire and her father lent her his tin hat so she could go outside to look. She had been there a few minutes, when her father called her back into the house – seconds later shrapnel fell on the very spot where she had been standing.

The school was closed in the war as it was used as a rest centre for the people in St Judes, Plymouth, to come in lorry loads to sleep. The headmistress Mrs Paddon asked the villagers to take into their houses the families that were sleeping in the school so that the school could reopen. The children's parents made trolleys for them to go around the village collecting the old iron for the war effort.

First-aid classes were given during the war and Marjorie Serpell recalled that the Hon. Mrs Parker (who was Lord Morley's mother) was her partner for bandaging.

'DAIRY COWS AT PLYMPTON, 30 AUGUST 1917'

Mr John Pearse held a sale of South Devon cows at Hemerdon Farm, Plympton, yesterday for Mr. Henry (Harry) Rowe, who has given up dairying. Thirty-one lots were offered and sold. The top price was £39.5s. for a cow stinted for her third calf. It was purchased by Messrs R. Cundy and Sons, Devonport. Bidding was very keen throughout. Ten cows renewed within the past two months, averaged £24.14s.6d. each. Seventeen cows in milk and stinted to calf averaged £28.9s.2d. Four fat cows averaged £24 each. The average of the 31 head was £26.16s.3d.

Jane Conran (left) digging at Blacklands, 1939.

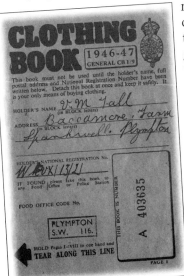

✿ FAMILIAR FACES ✿

Above: *Elsie, Margaret and Eva Wotton at Great Stert at Christmas, c.1930s.*

Far right: *Harry Masters at Baccamore.*

Right: *Jean and Albert Netherton with their Morris van which was bought for £200 and sold years later for £2000.*

Left: *Frederick (Ernest), Dora Tucker, Auntie Win and a friend at Mothercombe Beach.*

Below: *Ivan Hurn and Dave Barker on their bikes.*

Above: *Claude, Elizabeth and Deanie Hill.*

Far right: *Lawrence Baskerville, Francis Quest and Derek Reglar playing soldiers in Birchland Road, 1938.*

Right: *Jessie Reed, Florrie Mudge (née Kitts), Mrs Calloway and Mrs Taylor outside Lodge House, Beechwood.*

GERALD TUCKER'S MEMORIES

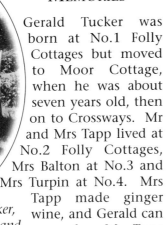

Frederick and Dora Tucker, Mrs Squibbs and Gerald and Dennis Tucker.

Gerald Tucker was born at No.1 Folly Cottages but moved to Moor Cottage, when he was about seven years old, then on to Crossways. Mr and Mrs Tapp lived at No.2 Folly Cottages, Mrs Balton at No.3 and Mrs Turpin at No.4. Mrs Tapp made ginger wine, and Gerald can remember Mr Tapp having a spittoon by his side as he was sitting next to the old cooking range. Mr Tapp liked a 'drop of cider' and very often Mr Tucker would put him across his bar on the bike and take him home. Of Christmas, Gerald says 'Mother would boil the Christmas pudding in a copper. She would get up four o'clock in the morning to get the fire going with paraffin.'

His mother ran the village Post Office for 25 years and Mrs Roberts (his mother's sister-in-law) helped until around 1973. He said 'people would make their own 'fun' – though nothing nasty.' He remembers, for example, when he and several friends picked up Mr Bradford's Austin 7 car and carried it to the other side of the road from the Treby Arms. Mr Bradford was perplexed as to how it got there.

He can remember looking out towards Plymouth, to see it lit up like daylight. The oil tanks in Plymouth had been bombed. Mr Lee (who was in the church choir 1939–40) told Gerald about something that he could see in the distance in a field near Moor Cottage. Gerald investigated and found two pure silk parachutes. Bombs were dropped between Voss Farm and Applethorn Slade. Gerald was a choirboy and remembers carving his name on a seat. He says it's probably still there.

Up Leggetts Lane there is a hollow oak tree. Gerald remembers that Christmas trees were grown around the area, and rumour had it that someone was going to steal some trees, so PC Plant hid in the tree and the culprits were captured.

Gerald was also in trouble once with PC Plant for not having lights on his bicycle, and was fined 10 shillings (50p) – a lot of money back then.

One day Gerald's brother had a 'backstep' off Mr Doney and they all ended up in the hedge.

He can remember the Indians being based at Chaddlewood House and bringing the mules to the village (Sparkwell) for exercise. There was one Indian to three mules.

Right: *Emily Wingett.*

Below: *Ernest and Emily Wingett with their children (left to right) Reg, Ida, Gerald (centre) and baby Ethel.*

Bottom centre: *Ethel was a 'Nippy' Lyons girl for a while in her youth.*

Bottom right: *Ida Hopper (née Wingett) and Gladys James.*

Far right: *Charles Hopper.*

❧ FAMILIAR FACES ❧

SUSAN FOSTER'S MEMORIES

Jack, Katherine, John and Susan Colborne-Mackrell came to live at Beechwood on 21 April 1955. The date is easy to remember being both the Queen's birthday and my late father's. The family arrived with my grandmother, Mrs Pollock, in our two old cars – a 1926 Humber tourer and a 1934 Rolls drop-head coupé.

At Beechwood we found Mrs Nancy Little, her seven-year-old son Edwin and Mr Short, who had been butler to cousin Wick, the fourth Lord Seaton. Beechwood is at its best in spring and that year was no exception. The garden was wonderfully tended by Mr Charlie Taylor, who had started years before. We believe that he was head-hunted from Blacklands. He told us that when he left school there was a choice of two jobs – to work for a wheelwright or as a gardener's boy. As the latter paid 3d. a day more that is what he did and this was a great thing as he was a quite wonderful gardener and friend to us all. When he was at Blacklands Mr James the head gardener made him whistle as he picked so that he could tell that he was not eating any berries! He was allowed to keep 6d. a week and after six months bought an Ingersoll crown watch.

Mrs Little had come to cook at Beechwood seven years earlier. She was a marvellous cook and her cakes were famous. Mrs Little had a fund of stories about her time in the WRAF during the war and of Balmaclellen in Dumfries where she was brought up. She believed in punctuality and kept us up to the mark with mealtimes. We also knew which guests coming to the house had her approval! Mrs Little advocated 'early to bed and early to rise' and scarcely stopped all day doing much more than she need have done for everyone – and every animal too! She loved cats in particular, but to be really approved of they had to be black.

When we came to Beechwood lilies of the valley were already being sent to Covent Garden by our cousin. We continued this and also sent up snowdrops, daffodils, anemones, polyanthus and other flowers – also strawberries and figs. We tried mushrooms too but with no great success.

Miss Mary Taylor, Mr Taylor's sister, came in to help for many years and Mr Taylor's wife Enid, who had long associations with the house, also did wonders. So Beechwood owes much to all that was done by the Taylor family over many years.

Edwin suffered from the 'early to bed' theory, but used to slip outdoors and meet his friends. Miss Taylor knew this but never gave him away. One never-to-be-forgotten day Edwin hurt himself and his mother wanted to cauterize the wound with a hot poker. Edwin took off and did not return till nightfall by which time his mother had been dissuaded from her intended course of action.

Mrs Kathleen Jenkins helped in the house after Mrs Taylor and Mrs Florrie Mudge came in August 1957 where she too did marvels for the next 38 years. Her mother had been a laundress and her daughter certainly inherited her skills. Before her Mr Walter Kitts, her father, worked in the grounds and remembered Edwin as a small child tipping over his barrow. Edwin also decided to re-arrange the name labels of all the rose bushes! Others who helped us in the walled garden included Mr Baskerville, Mr Marsh from Lee Mill and Mr Charles Taylor who came from Plympton and then from Plymstock. Mr Taylor had trained in gardening at Scotts of Merriott and was a fund of knowledge. Mr Gerald Tucker has long been a wonderful friend to us all at Beechwood doing great things in the garden and grounds as well as keeping the machines running sweetly, even in their old age. Mr Kenneth Pledge helps us too in many ways. In the last 15 years Mr Tom Alford has sorted out the many problems that arise in old buildings. He can turn his hand to anything and everything, leaving the place looking better than ever it did.

Memories of storms are vivid. There was the big freeze at the end of 1962... We were having a dinner party before a hunt ball, but heavy snow fell and we just succeeded in retrieving two guests from Plymouth Station – who stayed for days! One man walked from the village and fortunately no more came as a huge beech tree fell where cars would have been parked. We had the puddings, but all the main course was in Cornwood, made by our friends the Butlers. Mrs Taylor and Mrs Mudge had laid the table up beautifully awaiting all these guests and there were only about half a dozen who could get through. Mrs Taylor said her husband escorted Mrs Mudge back to Birchland Road and he had a job to get back home. My mother caused quite a stir on a Sunday when she skied down to the Roman Catholic Church at Plympton to attend the service! During that same period my father met a ram coming out of the boiler house. The ram made off into the blue with our flue brush firmly attached to his horns.

The Field Marshal was born on 16 February 1778 and we decided to have a party on the 200th anniversary. This proved to be a day of quite dreadful snow and wind. It sorted out the guests all right, as only the stalwart characters made it!

The great storm of 25 January 1980 nearly did for Mrs Little and me. We set off for Plympton during the morning. In Plympton a large piece of lead fell off the roof of Lloyds Bank and hit a woman who at first I thought was Mrs Little. We were thankful to get home but found a number of fallen trees, including a 200-year-old beech near the back door where we had been standing not long before. Too late we heard that people had been asked to stay indoors.

GEORGE MUMFORD'S MEMORIES

I was born on 7 September 1916 at No.5 Western Row, Hemerdon. Today the Cottage is known as Elm Cottage, named after the famous elm tree opposite the house, and is owned by Mr Peter Smerdon, a local taxi driver. My parents were Richard (Dick) and Elizabeth (Lizzy) Mumford. We were a big and a very well-known family in the village. We all grew up in a two-up-two-down cottage and my mother's father lived with us as well. We all called him Grandfer Woods. My brothers and sisters were: Alice, Tim, Frances, Richard (Dick), William (Bumble), Minnie and Kathleen.

I went to Sparkwell School and ran with a hoop and sloo. The blacksmith Mr Pillage at Sparkwell made the hoops and sloos for the children. After school I also went to the Cubs and Scouts at Goodamoor House and Miss Anstice was our leader. We played ping pong, table tennis and cards in the village hall at Hemerdon when we were young lads. The policeman who came around the village was PC Longman from Cornwood.

When I was 11 I went to the Ridgeway School until I was 14 and when I left I worked for a time at the Lee Moor Brickworks. My wages were 1 guinea a fortnight; I kept a shilling and I had to give the rest to my mother.

About 1940 during the war I worked on the land at the forestry at Cornwood which was owned by Jewsons the timber people. I was also a Sergeant in the Home Guard. After the war I worked at Lee Moor Clayworks then two years later I left to work at Marsh Mills drying sheds as a lorry driver.

I married my wife Daisy on 20 November 1944 at Sparkwell Church. She originally came from Lee Mill but moved to Gorah at Lutton. Her maiden name was Nicholson. My sister Kathleen married my wife's brother Bill Nicholson and they lived all their married life at No.5 Western Row, Hemerdon where we all grew up. Several years ago No.5 was owned by my niece Kathy and her husband Ron Shoplin; extensive alterations were made to the cottage including a large extension. My sister Kathleen lived there until her husband died and she then went to live with my brother Bumble's daughter Kathy and her husband Ron Shoplin at various pubs they ran. Kathleen died in January 1997 and we miss her dreadfully. We would sit and play her favourite game of cards, gin rummy, for hours on end usually for 5p to win. Kathleen was a very popular member of the village being on the committee at the village hall for a great many years and she also helped run stalls at the village ram roast. She also helped some people with their housework.

My brother Dick and his wife Ivy went back to live in the village at No.3 Western Row in the 1970s. When Dick retired he drove the cattle lorry for Jack Lambshead the farmer at Hemerdon Farm taking cows to Newton Abbot on market day and helping out on the farm.

When Minnie first got married she lived in Rose Cottage after my grandad moved out. She married Clifford Williams and today she lives in Cornwall.

I can remember Bill Penwill was the haulier and he would draw the clay from Galva using a cart and two – maybe three – shire horses. Ned Honey would sometimes give him a hand when he was very busy. The horses had a terrible time trying to get down West Park Hill as the weight of the clay in the cart was so great that it would rub the hedge all the way down the hill trying to slow it down.

My brother Bumble for many years kept horses at Ploughlands, Hemerdon, and it was a thriving riding stables. Not long after Bumble died the house burnt to the ground but the stables were ok and his son Richard kept them going for a few years. The stables are no longer running and the land where the house once was and the stable blocks have been redeveloped into a bungalow by Brian and Margaret Daw. Margaret is my niece, being the daughter of my brother Dick and his first wife.

Above: *Sparkwell's own postmark.*

Right: *A typical birthday card of the early 1920s. This one of Ida's is dated 1922.*

Right: *Another card of 1929 sent to Ida by a friend named Mary in Birkenhead.*

Below: *A 1909 New Year's card.*

An old postcard of Lee Mill on the Plymouth Road.

Main: *Another early postcard of Lee Mill showing the village shop.*
Inset: *The mill at Lee Mill.*

CHAPTER 11: LEE MILL:
A BRIEF HISTORY

by Christine Hartley

INTRODUCTION

Lee Mill was referred to as 'Leghbrygge' in 1414, as 'Lea Mill' in 1890, and today is known as Lee Mill. It belonged originally to Plympton Hundred and was part of the parish of Plympton St Mary. Always referred to as a hamlet in the early part of its history, along with Sparkwell, Venton, Hemerdon and Bottle Hill, it was eventually formed into an ecclesiastical parish from the civil parish of Plympton St Mary on 15 August 1884.

Lee Mill, meaning the mill in the lee of the hill (the associated bridge being the one that crosses the River Yealm) has seen many changes over the years. This brief history will begin with what a majority of people from outside the village perceive Lee Mill to be – the industrial estate. From there we will look back at what Lee Mill used to be, a thriving village centred around a paper mill.

LEE MILL INDUSTRIAL ESTATE

At the start of the Second World War, the Government's National Hostels Corporation was responsible for turning 60 acres of land at Lee Mill into a housing estate. Some 157 brick-built, red- and green-roofed homes were built to house what were classed as Plymouth's 'essential workers' – people living in areas likely to be blitzed by the Luftwaffe. During Plymouth's post-blitz housing difficulties, the estate was taken over by the Admiralty, and homes were used for Devonport Dockyard employees returning from overseas postings who could not find any other homes. These families stayed here until 1959.

In the late 1950s the need to bring industry to the area was recognised and Plympton Rural District Council was interested in the Lee Mill estate as a future development site. The estate was bought in 1959 by that body for £8000, but as Mr G.S. Thomson, Chairman of the Council, commented at a meeting of councillors: 'I hope you appreciate the fact that it was worth much more' (*Western Evening Herald*, 24 April 1959).

A recommendation by the Chief Medical Officer had already asserted that 'the Lee Mill estate should be demolished because the dwellings were unfit for human habitation' (*Western Evening Herald*, 30 January 1959). Council members spoke of clearing the site quickly so that active and virile industries could be brought into the area, and thus solve the problem of a rising tide of unemployment. In all 150 families were offered homes at Plympton St Maurice, in place of their sub-standard homes on the Lee Mill estate. A report in the local paper told of how eight out of ten families were 'glad to go to better homes nearer their work' (*Western Evening Herald*, 4 December 1959). In the opinion of the local people at Lee Mill today, however, many families would have stayed, and would really have preferred to have had their homes rebuilt on the estate. 'It was an absolutely wonderful place to live', recalled Mrs M. Butler of Lee Mill on 19 April 1996.

It was 1963 before industry took an interest in the estate. A plan had been drawn up for the development of the site. 'One or two firms are already waiting to see the plan' reported the *Western Morning News* on 7 August 1963. The paper noted that a planning application for industry had been submitted to Devon County Council and that when approval was received sites would be advertised.

By 1969 Lee Mill had an industrial estate. It also had a vacant 20-acre site that Plymouth's Consumer Group were eager to see turned into an out of town shopping centre. Plymouth and South Devon Co-operative Society had submitted an application for a shopping centre but the application was rejected on the grounds that it was contrary to the development proposals of Plympton town centre.

The site remained vacant until September 1978. Although a planning application from International Supermarkets had been approved, South Hams Council decided to accept Tesco's offer for the lease 'which was said to be in excess of the Council's reserve of £225 000' (*Western Evening Herald*, 5 May 1978). Tesco had also offered a substantial amount of money for ground rent.

Today Lee Mill industrial estate is home to many thriving businesses. Sadly, the old paper mill was demolished in 1995 to make way for 40 new houses.

Paper Mill

The earliest records of Lee Mill's association with paper date back to 1833. Owned by the Holmans, a family who originated in Cullompton (see *The Book of Cullompton*), it was until 1995 a focal point for the village. Its size and historical value were such that in 1988, when it was first suggested that it should be demolished, South Hams Council's Conservation Officer, Mr Alan Cheetham, described its 'visual significance being compared with a parish church'. He continued: 'The historical value of the building is due to the juggernaut proportions, being unique, in a district where such industrial complexes are rare' (*Western Evening Herald*, 23 August 1988).

Powered by water from the River Yealm until 1856, and then by steam, the paper mill turned partially processed material – 'half stuff' from Lower Mill, Ivybridge – into high-quality brown paper. For a considerable length of time the mill employed most of the men in the village, and housed several of them as well.

The mill's industrial life came to an end in 1908 when fire destroyed one of the two main buildings. 'Being too far from wind and tide' (Barber, T., 23 March 1996), rebuilding the mill was not viable. Times were changing, and the donkey and cart were beginning to become outdated modes of transport. Redundant mill workers and their families were, however, allowed to stay on in their cottages, and a number did so for many years.

Paper making is not the only thing that the mill has been used for. Since its closure it has played a part in both world wars, and has served as an agricultural machinery salesroom. During the First World War German prisoners of war were stationed at the mill and marched each day to Wolfram Mine, Hemerdon, to dig 'dig out'. Mr Harry Hill remembers watching them being taken up the road, all wearing uniforms with red patches on them. The prisoners had a grocery ration and Mrs Betty Coombes recalls how her father told her stories of Aunt Do' delivering the prisoners' rations to the mill by pony and trap. During the Second World War Brown, Wills & Nichols used the mill buildings as a food store. Local lady Mrs Ruth Huxtable worked for them. Brown, Wills & Nichols, originally of Finewell Street, Plymouth, were the main food suppliers in the area during the war and at their food store in Lee Mill they kept groceries; both tinned and perishable goods.

Mill Workers, early 1900s.

CHURCH

The Congregational Church has been in Lee Mill since 1810. It was started by Mr Collins, and he along with several other people met in the cottage behind what was the Smiths Arms (now the Westward Inn). In March 1996 Revd Cyril Short explained how in 1832 Mr John Windsor started prayer meetings in his home in Buttsford Terrace and that the names John Stranger, Robert Callard and John Langmead were among those who ministered at these gatherings. They ceased when Mr Windsor passed away in 1834. Mr Harry Hill, a former special constable of Lee Mill, also remembers John Wingett and Alf Kingwell as being involved with the chapel, and that they taught him at Sunday School.

Eventually Mr Benjamin Holman lent the Church a house in the mill yard which, as noted by Revd Short, became the 'place of worship for all those of the Independent and Congregational way.' Due to an increase in numbers it was soon realised that a more permanent place of worship was needed and members of the congregation set about the task or building a new church.

The following was recorded in the church book in March 1868:

After much deliberation and special prayer to God it was deemed desirable that a church should be formed in the 'Congregational Chapel' at Lee Mill Bridge.

After a meeting of the congregation in said chapel in 31 March 1868, presided over by Mr I.B. Thomson, it was proposed by Mr Coyte, seconded by Mr Farley and unanimously approved:

That a Church be formed in the Lee Mill Bridge 'Congregational Chapel'. At the same meeting the following names were proposed as members (received upon being interviewed by Mr. J.B Thomson and at meeting when the Rev. C. Wilson, F.E. Anthony and Messrs Polkinghorne, Thomson, Maitland & Clarke were present):

Mr Coyt
Mrs Coyt
Mr Bennett
Mrs Gandy
Mrs I. Sandover
Mrs Falkworthy
Mr Wyatt
Mrs Wyatt
Mrs Turpin
Mr Farley
Miss Rouse
Mrs Kingwell
Miss Jane Maddock
Mr Yelland

The building was designed by H.J. Snell Esq. Mr Abbott, a local farmer and Mr Holman, paper manufacturer, who had earlier made available the house in the mill yard, gave the stone and the land. Mr Horton, also a farmer, drew the lime, and Mr Barons of the Beach Estate gave the sand which he kindly hauled to the site. Work was completed in 1836 by Mr Crocker of Modbury at a cost of £700.

For many years Lee Mill Church was part of the Ivybridge Congregational Church and the Western Congregational College in Plymouth. In 1986, they made the decision to become Independent once more. In 1893 a code of rules was submitted as follows:

The doors to be opened ten minutes before the start of services.
The Chapel keeper or a trustworthy person is to remain in the Chapel to see that the Boys or no other persons molest or do any damage before the congregation arrives.

On 6 August 1889 the first marriage to be solemnised was that of William Edward Laverick of Leeds and Rose Cork of Ivybridge. As it was the first marriage at the chapel the bride was presented with a Bible and hymnbook.

In October of 1942 a letter was received from the Ministry of Demolition and Recovery stating that it was necessary to remove the railings from around the chapel as a contribution to the war effort. The February of the following year a service was held for the first time with electric lighting. Thanks and a gift were given to Mr H. Coombs and his son Bernard who were had sole responsibility for the installation.

Available records state that when the Wesleyan chapel was opened in 1874, there was 'a slight decrease in the numbers of the scholars of the Sabbath School, but the congregation appear[ed] to have been in no way affected. Little else is known of the Wesleyan chapel, although it is listed as being in existence in the 1890 volume of the *Devonshire Directory*.

As well as the Congregational Chapel (*below*) there was also the Mission Church at Lee Mill. Not a great deal is remembered about this building other than that the Sisters of Mercy lived in a caravan on a piece of land adjoining and prayer meetings were held there. During the winter months they were provided with logs by Mr Downs.

Lee Mill School, 1920s. Most of the names are unknown although Harry Hill is in the front row, a young boy with the surname Skelly is in the middle row (he was born in 1914) and Jack Hill is front centre.

Lee Mill School in the 1950s with the headmaster Mr Williams and the teacher Miss Williams. Those present include: Mrs Elliott, Roy Pearce, Ken Downs, Ivor, Terry and John Willis, Miss Matthews, Peggy Willis, Betty Downs, Julie Stevens, Betty Willis, Esmond Pearce, Edward Willis, Edward Glass.

SECOND WORLD WAR

During Hitler's bombardment of Plymouth, which was at its height during March 1941, the people of Plymouth became 'trekkers'. Up to 50000 people left the city daily to seek safe haven in the countryside. In the words of Mrs Ruth Huxtable 'people would come out on anything that moved.' Not only did the people of the village take in some of these refugees, Lee Mill Chapel also offered 60 places of safety.

On the night of 24 April 1941, recalled A. Clamp, 'there were a recorded 100 trekkers staying there.' Lee Mill was also a dispersal point for Armed Service vehicles. On some nights there were up to 45 of these vehicles located between Plympton and Ivybridge, each with up to 20 trekkers in them.

Although incendiary devices were dropped in the fields on the outskirts of Lee Mill, unlike Plympton nothing took a direct hit. The ARP warden during the war was Mr Downs, whose daughter, now Mrs Betty Coombes, recalls the war 'as an awful time', and remembers how you could hear the air-raid siren in Ivybridge, before the official signal was received by her father. The people of the village often heard Betty and her tin whistle running down the street, warning of air attack, before her father had received the official call.

Hitchcombe Farm was used during the war to house a searchlight and an anti-aircraft gun. Two Nissen huts were erected in a field close to the farmhouse. These huts are still standing, along with Mrs Cane's recently built bungalow. Mrs Cane remembers the war years well and recalled how the searchlight was used a great deal.

From 1941–45 No.7 National Fire Service Regional H.Q. was based on the estate. It had been an auxiliary fire station previous to this but during the war approximately 200 men passed through here as trained fire-fighters. It was a major training centre for the West Country. Canadian fire-fighters were also stationed here during the war, for training purposes.

THE THREE SCHOOLS OF LEE MILL

Records show that the Reverend Merton Smith of Plympton had wanted a school in Lee Mill for several years prior to it being built. Letters available in the West Devon Record Office show that his correspondence was sent to a Baldwin John Pollexfen Bastard, of Yealmpton and Plympton. In 1873, after several years of discussion, it was finally agreed and the Reverend Smith chose the site in the centre of the village. Mr Bastard was informed of this by way of a letter and a map. The

following year the school was built. Miss Fanny Louisa Luckey, and Miss Nicholls were the two mistresses until it was closed in 1896.

A second 'national school' was built in the same year, at the top of the village, now New Park Road. It had two classrooms and two teachers. A local lady was the schoolmistress for a time – Miss Sarah Abbott. Along with others, Miss Mabel Richards, Mrs Cornelius, Miss Thomas, Miss Turner and Miss Williams, she was witness to a yearly average attendance of between 54 and 86 children.

As there was no provision for cookery lessons in the school, the girls were sent to Ivybridge once a week – a time remembered with some humour by Betty Coombes. During the war years children often went to help farmers pick their crops instead of going to school. They, as many other children in the country, were issued with cards to be stamped by the farmer, as proof that they had helped with the war effort. It was a time that the children loved, far better than going to school.

In 1929 the school became a junior school but 20 years later it was closed down, and in its place a council school was opened in a temporary classroom on the estate. This, the third and last of Lee Mill's schools, was closed in 1963. From this time all the infants and juniors were placed in schools at Plympton and Ivybridge, as they still are today.

HOSPITAL

Due to the fact that it is not easily visible from the road, Lee Mill Hospital remains unknown to many people. Many of the hospital records are still classified information, but much that is known about the establishment comes to us through the older generation of the village.

Until the late-20th century the hospital was used for medical purposes and as an annexe of Mount Gould Hospital, Plymouth. It was originally used as an isolation hospital, for smallpox sufferers. The remains of that building are now used for storage.

American servicemen were involved with the erection of the building that we see today which was intended for use by servicemen who had been injured during the war. The plan was that they would be flown to here from France but it never served in that capacity.

The first time the new building came into use was as an orthopaedic unit for children with tuberculosis in the bone and after a brief spell of closure, it was re-opened as a geriatric unit. Devon and Cornwall Constabulary have utilised the premises for the training of police dogs and handlers and it is now a semi-secure unit for people with abuse problems.

PUBLIC HOUSES:
LEE MILL INN & SMITHS ARMS

Estimated to be approximately 300 years old, the Lee Mill Inn was certainly the first of the two public houses in the village. Now brewery owned, with Mary Lakey at the helm, it has changed little structurally over the years. Previous landlords and ladies have included such people as Philip Bartlet (from 1870–90 and also the village shoemaker), Thomas Vine (from 1890–97, previously of the 'Old Ring 'O'Bells') and Underwood and William Nelder (around 1902, whose family name was associated with the Treby Arms from around 1919). At the start of the Second World War Albert Vivian was in control. Unlike the Smiths Arms (or Westward Inn as it is now known), the Lee Mill Inn has always been a public house.

Although not as old as the Lee Mill Inn, the Smiths Arms has an interesting history. Built in 1835, it had a water-driven cider press, smithy (hence the name) and a wheelwrighting shop. It had a reputation for making cider of the highest quality. Mr Abbott owned his own orchard, pressed his own fruit and sold the end product to the locals and to shops in Plymouth, as well, of course, as in the pub itself. 'For a time they were only licensed to sell cider, no beer or spirits', remembered L.H. Gill.

In the early days local farmers brought their own fruit to the press and took away their own apple juice. 'Farmers from outlying farms brought their apple crop to the press by horse and cart and as children we helped whenever we could', said Mr Harry Hill. By 1964 Albert Abbott's health had deteriorated to the extent where he had to sell his property. The fifth generation of the Abbott family who had trained for the job decided that his own business was a 24-hour-a-day job. Roy Abbott owned a petrol filling station and café which is now operated by Mr Michael Lane under the name of Lee Mill Services.

Albert Abbott saw a great many changes in cider-making from the time that he started learning the art, aged eight, alongside his father. Not only did the press eventually become electrically driven, in place of the old hand press that the local children had loved helping with, but the way the cider was made became so much more technical. During the Second World War Italian prisoners of war were working at the press and amongst them was a wine chemist who was amazed by the process of cider making. As Albert Abbott said 'there is so much more to making cider than squeezing the juice from the apples and leaving it to ferment' (*Western Evening Herald*, 20 July 1964).

When the property was sold it fetched £5500 and along with it went over 100 years of cider making in Lee Mill. It was replaced by the Westward Inn, which after refurbishment now consists of four bars, kitchen, restaurant, family room and a five-bedroom flat.

Top: *Mr and Mrs Hoskin in the bar of the Smiths Arms.*
Above: *Cyreta Willcocks (née Mortimer) with her father.*

ONCE A THRIVING VILLAGE

Some 140 years ago village life centred around the paper mill and the farming community. The Holman family were for some time the central family of Lee Mill, for not only did they own the mill, they were responsible for the building of around 20 cottages, and employed most of the men in the village. The Abbott family of Beech Farm, previously known as the 'Beech Estate' owned by Mr Barons, were the main farming family of the village. They were also the village blacksmiths and publicans, as well as agricultural engineers, garage owners and electricians from the late 1920s to the early '30s. With two public houses, numerous shops (including a butcher's and a grocery shop, tea rooms and the Post Office), the village centre would have been a hive of activity during the late-19th and early-20th century.

During the early 1930s, Mr William Matthews came to the fore as the man who employed almost all of the men in the village. A haulage contractor and quarry owner, he ran his fleet of lorries out of various quarries, including his own based in Bittaford. His garage was situated where P.L. Bowker LTD refrigeration is now. Due to extremely heavy traffic through the village, and sadly the loss of lives on the road, Lee Mill was by-passed along with most of the towns and villages between Exeter and Plymouth. With new roads and buildings being erected in the area, there is still the need for a local haulage firm. Handside LTD, who operate out of Strashleigh Hams tip, filled the space left by Mr Matthews and have become the local haulage firm. They also employ a handful of local men. Lee Mill has had a sub Post Office since 1910. Mr Samuel Crocker was the first postmaster, followed by Mr William Luscombe from 1914–23, and from 1923 by Mr Henry Roberts. Brian Ward currently fills the post.

As well as the relaxation provided by the two public houses, there was also Millbourne Hall. What is now seen as a tin hut opposite the garage once boasted a football team who, as remembered by Mr Harry Hill, 'never lost a game one season'. The scene of the Men's Club and frequent dances, it is remembered as a lovely part of Lee Mill's history; days that the local people feel will never return. When the estate was used for homes, Lee Mill boasted its own cinema, a Co-op, Mr Brown's newsagency and a garage. The Townswomen's Guild had meetings there, as did the Allotment Association. At first the people on the new estate didn't fit in with the villagers. Mr William Kelly, who lived on the estate for several years, was reported in the *Western Evening Herald* of 2 May 1983, as saying: 'For a while we weren't quite accepted by the locals – being regarded as townies – but after a while we became friends with the villagers.' The view is accepted by the local people, but as time went on they eventually had organised cricket and football matches. A cycle track was built, and enjoyed by the children from the estate and from the village. A dance band was formed, which included two men from the village and an unknown lady from Lee Mill. They

Supporters out and about with Lee Mill's football team, 1950s.
The photograph includes: Mr and Mrs Brooking, Mr and Mrs Marshall, Mr and Mrs Ainsbury, Mrs Roberts, Doll Willis, Syd Burning, Harold Willis, Mr and Mrs Merton, Mr and Mrs Dockins, Mr and Mrs Ward, Mrs Willis.

LEE MILL COMMUNITY

Left: *Lee Mill ladies, catering for Sports Day, late 1950s. They include, left to right from the back: Mrs Goss, Mrs Brown, Mrs F. Matthews, Mrs Marshall, Mrs Willcocks, Mrs Downing, ?, Mrs Betty Hill, Mrs Abbott, Mrs Rossiter, Mrs T. Willis, Mrs Penfold, Miss A. Hill, the Misses Johns, Mrs James, ?, Mrs Wingett, 'Granny' Willis.*

Above left: *Sports Day Dance in the galvanised shed known as the Millbourne Hall, 1950s. Included are Les Naylor, Wally Gill and Margaret Willis.*

Above right: *Coach outing for the football and darts teams.*

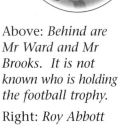

Above: *Behind are Mr Ward and Mr Brooks. It is not known who is holding the football trophy.*

Right: *Roy Abbott and Valerie dancing at the Millbourne Hall.*

Above: *Lee Mill Football Team, 1953. Left to right, back: S. Matthews, A. Phillips, ? Johns, F. Quick, W. Nicholls, G. Netherton, P. Turpin, B. Ellis, S. Phillips, R. Turner, H. Roberts; middle: H. Hill, ? Carter, ? Abbot, ? Painter, ? Simmons; front: G. Matthews, A. Hill, J. Hill, W. Bell.*

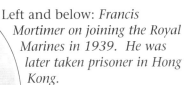

Left and below: Francis Mortimer on joining the Royal Marines in 1939. He was later taken prisoner in Hong Kong.

Above: Mr Alfred Mortimer.

Above right: *Lilian Mortimer.*

Right: *The wedding of Vera Mortimer to Les Brisenden (on the left) at Sparkwell Church, 1945.*

became so popular that people from miles around came to listen to them. Western National buses even ran special trips to the village on Saturday nights to hear the band play. Pantomimes at Christmas and plays throughout the year became a new part of village life. The townies were accepted whole-heartedly.

As with a lot of villages, not only in Devon, but throughout the country, Lee Mill has seen radical change over the centuries. There was hope, however, that some things would stay the same. In 1883 Lee Mill Independent Church commented: 'Lee Mill is a place which, owing to its position between two towns, and for other reasons, will probably remain ever a village.'

The older generation of the village have of course seen many changes over the years, not all of them for the better. Many people fail to see why they cannot have a village school again, why places like Millbourne Hall are used by table-tennis players from Ivybridge, and not the local community. But most of all, locals ponder why all of those houses had to be demolished to make way for an industrial estate? Unfortunately all the signs are that Lee Mill will not, in fact, 'remain ever a village.' There are plans to build a new town in the area and even if it isn't built at or around Lee Mill, it will probably be close by. A vast majority of people living here do not wish to see this happen. Lee Mill is a village like any other

and the people here form a community, as they do in any village, be it a pretty chocolate-box place on the moor, or one on the side of the A38, with an industrial estate as its closest neighbour.

REFERENCES

PAPERS AND BOOKS:
Bovett, R., *Historical Notes on Devon Schools* (Devon County Council, 1989)
Clamp, A., *Plympton During The Second World War 1939–45*
Unknown, *Historical Sketch of Lee Mill Independent Church and Congregation* (1883)

ALSO: Hutchings & Mason Printers, Plymouth.

Thanks to the following people for their reminiscences of Lee Mill (all from Lee Mill unless otherwise stated): the late Mr D. Abbott, Mr T. Barber (Ivybridge), Miss D. Brown, Mrs M. Butler, the late Mrs Cane, Mrs B. Coombes, Mrs B. Down, Mr L.H. Gill (formerly of the Westward Inn), Mr H. Hill, Mrs R. Huxtable, Mr B. Joce (Yealmpton), Mrs F. Kerton, Mrs M. Kerton, Mrs J. Matthews, Mr and Mrs R. Ryder, Revd C. Short and Mrs Willcocks.

The pictures were reprinted with the kind permission of Mr Harry Hill, Mr and Mrs Huxtable and Mrs Cyreta Willcocks.

Hemerdon House and the lake.

Beach party, c.1885. W.J. Woollcombe (founder of Woollcombe & Yonge) is in the white hat on the left and his nephew G.A.L. Woollcombe (1864–1947) is in the bowler hat next to his uncle.

CHAPTER 12: HEMERDON

HEMERDON HOUSE AND THE WOOLLCOMBES
by J.H.G.W.

William Woollcombe of Challonsleigh, later Mayor of Plympton (16??–1728).

The manor of Hemerdon (consisting roughly of the village of Hemerdon, Sterts and Hemerdon Farms, Bickfordtown (Sherwell and Sparkwell Farms), the eastern slopes of Hemerdon Ball, Hemerdon House and grounds and the western end of Sparkwell village), belonged to the Crockers of Lyneham from the late-14th century until 1632, when they were sold and divided between Peter Ryder, who took half of Hemerdon, and Tristram and Nicholas Avent, who took Bickfordtown and the other half of Hemerdon. The two halves of Hemerdon were reunited by purchase in the time of the first George Woollcombe, who acquired the estate by marriage in 1792.

In 1790 the Avent share was bought by Thomas Woollcombe, a surgeon practising in Plymouth who had the good sense to marry an heiress. It became the dowry for his daughter Maria who was about to marry her cousin George. Confusingly, his father was also called Thomas Woollcombe and was also a Plymouth surgeon. Portraits of both the Thomases are to be seen at Hemerdon House, one painted in about 1748 by Reynolds and the other in 1806 by Downman. The wedding took place in 1792 and the house was begun in 1793 on a new site previously used as an orchard. What are now the grounds of the house then contained the two farmhouses of Higher and Lower Bickfordtown, one of which was near the present pond whilst the other included the present stable buildings, the sole survivors of these two farms.

The house was originally completed and occupied as a simple rectangular structure on the Plympton–Cornwood road, but soon after Maria's father's death in 1799 plans were made to extend it. This required the road to be diverted and by an Order of the Magistrates of 1800 the old road became the drive to the house and the present road from the Lodge to Beechwood Cross replaced it. The house was then extended into the old road by the construction of the present entrance hall, library, drawing room, kitchen and outhouses.

There is evidence that the original expansion plan was more ambitious than that which was actually achieved. The library was an empty shell for almost 100 years and what seems to have been planned as a gallery ended up as three ordinary bedrooms. Whatever was intended the house has not been altered structurally since it was completed in its present form, although essential modernisation such as the installation of bathrooms has of course taken place.

The Woollcombe family has been resident in the Plympton area for at least 500 years and an unbroken line can be traced to William Wolcombe (sic) who died at Holland Farm (now in the middle of Langage Industrial Estate) in 1570. Evidence exists of Woollcombes in the parish as early as the 13th century. William's descendants moved to Challonsleigh in the 17th century, where a later William paid £30 to the Royalist General Digby for the maintenance of his troops during the Civil War and was given a paper protecting him from further demands. In the 18th century the family moved to Plympton, where they provided two mayors and a town clerk, who also supervised the building of Plympton House for Sir George Treby. From there they went on to Plymouth, the last move before almost completing the circle at Hemerdon. George and Maria's daughters led the typically dull life endured by unmarried ladies in

Thomas Woollcombe (painted by Sir Joshua Reynolds before he went to Italy). Thomas was father of Maria Woollcombe who married cousin George in 1792 and for whom Thomas bought the Hemerdon estate in 1790.

the early-19th century and died in their forties, probably of TB. Their only recorded excitements were a two-year visit to London in 1815–16 when Hemerdon was let, and a holiday in the Channel Islands in 1842.

The two sons both joined the Services, William the Army and George the Navy. After seeing action with the 71st Foot in the Peninsular War and at Waterloo, William died on a Greek island in 1829, unmarried and during his father's lifetime. George began his Naval career as a 14-year-old First Class Volunteer aboard the flagship *Caledonia* commanded by his uncle at the Basque Roads expedition in 1809. He was later wounded in the foot as a master's mate at the battle of New Orleans in 1815 (see page 84). He went on to command various ships engaged among other things in the suppression of the slave trade, and eventually retired in 1830 in the rank of Post Captain. He died at Hemerdon in 1865 as a Vice-Admiral, rising in the Navy list as his seniors died off. He was an active landlord and brought the slopes of Hemerdon Ball into cultivation. The present trees at the top date from the early 1950s, replacing an earlier clump which existed in his time and which may even have preceded the arrival of the Woollcombes, as trees there are mentioned as early as 1773. The Ball housed a military camp during the Napoleonic Wars. Admiral George is also credited with the foundation of the Miners Arms as a safeguard against his tenants drinking cider in their cottages – an offence which was punishable with the loss of the culprit's allotment.

Henry and William Woollcombe were younger brothers of the builder of Hemerdon and both are distinguished in the history of Plymouth. William was a much respected physician who died prematurely in 1822. There is a memorial to him in St Andrew's Church. Henry was a lawyer who became Mayor and Recorder of Plymouth and was active in the foundation of many Plymouth institutions, including the Athenaeum, the Proprietary Library, the Mechanics' Institute and the Chamber of Commerce. He left a diary and a manuscript 'History of Plymouth' which has never been published but which is the source of much material in later published works. He died in 1847, leaving his books and pictures to his nephew at Hemerdon where most of them remain.

Admiral George's children, six sons and three daughters, led the usual life of their kind. The eldest son was a clergyman, and the others respectively a Naval officer, a solicitor (the founder of Woollcombe & Yonge in Plymouth), a Royal Marine, an Artillery Officer and another solicitor. Two of the daughters married clergymen and the third lived all her life unmarried at Hemerdon. The Reverend G.L. Woollcombe, the Admiral's eldest son, moved to Hemerdon on his mother's death in 1889 and in his time completed the

HEMERDON BALL BEING REPLANTED

CEREMONY AT HISTORIC S. DEVON LANDMARK

PEOPLE living in Plympton and for many miles around will be interested to know that steps are being taken to preserve Hemerdon Ball, the well-known and historic land mark, planted many years ago by ancestors of the Woollcombe family, of Hemerdon House.

Time, age and the exposure of the trees which are about 700 feet above sea level, has told, and for several years, they have gradually been disappearing.

The owner is Mrs. George Woollcombe, widow of the late Mr. George Woollcombe, of Hemerdon House from whom permission for the replanting has been obtained.

The general "lay-out" of the plan has been prepared by Mr. T. Brown, forestry expert, of Totnes, and the variety of trees, pine and beech most suitable for the site has been recommended by him.

The First Tree

The replanting has been undertaken by Mr. Humphrey Woollcombe, and his son, Mr. James Woollcombe, of Hemerdon House, both of whom are taking a pride and interest in seeing this historic place preserved, for it can be seen from many parts of Plymouth and from as far south as Churchstow.

To mark the commencement of the scheme, an interesting ceremony took place there on Saturday morning, when Mr. Humphrey Woollcombe, heir to the estate, planted the first tree. He was followed by his wife and by Mr. H. Rowe, of Lowdamoor, Hemerdon (one of the oldest inhabitants of Hemerdon), and Mr. Allan Scott of Hemerdon Farm (one of the youngest).

Appeal To Visitors

Mr. Charles Strong, very interested in the movement, also planted a tree, as did Mrs. Konev and her brother, Mr. Norman Perry, who is in charge of the whole of the tree planting taking place on the Hemerdon estate.

As this is a favourite place for visitors during the summer months the owners ask for their full support and co-operation in seeing that no damage is done to the young trees.

In addition to this planting of some 1,200 trees on Hemerdon Ball, between 11,000 and 12,000 trees have been planted during this last season in an area of ten acres close to Beechwood Cross, from which timber was taken during the recent war. It is also intended next season to replant a further ten acres.

A great writer many years ago said "he that plants a tree doeth a service to his country, and shall be praised by many he hath never seen."

library, dug the pond and consolidated the land holdings. On his death in 1902 his son George took over. His daughter Edith married John Nicholls and lived at Galva for many years.

In the 1920s Hemerdon Farm was sold to its tenant Harry Rowe and in 1930 a large legacy from an old friend in Torquay repaired the finances of the estate. Towards the end of the Second World War a military camp was built in the grounds and occupied for a short time by Americans preparing for the D-Day landings. George died in 1946 and his cousin Humphrey Woollcombe, a well-known solicitor in Plymouth, moved to Hemerdon in 1947. During his time the ravages of the war years were repaired and the Miners Arms and the cottages in Sparkwell and Hemerdon sold to their occupants. The farmhouses and remaining house property were modernised and the woods replanted after wartime felling (*see the report from the* South Devon Times, *10 March 1950, above*).

Until her death in 1954 George's widow Edith occupied the main part of the house which was temporarily divided into two to accommodate Humphrey and his family. Afterwards the house was thoroughly repaired and brought up to date, and the 'flat' was let. Humphrey died in 1968 and his widow Dorothy died in 1977. The partition was removed and the house restored to a single unit in 1984. Hemerdon contains many reminders of all the family, including portraits, photographs, letters, diaries and notebooks.

In 1948, it was decided to sell off a number of properties belonging to the Woollcombe estate, because it would cost too much to renovate them bearing in mind the low rents. The following is a correspondence from that year sent to Messrs Woollcombe & Yonge by C.S. Holditch:

1st April, 1948

Messrs. Woollcombe & Yonge,
2 Queen Anne Terrace
Tavistock Road
PLYMOUTH

Dear Sirs,

RE: HEMERDON ESTATE.
1 & 2 JUBILEE COTTAGES & COTTAGE OCCUPIED BY
MR. PAUL.

Mrs. Perry's son is desirous of purchasing either the cottage occupied by Mr. Paul or all three of the block. As you know his mother occupies No.2 Jubilee Cottages and Mr. Rowe of Sterts Farm No.1. I have been thinking over this proposition having in mind the cottage requirements of Sterts Farm and my conclusions are that it is necessary to keep two cottages for this farm pending, at some future date, the building of two modern cottages.

Now, Mr. Rowe has No.1 and also No.1 Rose Cottages. This latter cottage is poor and the Jubilee Cottages are the better to hold. On the whole I think it would be best to keep 1 & 2 Jubilee Cottages for letting with the farm/and to sell Pauls cottage only of this block. I could arrange a division subject to the purchaser's approval.

Pauls Cottage rent is £13.14.0d. per annum but it is worth more and I think £20 would be fair rental value and £300 a fair selling value but with vacant possession probably £500.

If you approve I will get negotiations in hand.

Gran Perry and granddaughter Mary at the rear of No.2 Jubilee Cottages.

GALVA COTTAGE, IVY COTTAGE & ALMA COTTAGE.

The tenant of Galva Cottage wishes to buy and might possibly purchase all three. Division is somewhat difficult but I think I could work out a scheme to divide off Galva Cottage.

The rents are:

Galva Cottage	£6.0.0.
Ivy Cottage	£5.0.0.
Alma Cottage	£9.0.0.

All are in very poor condition and maintenance repairs are bound to be heavy. I think the values are: Galva Cottage: £150. And if you approve I could get in touch with the tenant of Galva Cottage.

GALVA COT, DRAKELAND ROAD.

This cottage is let to Mr. R.J. Mumford who wishes to purchase. The rent is £7.0.0. (sic) per annum. I have been considering the advisability of keeping this cottage for Sterts Farm, the lands of which adjoin, but my conclusions are that it is rather far from the village and the farm would be better provided for with Jubilee Cottages. The cottage is by no means good but it is detached, has a very good garden and the position is attractive. Subject to tenancy it is worth £200 but with vacant possession it would make £400 and I think the tenant should pay a little more than £200. If you approve I will approach the tenant.

HEMERDON COTTAGE OPPA. MINERS ARMS.

This cottage is let to Mr. A. Bawden at £6 per annum. It is in very poor condition and will be expensive to keep. From an income point of view it would be best to clear it at £100 but it is at the only entrance to the field behind let to Mr. Honey (who would like to buy both the cottage and the field) and I am wondering if selling would be advisable. The cottage is on the narrow part of the road and should be removed rather than reconditioned and the garden thrown into the field. This would make the field good for building development if, and when, such would be possible. Building development might be somewhat prejudicial to Sterts Farm house from one point of view and the field would form the key to further development from another point of view. I am perhaps looking very far ahead. The point against holding the cottage is its condition; the roof is really worn out and parts of the main walls require pointing up and making good. To hold and continually patch means spending the rent and to recondition properly say £150. However, from a long-term point of view it might be best to hold the cottage, keep it going until it becomes vacant and then demolish it to improve the field behind. Before deciding you might like to consider this on the spot.

No.1 & 2 Rose Cottages & Western Row.

These are poor and cannot be divided to offer to the tenants. It will come to a question of trying to find outside buyers for each parcel.

Sparkwell.

I have not seen Mrs. Kingdon but understand she would like to buy her cottage on the main road. I could arrange a division but am thinking of the other cottages.

I enclose a rough plan. All the cottages are poor and must eventually come under review by the Local Authority.

Really the whole should be in the hands of an owner who would keep them going until such time as a re-development scheme could be carried out when sites for eight good cottages could be made; another long term view!

This I feel would be the real scheme but it is so remote that to save the maintenance expenses against poor rent returns and the fact that severance would not prejudice the land behind. I think probably it would be policy to sell and as it may be difficult to sell the whole, work out a letting scheme as best I can with a view to piecemeal disposal.
Yours faithfully,

C.S. Holditch

Left: *Jack and Florrie Stancombe at No.4 Western Row.*

Below: *No.5 Western Row, known as Elm Cottage and, at the time of writing, owned by Mr Peter Smerdon. In the 1940s it was tenanted by Dick and Lizzie Mumford and owned by the Woollcombes.*

THE SHRIEVALTY

Mr James Woollcombe of Hemerdon House was High Sheriff of Devon in 1995/6, and in discharging the duties of this ancient office was presented to HM the Queen when she visited the centenary Devon County Show. The High Sheriffs of England and Wales hold the oldest secular office under the Crown, and celebrated their millennium in 1992. Originally they were very powerful, performing all the functions now shared between the County and District Councils, the Police, the Inland Revenue, the Magistracy and to some extent the Army. Robin Hood had some experience of this in Nottinghamshire.

The only surviving part of these duties is the enforcement of High Court judgements, which is carried out under the High Sheriff's authority by the Under-Sheriff and his officers with the help, where necessary, of the 'posse' – well known to all fans of Western films. It is the High Sheriff's right to summon the support of able-bodied people to assist in the enforcement of the law and nowadays this right is often exercised by the Sheriff's officers when they meet with resistance in seizing property required to satisfy a judgement. Eventually the High Sheriffs became so wealthy and powerful that King Edward III limited their tenure to one year. Modern High Sheriffs are quite glad of this restriction as the office is in no way subsidised and they have to foot all expenses.

Apart from the enforcement of judgements, their present functions are to attend the High Court Judges when they visit the county, by sitting with them in court at Exeter and Plymouth and by entertaining them at home to make them better acquainted with local people, to attend visiting Royalty in company with the Lord Lieutenant, and increasingly to make whatever contribution they can to the maintenance of law and order in the county. A nationwide campaign called 'Crimebeat' spearheaded by High Sheriffs was joined by Devon in 1999 and is proving effective in fostering good citizenship among young people.

Over the centuries the High Sheriff's duties have changed and so has the composition of the Shrievalty. Today the office is shared between the sexes (four of the last nine in Devon have been women) and steps are being taken to broaden the base ethnically and socially to include anyone capable of the job and able to afford it.

Left: *Queen Elizabeth and Prince Philip with James Woollcombe (far right), High Sheriff of Devon.*

INDUSTRY IN HEMERDON

Mining on Hemerdon Ball Interest in the mining possibilities of Hemerdon Ball dates back at least to the second quarter of the 19th century and the overgrown pits (now occupied by badgers) on the way up to the summit reflect the efforts of individuals with elementary equipment to make something of the metals to be found beneath the surface. Their hopes were concentrated on tin and copper with arsenic also present – the Bottle Hill chimney served as an arsenic burner. Tungsten was unknown until late in the 19th century and not discovered at Hemerdon until early in the 20th. Nevertheless, the interest was enough to generate heated disputes amongst the landowners and would-be miners and between the landowners themselves. The three estates of Newnham (Strode), Hemerdon (Woollcombe) and Goodamoor (Treby) all laid claim to mining rights in the area and some of these claims conflicted. A settlement between the Strodes and Woollcombes was reached in 1834, under which the mining rights on the Ball are held jointly by the two estates, but even this did not prevent further trouble in the 1840s when George Strode of Newnham wrote to George Woollcombe of Hemerdon in terms of firmly controlled politeness which left no room for doubt about his feelings. He began by saying that the right of using the Drakelands stream for mining purposes involved a difficult point of law which 'to avoid the possibility of an angry discussion would be best left to the professionals'. 'Both you and I, my dear friend', he wrote:

... are of rather an excitable Temperament, and such being the case, I should be sorry truly sorry to place myself in a situation where, on the impulse of the moment, some unguarded expression might escape my lips, which on cooler reflection would be much to be regretted; and I should never forgive myself were I so far to forget the rules of propriety as to say or do anything likely to disturb that friendship which has for so long a period subsisted between us.

He said firmly that the matter should be left to the advisers and continued:

I need say no more to assure you of my unaltered friendship, to maintain which it will be well to avoid a personal interview lest a feeling might be induced which would not readily subside.

There is no record of the outcome, but tradition has it that relations between the families were cool for some time.

The first serious attempt to mine the tungsten was made during the First World War, but by the time that the plant was operational the war had ended and the tungsten price fell to the point

Mine workers, 1940s.
Left to right: Florrie Mudge,
Gwen Clemo, Doris Higman,
Blanche Lee, Betty Mudge.

where the mine was forced to close after yielding only 16 000 tons of ore. Nothing more happened until 1936, when a mining company took a lease and built a small plant which went into production in 1941. The Government then became interested and commissioned a much larger plant (still standing but mostly derelict). This plant started production in 1943, but ran for only eight months as it became more attractive to buy supplies from abroad. After the war, apart from an abortive attempt to restart production in the Korean War, nothing happened until the 1960s when a Canadian entrepreneur took a lease which later passed into a succession of hands including the American mining company Amax.

In the late 1970s came the first full exploration programme, resulting in the discovery of substantial reserves which make the Hemerdon mine Western Europe's largest source of tungsten. Planning consent was eventually granted for the exploitation of the deposit, but before any significant work could be done the tungsten market collapsed and the mine was mothballed. It is now without a tenant. Future prospects are uncertain, but it is hoped to find suitable uses for the land pending any revival of interest in the tungsten.

Smallhanger and the China Clay Works

Smallhanger was purchased in 1869 from a Frederick Bishop, being in the parish of Plympton St Mary and in the manor of Lyneham by John Olver, China Clay Merchant of St Austell. The farmland comprised about 40 acres, but when Claymoor was built, the remaining land amounted to about 32 acres. It is believed that Smallhanger was at one time used as kennels for the Kitley Estate (Yealmpton). The farmhouse when purchased by John Olver was a typical four-roomed building, and to house his increasing family he built on another four-roomed cottage, adding also a kitchen and wash-house. John Olver sold Smallhanger to his son Arnold early in 1900 and it was let as two cottages for a time to farm workers.

John Olver had been working the Stockers Clay Pit (adjoining Smallhanger) on a lease, with the clay stream running about one and half miles to the dries at Galva, situated above the village of Hemerdon. Until the late 1900s, the only supply of water to all the dwellings on the higher side of the road from Drakelands was piped from a stream/spring at Stockers. The last house was Galva and the overflow supplied the top field of Sterts Farm, Hemerdon. The clay on Smallhanger at that time was an unknown quantity although it was said John Olver only needed to walk over land to know what minerals were beneath the soil! He was proved right even in the 1980s when drilling took place. Having purchased the farm at Smallhanger and a considerable area of 'waste' he built a dry-stone boundary wall dividing his property from the neighbouring land and proceeded to mine an especially good quality of china clay –

Clay workers in 1920, from left to right: Lew Bawdon, Joe Collings, Alf Calloway, ?.
Main: *Loading the clay.*

which is a mineral made up of decomposed granite and found only in a few areas in this country.

The process from the time of John Olver in 1869 until his son, Arnold Olver, retired in 1952, at the age of 80 years, remained the same. The very first claypit, having been worked to capacity, was flooded; a spring constantly flowed into the deep end and leats were made to catch water from Headon (or Heddon) Down and the surrounding land to channel all surface water into the pond. Over the years this process was repeated with another pond being made and two claypits worked. Mining obviously had to be where the china clay was.

First the burden had to be removed; this was the soil, mainly peat and, under this, a stony clay soil, to a depth of a few feet on the Smallhanger works (the only machine ever used was a bulldozer brought in to remove an area of burden soon after the end of the war in 1945). The whole area of the claypit had otherwise, over many years, been dug away by men using a pick and shovel, with the soil being loaded into a wagon and manually pushed on tramlines to the top of a burden tip (this being separate to the sand dumps or tips). The empty tram wagon would then run back to the start for another load, the man usually riding, but ready with the brakes (it was great for children to enjoy).

The next stage of working for clay was to channel the water from the pond to the top of the pit, from the area where the burden was removed, down over the stopes or ridges. The water ran down the side over the clay where a man with a pick would work lumps into the running water, this (by now white) water ran to the bottom of the pit into an oblong area about 20ft by 15ft with the sides boarded and the outlet for the water in one corner. The clay stream from the pit side flooded across this 'tank' and the sand settled to the bottom. The particles of clay carried on in the stream. The sand accumulated over a period of days, and when one side was deep enough, the boards were removed to start the process again on the other side.

The white sand which collected each day was removed with a horse and cart, being loaded with a shovel into the cart and pulled about 400 yards to the top of the sand dumps, where the horse would back to the top of the steep slope, the cart would be tipped up, the sand sliding down the slope and the man, horse and cart returning to the china clay pit for the next load.

The clay stream ran for about half a mile through underground pipes to the mica dregs. There were lengths of planks (on edge) about 30 feet from end to end and with about 8–10 channels, spaced about 3 feet apart. The stream of water with the particles of clay flowed through two or three of these each day, where the rough clay settled and was then diverted into a settling tank ready for the mica shed, to be separated from the best clay.

The stream with the fine clay particles then flowed further to the next stage, large settling tanks, about 20 feet square and about 10 feet deep. The stream flowed into the appropriate tank until it was full, to the required fathoms, and then left until the clay had settled to the bottom, leaving the water on top to be gradually run off.

On one side of the tanks was an opening about 4 or 5 feet wide where planks formed a block, being removed one at a time to drain off the water and leave the clay in the tank, at this stage being very sloppy. The settling process took several weeks, longer if it was wet and stormy.

Next, the clay was run into a shallow tank where it stayed until it was firm enough to be dug into cubes with a man using a shovel, put into flat-top wheelbarrows (iron wheels) and wheeled into the adjoining sheds for drying. The cubes (shovel size) were placed on shelves, well spaced out, and left to dry with the elements (a northwest wind providing the best conditions).

When the clay was dry enough, depending entirely on the weather, a lorry was ordered. Usually two men threw the clay up into a lorry and it was taken to Plympton Station, when the tonnage for the required order was complete. It was then loaded onto a truck (with a cover, which was very important to keep the clay dry) and transported to the potteries in Staffordshire.

This was the process employed until the time of Mr Arnold Olver's retirement in 1952. Until lorries were available, horses and wagons would take the clay either to Moor Sidings, between Beechwood Cross and Langage Cross, or to Plympton Station.

At one time, some clay would be dried by the heat from a coal furnace in a stone shed at one end of the settling tank and flues under the tanks with the smoke coming up through a tall chimney at the other end. After all the clay had been drained into the tanks, the clear water carried on in a stream to the Smallhanger brook which eventually runs into the River Plym. Before selling the clay, fired samples would be sent to various firms; these were cubes of clay about one inch, from different sheds labelled ED or DX2, etc. and orders would be dispatched accordingly.

John Olver, having a large family, purchased dinner and tea sets of 24 pieces, first choosing the design and then having each one made from Smallhanger clay. Afterwards the designs were destroyed and several pieces of these sets are still treasured by the family.

In 1919 John Olver died and his two sons, Fred and Arnold Olver, became the owners of one

THE OLVERS

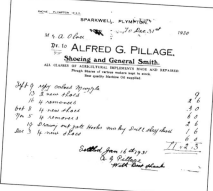

Top left: *Smallhanger, 1962.*

Top right: *John and Mary Olver at Claymoor, c.1890.*

Above: *Arnold and Gladys Olver with a friend. Behind them are the lumps of clay stacked in cubes.*

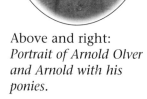

Above and right: *Portrait of Arnold Olver and Arnold with his ponies.*

Above centre: *A receipt written out to Arnold Olver by local black-smith Alfred Pillage, 31 December 1930.*

half each of the Smallhanger China Clay Works. In 1929, following his marriage, Arnold and Gladys Olver lived in the original house, and in 1935, Fred and Chrissie Collings occupied the smaller side of the house. A bathroom was added in 1936 (built by Bill Lee of Drakelands) and electricity was connected 20 years later. A telephone was connected in about 1930 (the number of which was Cornwood 12). Brief chats to either Mrs or Miss Vivian at the exchange were normal when the receiver was picked up, before being connected to the number asked for.

Deliveries by van were made shortly before the war and continued afterwards – the goods of Mr Bill Damerell, butcher of Colebrook, were usually delivered by Jack Martin or Mrs Gwen Honey, and Mr Tom Cannon (employed by Plymouth Co-op) delivered bread and cakes twice a week. Mrs Griffin brought bread once a week until about 1943. Alf Collings used to bring milk from Mr Sid Sandover of Birchland each morning on his way to work, together with the *Western Morning News*. Mr George Townsend from the shop in Sparkwell used to either walk or ride his bicycle to deliver the post, sometimes making two deliveries, but in about 1940 post was brought by a red van from Plympton – there were still two deliveries, and it was collected! Mr Cannon also collected laundry which would be returned two weeks later.

There was a small hut built next to the Hemerdon hut – a Co-op shop which used to sell most things, and Jean would order anything required to be there the following day. People from Sparkwell used to catch a bus to Hemerdon, have a cup of tea with Jean and return with their purchase on the next bus.

Mr Arnold Olver used to ride a pony everywhere until 1934 when he purchased his first car. Although he never drove Mrs Gladys Olver learned to drive in the fields and in 1936 they bought a Morris Oxford which was used until 1954, and a smaller Ford Popular became the family car. Before and during the war, Mrs Olver drove to Plymouth once a fortnight to get the wages for the clay workers and to buy household provisions. Other than what could be consumed quickly, things like dried fish were bought because everything had to be kept outside in a 'safe' as there was no fridge until 1956.

The car was never used if it was possible to walk anywhere. Mrs Olver and Heather Harvey (née Olver), together with Miss Winifred Olver from Claymoor, used to walk regularly to Venton Chapel for the afternoon service on a Sunday.

Arnold Olver retired from farming and a sale was held in 1942, when Mr Fred Collings rented the land until his death in 1964. Shortly after this, Smallhanger again became one house, with several alterations being made. A large water tank in

the field provided water in the taps instead of using the hand pump to draw water from the well. The yard was levelled and tarmacked and the shippen and stable made into a double garage and a DIY area.

Vegetables were always grown and hens provided eggs and meat. Until several years after the Second World War had ended, a fat cockerel was killed for Christmas dinner, more cold meat and chips followed, the giblets were another meal and the bones made a stew.

Smallhanger was sold to ECLP in 1975 (by Jack Harvey of John Pearse and Sons of Plympton). Originally the firm name had been John Olver and Sons. In 1937 Fred Olver died, leaving his son Frank to continue in the name of F.N. Olver, and Arnold Olver his uncle carried on from the death of his father, in the name of Olver & Co.

During the Second World War, Frank worked at the Wolfram mine, adjoining Smallhanger land, and his uncle kept the works ticking over. The men working for Olver & Co. were exempt from call up as it was considered essential that clay continued to be produced. Only one man asked to leave to serve. A Professor Jones from St Austell came in 1941 to inspect the Smallhanger Works, and declared it to be 'the most economical works in the whole country', and a facility which was to be kept open.

In about 1910 a canon ball was found on the clay works below Claymoor House which was thought possibly to date from the battle said to have taken place on Hemerdon Ball in 1646.

Top: *Clayworks, 1953.*

Above: *The Olvers' letterhead.*

Left: *Chimney stack at Smallhanger in the 1960s.*

Claymoor House and the view from the house over Drakeland Corner and Bottle Hill with the River Plym at Laira and Mount Edgecombe and Cornwall in the background.

Wolfram Mine workers, 1940s.
Left to right, back: Arthur Baskerville, Marjorie Jones, Doris Taylor, Florrie Kitts, Gwen Taylor;
middle: Joan Tucker, Audrey Willcocks, Betty Mudge, George Lee, Blanche Lee;
front: Norman Lee next to dog.

Claymoor The house, almost a mile from Sparkwell, was built by John Olver, owner of Smallhanger China Clay Works, for his family of eight children. They included John (who died in Denver, Colorado, at the age of 21), Wilsie, Fred and Arnold, Ellen (Nell), Fanny, Winifred (Winnie) and Christabelle (Chris). Claymoor was built from stone extracted from a quarry at the entrance to the drive, now a field. The floors were tiled in the porch, hall, kitchen and dining room – probably with some thought of boots carrying clay into the house! The floors of the breakfast room and sitting room were of wood. Pitch pine panelling covered all four walls of the breakfast and sitting rooms, with marble mantles and surrounds for each Victorian fireplace. The sitting room boasted an ornate ceiling and white marble fireplace. Upstairs three bedrooms enjoyed wonderful views over Plympton, Laira and into Cornwall, the other three main rooms overlooking the fields of Smallhanger.

John and his wife Mary moved with their family into Claymoor in November 1881 on completion. Although the girls did housework, one maid was employed and a coachman/gardener was paid for outdoor work, as the sons worked for their father or left home later. The stable building was completely separated from the house with a walled courtyard and small door to a path leading through the shrubbery to the house. There were two large stalls/boxes for horses, a harness room (with fireplace), a hay loft and at the end of the building an enclosed shed for a carriage and a trap.

Many trees were planted on Smallhanger and Claymoor as windbreaks (a wise move). Poplars lined the drive, copper beech shaded the lawn, and there were also beech, larch and scotch pines. Many lovely coloured rhododendrons and azalea crowded the shrubbery together with holly and other shrubs. The vegetable garden was very sheltered being lower than the adjoining land, and about 200 yards away from the house there was a 'secret passage' between two privet hedges leading from the corner of the orchard to the garden. The orchard was below the terraces at the edge of the lawn at the front of the house and some of the original trees are still to be seen, notably a cider apple tree. Several young fruit trees were planted here by Mr Jack Harvey in 1980.

The only water for the house was collected from a stream at the end of the Smallhanger meadow, but in 1958 a large 4000-gallon tank was built and, together with a small pump, this supplied water for the needs of the household. Until 1958, all water was carried to the place of need! Large 2-gallon (or more) galvanised cans with a pouring lip for water were used to flush the closets (a small hole to sit over surrounded by an expanse of wood each side and a round wooden lid to lift to the side). Thick earthenware jugs with lids were used for hot water for the bedrooms, where there were wash stands with large round bowls and jugs of cold water, permanently filled, and matching covered soap dishes.

All rooms were furnished with four-poster beds – drapes keeping out the draughts – and feather ties and feather pillows, built-in wardrobes with pitch-pine doors (matching the pattern of the downstairs panelling) provided hanging space, and with the dressing table, washstand, a chair and possibly a wooden chest, the room was complete with necessary furniture. Most of the furniture was made for John Olver by Stephens of Plympton. In the breakfast room, at about shoulder height, just a few feet from the left of the door, there is a round hole in the panelling which was caused by a gun firing when Wilsie was cleaning it on the large table, nearly shooting his brother Fred – a narrow miss.

Rooms were lit with candles and single candles were carried when it was dark. Later lamps used paraffin oil, the same as that used for small stoves. Miss Winnie Olver lived alone at Claymoor during the war until moving to Smallhanger at the age of 86 to live with her brother Arnold and family. She had never used electricity and insisted on using a candle in her room at night. The electricity supply was brought to Claymoor in the late 1950s by Mr Jim Carter.

Some of the children were educated at boarding school, travelling by pony and trap to Plympton Station and by train to St Austell. Chris was at boarding school at Plympton (between Ridgeway and St Maurice) and one afternoon she was so homesick she ran away, walking up the turnpike and back to Claymoor, arriving at tea time, little knowing that the town crier of Plympton had been alerting the area as to her disappearance. Arnold Olver attended the old Plympton Grammar School at Plympton St Maurice, riding a donkey to and fro.

Although fruit and vegetables were grown to supply the house, it was necessary for Mrs Mary Olver to travel into Plymouth by carriage at times. As she did not wish to drive through the clay works to Hemerdon, John Olver made a special road from Claymoor to join the track at Goodamoor Clump and made up the road to Beechwood Cross.

Miss Winnie Olver used to walk into Sparkwell three times every week until the early 1950s, taking a gallon enamel can for milk from Mr Lawrence Hooper at Bank Cottage, Sparkwell, and two large canvas shopping bags to purchase all necessary food from Mrs Susie Townsend at the shop, on the way collecting newspapers from Mrs Bawden from the shed next to her cottage (now Wayside). At every stop, she would pause for a long chat, then return through the pathfields from the Treby Arms to Goodamoor Clump and home.

The blizzard of 1891 caused great problems for everyone. To go outside, Arnold Olver had to open the upstairs window and walk on the frozen snow from there; it was very dangerous and one life was lost at Bottle Hill.

In the kitchen was a large black kitchen range for cooking, a long table with a bench under the window on one side and adjoining a laundry with frosted glass in the window, so that visiting horseriders would not be able to look in and see the daughters working at the mangle or otherwise! Down a short passage was the wash house where a copper was built with a fire under and a round cavity above where the water and clothes were boiled. A telephone was connected in 1975 when Claymoor was purchased by John Olver's granddaughter Heather.

Galva House (by Mr Richard Silverlock, son of Leonard Silverlock, who lived and grew up at Carthew House). Built around 1780 as a row of cottages for china-clay workers and converted into a house in about 1880, Galva was extended in about 1908. The lower china clay works were formerly used in connection with the mine at Hemerdon Ball and the Galva Cottages were occupied by miners. The leasehold of the works and house were owned by John Nicholls & Co. Ltd, the freehold being owned by the Hemerdon House Estate (Woollcombe family). John Nicholls' son

Galva House from the front and the side.

married Edith Woollcombe, the daughter of the rector of St Mewan near St Austell, Cornwall. The company converted the house into a large single dwelling for the Nicholls family. The house comprised: six bedrooms, a dressing room, bathroom and three servants' bedrooms on the first floor, and a large drawing room, morning room, dining room, large kitchen, scullery, pantry, butler's pantry, large front hall and WC on the ground floor.

Captain Leonard Silverlock, late Captain of the Sherwood Foresters and Captain of the Mines.

The large garden comprised a pond area, a lily pond and tennis court. The lower garden was for fruit and there were two greenhouses (vinery and peach) and two garages (old coach houses). Behind the house and adjoining the china clay dries were a coach house stable and workshop. Below the lower garden was the lower china clay dry.

In 1919 the Hemerdon Works was acquired by English China Clays Ltd being the first company to be acquired by that firm in a long series of acquisitions. They subsequently acquired the freehold. During the 1940s they converted the house back into cottages. Before the acquisition by English China Clays, John Nicholls junr was joined by his nephew Leonard N. Silverlock (late Captain of the Sherwood Foresters) who, after his marriage, lived at Carthew House, Hemerdon.

Carthew House Carthew House was built in 1908 (using granite from the quarry at Hemerdon Ball) to house a China Clay Captain, Mr Sam Perry, who was being transferred from the China Clay Works area of St Austell to be the Captain of the Hemerdon Works. As he came from Carthew near St Austell he called the house 'Carthew'. When he retired the house was occupied by Leonard Silverlock until he retired and moved with his wife to St Austell in 1954. They had two sons, John Vivian and Richard. The former joined English China Clay in 1946 in its production department and Richard joined them in 1948 to be head of its estates department.

Mr and Mrs William (Bill) Stevens have lived at Carthew since the early 1960s (see page 169). Mr Stevens has now retired from ECC (English China Clays) and with his wife Eileen, a talented artist, has four children all of whom grew up at Carthew – John, Theresa, Yvonne and Christopher.

OTHER HEMERDON PROPERTIES

Crownhill Down Cottage, **Drakelands**
Crownhill Down Cottage was built in the 1800s for £32. It was reputed that the floor of the cottage had been lowered and that a ghost could be seen walking across the room at the old floor level in this cottage. For many years until the early 1960s Mr and Mrs Wilsie Olver lived there (not the family of John Olver of Claymoor). He did odd building jobs and kept one or two cows and pigs, as well as some poultry. Mrs Olver used to take eggs to the Plymouth market, walking to the bus stop at Bottle Hill. Mr Olver rented two of the fields belonging to Claymoor for grazing during part of each year. Pat and Bob Burns bought the cottage and almost rebuilt it following the deaths of Mr and Mrs Olver. Tragically Bob was killed whilst digging a trench for a water wheel.

Higher Drakeland Farm   Philly Luscombe farmed Higher Drakelands. The land between the farm and Drakelands leading up to the top of Crownhill Down was always known as Luscombe's Lane. Philly's daughter Emily and her husband Stan May farmed there for several years and now Sid May and family live there, with Richard farming.

Drakelands   Mabel Lee, resident of Drakelands, lost her husband in the early 1940s, which left her with four sons and a daughter. She kept a cow, a few pigs and poultry. The cottage was sold in the mid 1950s to Mr Palmer of Joshua Rendle, builders, who lived there with his wife Doreen and their children John and Jane until the Havillands bought it. Then in about 1967, Peter Bloom, wife Muriel and children Mark and Mandy purchased it. The cottage originally had two rooms downstairs and two upstairs with a separate shippen and pigs' houses backing on to Luscombe's Lane. Mr Palmer extended the house and joined it to the shippen and Mr Bloom built out even further.

EMARCO (now Lyndenfell)   This attractive cottage was built by Bill Lee for his eldest daughter Dorothy and husband George Lee.

Lower Drakelands   Sam Farley with his wife and son George lived at Lower Drakelands for many years, keeping some cattle, pigs and poultry. A few fields went with the smallholding and as well as keeping stock, vegetables were produced for sale in the market at Plymouth. The Farleys also purchased fruit wholesale.

Plym View   Mr and Mrs Phillips and Mr Phillips' brother lived at Plym View until the mid 1960s. There were fields belonging to the property and they also kept cattle, pigs and poultry.

From top to bottom: Tom and Sarah Lee, with children including Arthur standing to the far right; Russell Lee with his car; Gladys Lee eating a pasty for lunch at the back of Rose Cottage (Mousehole); Bill Lee in Naval uniform outside Rose Cottage. He served on HMS Thunderer *during the First World War and was also in the gun crew; Bessie Lee riding a relative's motorbike.*

High Post Before the war the Miller family lived there. A small window faced the road and Ida used to sell cigarettes to anyone (work men usually) on request – and probably sweets also. The property was sold during the 1950s to a young family called Hoskin (daughter of Mr Coombes, the barber in Colebrook and sister of Dennis Coombes of Shaugh Prior, now retired barber).

Elfordleigh Hotel In 1880 a Mrs Bainbridge lived in the then private residence – and kept a pet monkey. When Arnold Olver (then a young boy) was playing on the Hemerdon incline embankment, he found this monkey and returned it to its owner! The Elfordleigh Hotel, together with other properties then belonging to the owners, was sold off in 1928. It is said that somewhere around this area there was a hydraulic ram. In 1937 the hotel was sold again with the addition of a nine-hole golf course (which was designed by J.H. Taylor).

Mrs Dorothy Woollcombe remembered that as a young girl, she loved going to dances at the Elfordleigh with her aunt.

During the war years the golf course was ploughed up for the war effort. It is reported that Amy McDonald stopped off at the hotel, during her round-the-world trip.

The hotel comes complete with its own alleged ghost which some say roams the Reynolds Bar. The hotel has recently been refurbished and an 18-hole golf course added with extra bedrooms being built on.

Elfordleigh Farm This farm was owned by Mr Edwards, who sold part of the farm to Mr Rob Skelly of Wotter Farm, and the remainder to the Newnham Estate, which has since sold the land to the Elfordleigh Hotel to enable them to enlarge their golf course (1990s).

Boringdon Camp The Camp is now owned by South Hams District Council, and for many years prior to that was owned by the Luscombe family of Brixton Barton, Shaugh Prior.

Higher Elfordleigh Now known as Heath Farm, Higher Elfordleigh comprises the farmhouse and buildings, together with four houses known as 1, 2, 3 and 4 Staddon Close and a separate dwelling known as The Bungalow.

Heathdown Cottage Approximately two miles from Colebrook Village, on the Shaugh Prior road and opposite Cann Woods, sits Heathdown Cottage. Part of a 231-acre marriage settlement in 1876, from Margaret Holford on her marriage to the Earl of Morley, the cottage was eventually sold to the Damerell family in 1920. Originally two cottages, Heathdown was once a mine captain's home and was passed daily by his miners on their way to Wheal Sydney, whose stack is still clearly visible across the fields behind.

Now a comfortable private home, Heathdown Cottage sits on the threshold of one of Devon's most progressive charities. Less than 100 yards further along the road is the entrance to the Woodside Animal Welfare Trust, the nerve centre for the care of abandoned and abused pets. After coping for years with a shanty town of slowly disintegrating sheds and outbuildings, Woodside finally managed to raise the funds for the start of a replacement sanctuary. This was to be no mean feat, involving endless negotiations for planning permission and noise level restraints. Compromise was finally reached and Phase One of the New Woodside arose (and was forged below ground) during 2000. Amongst the sanctuary's environmentally-friendly manufacture is camouflage in the shape of a grass roof, and reed bed ponds for waste water recycling. Although slow to mature, the ponds now offer a home to wildfowl, insects, frogs and a variety of wild flowers. Because of its ground-breaking community welfare programme, reducing unwanted pet pregnancies in Plymouth's most deprived areas, Woodside won a rare, animal-related grant from the National Lottery. This was designated for the refurbishment of a spay and neuter clinic in the city. Another prestigious award arrived in late 2000 from Sir Paul McCartney in memory of his wife Linda.

As well as unwanted domestic pets, the sanctuary is home for a small number of goats, sheep, fowl and pot-bellied pigs and is very popular with the press. Its founder Carole Bowles is regularly interviewed on animal-related problems and Woodside even had its own six-part documentary on Carlton TV. Only euthanasing terminally ill or dangerous pets, and caring for over 1700 others annually, Woodside's reputation for compassion ensures the respect of many Plymouth people.

Loughtor Mill   Loughtor Mill was part of the Newnham Estate and was a flour mill. There was a serious fire at the mill.

Lobb Farmhouse   Many years ago the tenants of this farm were called Maddock, who claim to be related to the Martin family, who originated from Coldstone House (Shaugh Prior Parish) and who emigrated to America, Mary Martin being the mother of Larry Hagman (J.R. Ewing of Dallas fame). The farmhouse has now fallen into disrepair and is owned by the Cobbold family. It is farmed by Cundy & Sons.

Windwhistle Farm   The farmhouse, buildings and land at Windwhistle were occupied for several years by the Tucker family as tenants. Bob and Fran Tagert live there and developed the barn. For several years it was the home of the Elfords, butchers, the land being farmed by Newnham estate tenants. Now there is a guesthouse at the farm.

Lowdamoor   Lowdamoor was built and occupied by Mr Harry Rowe. On his death it was purchased by Stan White.

The men who built Lowdamoor in the 1930s as a retirement home for Mr Harry Rowe when he gave up farming Hemerdon Farm. Today it is owned by Mr and Mrs Julian Taylor whose sons are Scot and Glen.

Above: *Beattie Tucker and Joe Hutt at Lobb Farm, 1959.*
Left: *Photo of Beattie Tucker aged 21 years with her baby son Jack. Beattie lived with her husband at Lobb Farm. At the age of 16 she was taken very ill and was sent to her aunt in North Devon to recover. The doctors said that she 'would never make old bones.' Beattie died in February 1998 aged 104 years. Jack grew up to be 6'1" tall and was so big that his parents had to dig out the floor of the house so that he could stand up straight!*

Hemerdon Farm   For many years Hemerdon Farm was run by A.R. West as tenant, then by Mr Scott, and recently (since the late 1960s) by Jack Lambshead, who purchased the farm. Mr Lambshead has now retired and the farm has been bought by Arthur West's grandson, Nicholas. Contained within the farmhouse is a private chapel although it is believed that this has not been licensed for some considerable time.

DOR–GLAD–DEL–BET (now 'The Bungalow') Drakelands   This was the office for the wolfram mine during the First World War and was purchased by Bill Lee for his wife, Ella, and daughters, Dorothy, Gladys, Delcie and Betty (hence the name). Ella used to live in Sparkwell and remembered walking to Claymoor on numerous occasions with telegrams for John Olver. Bill Lee was a builder and did many local jobs. Just before the wedding of his daughter Dorothy (to George Lee), Bill Lee put a new wooden ceiling in Sparkwell Church.

Val Evans Recalls Bottle Hill since 1968

You could go all day without seeing any traffic unless it was one of the locals going or coming as there was only me and the Harris family in Bottle Hill Cottages and down the lane at Little Drakelands were John and Winnie Coles. We never saw the Tretheweys who lived above us near the mine in Merrywinds or John and Kim Vane in Mine Cottage unless they were going for a walk as their lane led them straight down to the main road.

Where the scrap yard is now there was a disused quarry that was full of water. We used to have wild ducks nesting and frogs and tadpoles. On the side of the quarry were kestrels and buzzards and in the copse above the quarry was a badger set.

I can remember when we had hard winters and were snowed in several times. My daughter Ann was taken ill during one of these winters and we had to call a doctor, he could only get as far as Lobb Farm barn on the Lee Moor road and had to struggle through some very deep snow to reach us. We used snow chains on our cars in those days during the winter; very few people had four-wheel drive vehicles then.

There were lots of rights of ways over different fields, etc. which have all gone now. There was a stile down by the bridge which took you past Henry Elford's house up across the road at Drakelands, over Hemerdon Ball through the mine and down to Sparkwell School. Mrs Trethewey used to tell me she walked to school that way and another was via a little bridge over the stream near Little Drakelands almost through their back garden up over the big field behind the house and you could walk down to Lobb Farm below us.

The cottage that I live in was just one cottage years ago (built

Main: *Charlie and Hilda Jenkin (née Farley) at Bottle Hill. The two cottages belonged to Hilda for life but on her death reverted to the Strode family.*

Above: *Hilda Jenkin with friends. Mr and Mrs Jenkin lived to a very old age.*

Both photographs date somewhere between 1900–1910.

in 1841), with the one next door added at a later date. The garden here was known as the earliest garden around with everything growing earlier because it faces south. When the cottage was refurbished and the wallpaper was taken off the bathroom walls there was an imprint of ivy that used to grow up the side of the cottage.

HEATHER HARVEY REMEMBERS SPARKWELL

Boxing Day, 1962 [There was] heavy snow, shoulder height or over, and what was not cleared that day froze solid for weeks to come. Roads were blocked with high drifts. Animals had to be brought in – fortunately both telephone and electricity remained connected and we had a supply of calor gas and oil in stock. Eventually some roads were cleared to Hemerdon and Bottle Hill and the postman, milkman and baker all left what they considered to be the usual supplies at the end of the road nearest houses and each house took their supply. There was still snow up until June 1963...

Wartime During the war Daddy (Arnold Olver) let the Sparkwell Home Guard, with Colonel Conran, use the waste above the clay pit for firing practice. We always had notice (the men who worked on the clay works for Daddy were also members of the Home Guard). My cousins and I used to go looking for the brass cartridge cases, usually after a Sunday firing. There were tall poles on Headon Down to stop enemy planes from landing I believe, and after the war ended Daddy bought these, they were piled outside the farm gate and Harry Roberts from Bickfordtown Farm brought his tractor and saw bench and cut them into logs; it was my job to bring them with the wheelbarrow into the shed and split them... ready for the fire. I was only 10 years old then; children would not be allowed to use an axe now.

Mum and I used to walk to Venton Chapel and anniversary teas. One day we were going to tea with Mrs Gladys Sanders at Moor Farm (sadly now called Parkside). She took us the quick way, down to the bridge, through the rails, up the side of the embankment and down the side of the line to the signal box where the signal man advised further progress! A train was going 'up' full of American troops, and when they saw me, chocolate, sweets and cigarettes were thrown out of windows and they called loudly and waved. The signalman told us it was safe to collect everything and then we went for tea.

During the blitz, many people left Plymouth at night. The Munro family would walk out to Mount Pleasant to stay with Granny Munro away from the bombs. Three or four bombs fell at the top of Crownhill Down and several were found over the years at... Smallhanger.

Tollgates Daddy told me stories of when he was a boy, and later, when he was older and he used to ride into Plymouth for 'Saturday nights for 6d.' paying a toll for the privilege. On one occasion he was coming home across Friary Bridge when a train passed underneath. His horse had never seen a train before or heard one; luckily he was a good rider and managed to stay on the frightened animal.

Blacksmith The horses from Smallhanger, both the clay works and the farm, were always taken into Sparkwell for Mr Pillage, the blacksmith to shoe. Mrs Pillage used to sing solos at local concerts.

Wheelwright Arch Reglar had his workshop next to the blacksmiths. He used to do local painting and decorating jobs too.

Cobbler Mr Macbean was very disabled, but managed to ride a bicycle to Colebrook where he had a shop, although he used to do a lot of his work at home at Bottle Hill.

Local Sports Cricket: Sparkwell had a good team before 1939. The cricket field belonged to Birchland, but was only across one field and two hedges from Smallhanger (which was very convenient for catering).

Sparkwell Council Houses In the 1920s there was an avenue of elm trees from the Treby Arms along the Cornwood Road before the council houses were built. Mr Arnold Olver (Daddy) proposed that council houses be built in Sparkwell; he approached Mr Sid Sandover of Birchland and got a site approved. His original proposal was for 20 houses in Sparkwell, 10 at Hemerdon and 10 at Lee Mill (about 1930) but the Plympton Rural District Council (of which he was a member) were so pleased with the Sparkwell site that they insisted all 40 houses were built – hence Birchland Road.

Church Gladys Lee remembers in the mid 1920s an occasion when the collection bag was being passed around and there was a commotion in the front seat where Mr Kenyon Slaney was sitting with his aunt, Miss Whitmore. He was obviously looking through a handful of change for a coin, but then Miss Whitmore took his hand and tipped the whole lot into the collection bag.

John Lubman, Derek Honey, Heather Olver and Ann Mansfield at Elfordleigh Dance.

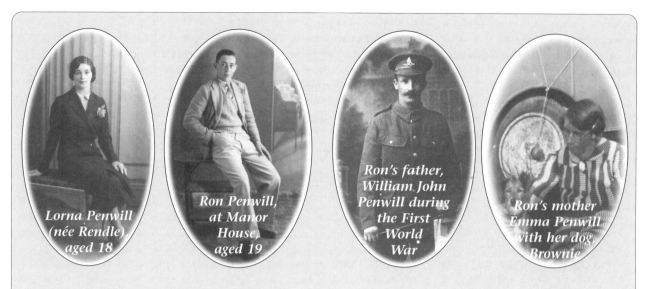

Lorna Penwill (née Rendle), aged 18

Ron Penwill, at Manor House, aged 19

Ron's father, William John Penwill during the First World War

Ron's mother Emma Penwill with her dog, Brownie

MEMORIES OF LORNA PENWILL (NÉE RENDLE) OF LIVING AT LUTTON, SPARKWELL & HEMERDON

I moved to Hemerdon Village 58 years ago in 1942 when I married my husband Ron Penwill. My maiden name was Rendle. I was born at Moorcross Cottage, Cornwood, the home of my Uncle Bill and Aunty Sarah Lillicrap [see also The Book of Cornwood and Lutton]. My uncle was a blacksmith on the premises. I am the eldest of seven children, four brothers and two sisters. We all had nicknames; I was known as 'George the giraffe' because I was tall and had a long neck. Charles was Trouty, Fred was known as Freddy Frog, Edna was called Jipper, Albert was called Polar bear because of his very blonde hair and Amy was affectionately known as beady eyes (because she didn't miss a trick and still doesn't to this day). [Then there was] John – he is the baby of the family – I can't remember him ever having been blessed with a nickname. We were all delivered safely by the village midwife, Nurse Thompson. She would always arrive on her pushbike wearing a long black dress and white apron. Large families were a thing of the times and my mother kept her very busy indeed. Our parents were Leonard and May Rendle. My

family lived at No.3 Gorah Cottages, Lutton, and later moved to 31 Birchland Road, Sparkwell.

We went to Cornwood School and at school lunchtime my brothers and sisters and I would visit Aunt Sarah who was always waiting with a mug of hot fresh milk. She also made her own cream which was absolutely gorgeous. Uncle Bill spent a lot of his spare time in the cellar below the house. He always had a huge jar of cider on the go and in the winter time we would watch him heat a red-hot poker on the fire and pop it into the cider. It would fizz and spit but it tasted wonderful. As children we loved to watch him take a big mouthful of cider and when he swallowed it he would twist his bushy moustache around and around until it curled up each side of his mouth. He also had a huge bushy beard that was nearly touching the top of his trousers.

On the way back to school my friend Barbara's mother, Mrs Drew, would be standing at the front door armed with a dessert spoon and a jar of viro which was a malt extract; it looked like tar but it tasted nice once you got used to it. We all lined up with mouths open as she administered the tonic. It must have worked – we were all as healthy as trouts.

My father and grandfather grew the famous Lutton Broccoli. I've never been sure how you would pronounce it but it had huge cabbage leaves with a cauliflower heart. It was a tradition unique to the Rendle family and people would come for miles just to get the seeds. Grandad and Dad would grow hundreds of them in the back gardens and my brother Charles and I would walk to Sparkwell pulling a trolley to sell them around the houses. The people that lived in the new council houses at Birchland Road were always glad to see us as their gardens had not been constructed and were still in a state of rubble. We also sold spring cabbages and rhubarb. It didn't take no time at all before we sold everything and we had to go back home and re-stock the trolley. Father also kept honey bees and Charles and I did the rounds selling clover and heather honey. The clover season was around May time and the heather came into season in the Autumn. The proceeds from the goodies we sold went on buying new shoes for one of us. Before my mother married she used to deliver bread around the Cornwood area for Vivienes the bakers with a pony and trap. Her maiden name was Venner.

Although during the war food was rationed we always

had plenty of food to go around. My mother was a wonderful cook and we lived on the best fresh fruit and vegetables.

During the war food was rationed and the weekly allowance per person in May 1941 was: 3 pints milk, 9oz jam, 7oz butter, 1/2 lb sugar, 2oz tea, a shillings worth of meat (rationed by price), 4oz bacon, 1 1/2 oz cheese, 2oz cooking (oil?). We couldn't get any bananas so we would boil parsnips and mash them to a soft consistency and flavour them with banana flavouring. It was delicious spread on bread and we couldn't tell the difference from the real thing. A lot of people lived on whale meat which was sliced with onions and cooked in a little fat in the oven.

At 14 years old I worked for Reverend Horten and his wife at Lutton. He was the preacher at the Congregational Church, Lutton. My work included domestic duties. My wages were 5 shillings a week. After about 12 months I went to work at the Ivybridge Orthopaedic Children's Hospital. It was while I was working there I contracted the deadly virus diphtheria and nearly lost my life. A very sick little boy was in need of caring and feeding so I volunteered to nurse him and caught the disease from him. I was extremely ill for quite some time, which meant I had to be isolated from my entire family.

After two years I then went to work at Moorhaven Hospital. There I worked as an assistant cook. My wages leapt to 18s.2d. a week and gradually went up more. Mr brother Charles introduced me to Ron as at the time they both worked at Lee Moor Brickworks and were very good friends. Also working with them was my Uncle Alvin. Fathers and sons mainly worked at the brickworks.

Ron and I like so many of other teenagers went to the Treby Hall dances. It was nicknamed the sweat box because it was so small hot and and stuffy in there. During the war years the hospital at Sparkwell was situated in the woods and used by the Navy lads for rest and recuperation. They also came to the dances and quite a few of the local girls ended up marrying Naval lads. My sister met and married Alan Wicks; he came from Norfolk originally. Ron's sister Edie also met and married Jim Alexander who was Irish and came from Ballymena. Before the war everyone seemed to marry within their own little community; the war certainly broke up this habit. Couples met and married their partners from all over the world.

To this day everyone who knew the famous sweat box remembers it with great affection. The atmosphere was always lively. The yanky lads could certainly teach the locals a few snappy dance steps – they were amazing to watch and great fun to imitate. Nylons were in very short supply so girls would use gravy browning to tan their legs. To make our nails shiny we used 'Amami'; it came in a little silver tin. I can remember we had to wet the palm of our hands with it, let it dry and rub our nails over it. Two perfumes that were really well known were 'Evening In Paris' which came in a little blue bottle and 'Californian Poppy'. To curl our hair we had metal clips with teeth which we heated up on the fire and this gave a crimped look. In her younger days my mother-in-law had long black hair half way down her back and she would use the legs of chairs to curl her hair. Clothes rationing came into effect on 1 June 1941 and finished in July 1949. Mothers seemed to be geniuses with a needle and thread. They would turn collars to get more use out of men's shirts and darn socks. They also had the knack of unpicking a few garments and coming up with a completely different looking outfit.

Ron and all the lads from Hemerdon had to walk across the moors to Lee Moor to get to work. My father and brothers would also walk across the moors from Cornwood. My brother Charles can still tell the story today of how our grandfather and his friends were walking across the moors one night going to work (it was a dreadful night, freezing cold and very very misty) when they saw a large figure looming in front of them. It was the shape of a man carrying a lantern and it appeared to be completely lit up. Needless to say they were completely startled by this and our grandfather talked about it frequently. It would appear they were not the only ones to have seen it, today it is referred to in books about Dartmoor as 'Jack O' Lantern'.

The Second World War broke out in 1939 and Ron was called up in May 1940 for the war. He went into the Royal Artillery. I recall one miserable evening before Ron went into the Army; it was raining very hard and was completely dark everywhere as there was a blackout on. Ron arrived on his motorbike to give me a lift back to the hospital as I was going on night shift. We couldn't use the headlights on the bike because the German planes would have seen us.

We hadn't travelled more than a couple of hundred yards from the house when we hit a huge stone that had been washed out of the hedge by the rain. I came off the bike and landed on the side of my face. We had to get back to the house and call Dr Trumper who had to come from Ivybridge. He put five clips into my head wound. I still have the scar to this day – a permanent reminder of that horrible night.

Ron and I married on 3 January 1942 at Cornwood Church and we had our reception at Treby Hall, Sparkwell. I had a frantic job trying to buy a gold wedding ring as they seemed to be in short supply. I eventually found one which was the last one in Plymouth. As the war was on and food was rationed our parents had to save their coupons for the reception food. I remember Grandad Rendle lived next door to us at Lutton and my brother Fred slept in his house because our house was a bit crowded with nine of us living there.

My mother would hide packets of jellies intended for the reception in the top of Grandad's wardrobes. Fred was very crafty; he never missed a trick and gayly tucked into them as soon as Mother's back was turned. Although it was a bitterly cold day the wedding went off beautifully; in spite of the jellies the reception was a wonderful do with plenty of food. Lewis Lock had a big black taxi which we used as our wedding car. He was a very well-known man who lived at Fosters Tenements, Hemerdon (in recent years it has been renamed and was later known as Ploughlands but it was destroyed by fire in about 1980).

After we married I still worked at Moorhaven Hospital for another eight months. Ron was away in the Army and I would live for three months with my mother-in-law Emma Jane Penwill at Hemerdon and then for three months at home with my parents and the rest of the family, who by now were all gradually leaving home and going off to war. My brother Charles was in the Royal Marines and he was sent to the jungle area of Burma. Brother Fred was stationed in the Krefeld area of Germany with the Army and my other brother Albert was in Eygpt in the Army.

My sister-in-law Edie worked at the hospital with me as well. We lived in the staff quarters and we had one and a half days off a week to go home. Sometimes Edie and I would manage to have the same time off.

One particular evening we were cycling back to the hospital as we had been home for a day off and we were frightened witless as a huge explosion in Plymouth lit up the sky for miles. The Germans had bombed the oil tankers in Turnchapel. No matter how fast we pedalled it felt as if the flames were licking across the sky chasing us. In fact the

brilliant red sky over Plymouth could be seen as far away as Torquay.

I had been at the hospital for 6½ years when I decided to leave. My friends Amy Mudge and Muriel Folly convinced me to go and work at the Wolfram Mine with them. It seemed a very good idea as it meant I wouldn't have to cycle to Bittaford from Hemerdon in all winds and weathers and it was only up the hill. Not long after I left Edie also left and came to the mine to work.

At the mine three shifts operated; A, B and C. I was on the B shift. Dick Sanders was the boss of our shift. He was a lovely man – he must have been in his sixties at that time. He was injured by a grenade in the First World War and suffered a leg injury. He would turn up for work with his motorbike and side car. He was a bachelor and lived at Moorbridge in the cottage by the railway line.

Some of the girls working on B Shift were Muriel Macbean (from Bottle Hill), Violet Phillips (from Cornwood) and Molly Harris (from Spring Cottage, Hemerdon). There were a couple of girls from Padstow who lodged in Plympton and another couple of girls from Plympton as well. The men on B Shift were: Reg Lee (Drakelands), Jack Mumford (Galva Cottage, Hemerdon) and Joe Bull (Sparkwell). We supplied our own bib and brace overalls.

We mainly worked on what were called jigging tables. Men outside of the mill dug up quarry stones and materials with big machinery which was then loaded on to a conveyor belt system which took it up very high. It then dropped down into a cone inside the mill. Every two hours we had to all shift around and take it in turns using the trap door. There was a knack to this – you could only let just the right amount of material through at once. If too much

'A' shift Wolfram Mine Workers, 1940s.

passed through the trap door it would certainly choke up the system and everything would have to be switched off and sorted out before starting up again. It was quite heart stopping to hear enormous pieces of stone travelling up the outside because you knew it would have to come crashing down inside the cone to be let through the trap door. Maybe once or twice during a shift we would encounter huge pieces of stone that just wouldn't come through the trap – everything had to stop and usually Jack Mumford would arrive with a group of men and have to break it up by hand until it was small enough to pass through the trap.

As the material passed through various stages of processing it became finer in texture. Waiting for its arrival the girls would be standing at the jigging tables. The tables would be vibrating and this action separated the minerals. Water jets were used to wash the wolfram out of the sand and silt. A line of black shiny wolfram was called a seam. After this it ended up in a drying shed and was later bagged up. Muriel and Dick worked in the bagging shed which was a filthy job. They

First World War lorry converted by Bradford & Co., Plympton, in Hemerdon Ball Lane at the back of Galva.

were issued with face masks but by the end of the shift they were completely black from head to foot. The only way we could tell which one was which was by Dick's little silver rimmed glasses. It was very hard work. Although the bags were not that big they were extremely heavy. Wolfram was used to strengthen steel, especially in the making of artillery guns for the war effort.

The discarded waste from the mill went out on another conveyor belt and filled giant mechanical buckets that went around on overhead cables. These were emptied out onto a tip in the field away from the mill – near to Hemerdon Ball Lane (see bottom left). Massive tips formed during the war years. In the 1960s Devonport Motor Cycle Club used these tips for scramble bike riding.

One evening B Shift was on night work when the staff canteen was hit by incendiary bombs. We were all in a panic to say the least; the Jerries had a direct hit on the canteen and it was well and truly alight. Reg our boss decided it would be best to turn off all the machinery. In so doing his arm became entangled with the machinery. We all rushed to his aid and he was really lucky he didn't lose his arm.

After the mines I went to work at the American Food and Clothing Depot at Coypool, Marsh Mills. Edie (my sister-in-law) and Kath Nicholson also worked with me. Part of the task here was to press the uniforms when they had been laundered and send them back to the American troops. In other workshops girls would be sewing buttons on uniforms and doing all kinds of repairs and stitching. The girls would have the terrible job of taking all the personal belongings out of the uniforms of the soldiers that had been killed in the battle fields. Lockets,

rings and photographs of their wives and girlfriends that they carried all had to be listed and packed up and sent back to America to their families. It was a heartbreaking job just knowing these poor lads would never be going home.

We didn't stay that long at Coypool as we were sent into the Dockyard to work. I worked as a shipwright's assistant helping to make metal helmet racks for Naval personnel on the ships. This was a tedious job to say the least. Strips of metal had to be measured and guillotined which I hated doing and then flanged (rounded off) by a grinding machine. It was then rivetted together to make four helmet racks. They were then sent to the fitters to be fitted on the ships. I left the Dockyard when the war ended and went to work at Spooners Restaurant with my sister Edna. I left after six months when Ron was demobbed from the Army.

Manor House is a smallholding. We have almost an acre of field plus a large garden. Evacuees from Plymouth lived in the field during the war in caravans and chalet-style huts. As Ron was away in the Army Mr Mumford senr (Mousey) helped to tend the garden.

Our amusement was listening to crystal radios which ran on accumulator batteries. They didn't last that long as they had to be charged up. Bob McNeil and Sid Gulley would come around the villages in their van, usually on a Saturday evening and swap the empty accumulators for a full one. Families would gather around the radios to find out the latest information about the war.

We had an Anderson style air-raid shelter outside the house which would take up to about six persons. People would grab their prized possession (usually a tin box with deeds of their houses and life savings).

Aerial photograph (1997) of Manor House, Hemerdon.

Aerial photograph (1997) of Western Row, Hemerdon. Back left is Hemerdon Farm Cottage. The row of cottages left to right are Nos 1 and 2 (formerly Plymcot and now called Florence Cottage), No.3 (Toad Hall), No.4 and No.5 (Elm Cottage). The lane at the front of the photo leads to Hemerdon Farm now owned by Mr and Mrs West. Sterts Farm is on the right hand side of the road leading up the hill towards Galva and Drakelands.

Ron's mother Emma was a lovely kind and very hard-working lady and she was known as the Florence Nightingale of the village. I remember she would visit some really elderly ladies twice a day, morning and night. She would help them get dressed in the morning and help to put them to bed at night as well as doing little bits of shopping for them and any chores that they needed doing. I suppose today this would be called 'Care in the Community'. One of the ladies, Gran Jones, lived at No.3 Western Row, Hemerdon; she lived well into her nineties. The other lady was Mrs Lee and she lived over the other end of the village at Rose Cottage now known as Mousehole.

Ron's grandparents William Thomas and Emma Jane Penwill came from Gunnislake original-ly. He was in the First World War and after they lived at Central Farm Gunnislake. They moved into No.2 Western Row, Hemerdon, and they had eight children:

Emily Jane (born 25 May 1878). She married Frederick Bawden of Hemerdon. After the First World War they moved to Drakewalls and St Anne's Chapel. Emily died on 5 December 1950. They had one daughter called Rosina.

William John (born 29 July 1879). He married Emma Jane (Warne) of St Austell and they lived at Rose Cottage (now Mousehole), Hemerdon. They had four children, including Myrtle who died aged 13 from pneumonia, Norman who died at about two years old from pneumonia, Ronald John, and Edith. They moved to Manor House in about 1925.

Mary (born 17 February 1882). She married Harry Perry and they had one son, William.

Above: *Photo of a Bawden family wedding at Muttram Cottage (later 'Ploughlands'). Left to right, back: Fred Bawden, George Bawden (bride's father), Charles (bridegroom), Lizzie (bride), Maria Bawden (in black bonnet, bride's mother), ?, Archie Bawden; front standing: Minnie Bawden; seated: Hettie, Rose and Eliza Bawden, Alice Kingdom.*
Top right: *Winifred and Hedley Mumford.*
Right: *Bobby Elford and George Mumford.*
Centre: *This family of all first cousins was taken in the garden of Alma Cottage, Hemerdon.*
Left to right, back: Harry Perry, Joe Bond; front: Russell Lee, Doris Penwill, Ron Penwill.

Edith (born 22 April 1884). She married Alf Mumford and they ran the village shop before the Co-op. They had three children, Dorothy, Cecil and Hedley (who lived at Ivy Cottage, Hemerdon).

Thurza (born 2 May 1886). She married a man named Bond and they had one son called Joe.

Kate (born 25 May 1888). She married Arthur Lee and they had one son called Russell. They lived at Penlee (abbreviated from Penwill and Lee) and later at Alma Cottage, Hemerdon.

Joseph (Ned) (born 26 September 1890) who married a girl called Bessie. They had three children, Marjorie, Robert and Leslie.

Samuel (born 5 March 1893). He married Florence and they lived at Heath Down, Elfordleigh. They had two children, Doris and Jimmy.

Jimmy was killed in Second World War parachuting into Arnhem.

I also remember how my mother-in-law would kill pluck and clean chickens ready for the oven and then walk all the way to Plymouth with them to sell to the hotels and guesthouses. She would tell me how she would walk to Plymouth carrying her goodies walking along the tops of hedges when the lanes were snowed over. The feed for the chickens and pigs would simmer away for hours in a big pot which hung on a crook and sat over an open fire. This was situated in a nook in the granite garden wall. After my mother-in-law died I also took on this task and would take eggs into Mutley Plain guesthouses. We were allowed to sell so many eggs but the remainder had to be packed up and sent to a packing station – I believe it was either in South Brent or Totnes. Ron and

I also kept pigs which kept me fully occupied as he was now working for the South Western Electricity Board (this was after the Second World War). I would feed them and look after the little runts (which were usually the last born); a watchful eye had to be kept on the sow pig as she would probably have such a large litter she would lie on a couple of the little piglets and kill them. I would also rear them by hand using a bottle. Having got completely attached to them they had to be sent off to Harris' bacon factory at Totnes.

In the early 1920s I can recall a Captain Barrel in the Plymouth market. He would stand on a soap box at the back of his lorry and administer all kinds of medicines and potions. He had a knack of manipulating bones and was a wizard with back complaints. A lot of people from this area would pay him a visit to get put right. Also if we

Aerial photograph (1997) of the centre of Hemerdon.
Top right corner West Park Hill, entrance to village and bus stop.

Villagers outside the village hut and little shop, c.1924. The little boy in the centre at the front is Sid Clague, the little girl on his right is Kathleen Mumford. The others names known are Edie Mumford, Gwen Taylor, Mary Richmond, Francis Mumford, Mrs Hacker, Annie Mearns, Jessie Simpson and little Jessie Simpson.

had a cold we would go to see Fred Bates [Ron's relative] also in the Plymouth market. He had a sign above the shop saying 'Cough No More'.

Before and during the war Ron's mum and I would go up on to the moors and collect 'smutties'. The commoners would set fire to the gorse and bracken every March. This practice would let new grass grow and the smutties were the burnt sticks that were left behind. Mothers would take their children and load up trollies full of smutties. The children loved this as they would have a competition of who could get the dirtiest. We would also collect fir cones from the woods [which] were dried [and] mixed with coal to make the fire burn longer.

Before we had freezers meat and vegetables were preserved in salt. For example, runner beans were packed into earthenware jars and layered with salt. They would keep well, especially for Christmas. Root vegetables, carrots, beetroots and parsnips were lifted out of the ground and stored in buckets of sand. They would keep dry for a long time. Turnips were pulled and 'caved'; this meant they were stored in a big heap and then covered in straw. Potatoes were treated the same to protect them from frost.

Ron's mum and I were very successful in making our own wine. Sloe Gin was made by packing layers of sloeberries and sugar in a stone jar tied down tight with a waterproof material and stored for approximately three to four weeks. The juice was then strained through a muslin cloth and some yeast was added. It was then bottled and left to stand for two to three weeks in a dark cupboard. We also made lovely elderflower champagne, blackberry wine (sugar ration allowing during the war) and we also made jars of mint jelly. I also recall that during the war local women picked lbs and lbs of rosehip berries which were then passed over to the Women's Royal Voluntary Service to make rosehip syrup to provide Vitamin C for children. Its commercial name was Delrosa but I believe today it is said that it rotted babies milk teeth so it is no longer available. It is such a shame really because it was really pleasant to take. During the war rabbit trappers came around door to door [and] French onion boys came over from France selling strings of onions door to door riding bicycles. Tinkers (gypsies) came around selling all kinds of ironmongery. After the war an Indian man came around in the summer time selling lovely men's silk shirts [and] Mr Tom Maddock from Ivybridge also came around... selling lamp oil and methylated spirits and... ironmongery.

When I was first married there was a Co-op shop situated next door to the village hall. I remember it closed some time after my daughter was born in 1955. It sold groceries and odds and ends. Ern Damerell the butcher came around on Tuesdays and Saturdays – he had a shop at Colebrook. John Clinick from Wotter had a mobile butcher's van and delivered in the l960s. Mr Almy, a baker and confectioner from Ridgeway Plympton, also delivered here. Uglows Bakers came later in the 1960s. Norman Nelder also had a mobile van and delivered groceries, etc. He and his wife Violet had the shop at Sparkwell. We certainly had more mobile tradesmen back in the olden days than we have today. Millbay Laundry also came around weekly for dry cleaning etc. Most of the women sent their large items for cleaning, especially sheets. Corona soft drinks had a weekly round as well in the 1960s to early '70s. Mr Foster came twice a week with groceries in a van from Underwoods at Plympton. He was also the preacher at the Hemerdon Mission Hall.

Our bus service was very good. The bus came from Breton Side Bus Station and turned around at the Cornwood Inn... if we missed one we could always run out through the woods to the Lee Moor road and catch it. Nowadays it is a combined route covering miles and of course there are no buses after 7p.m. which means if the youngsters want to go out the Mums or Dads have to do a taxi service.

Mrs Annie Lee delivered the Evening Herald newspapers for many years. The papers arrived by the tea-time bus from Plymouth and the bus conductor would jump off the back of the bus, nip across the road and throw the... newspapers on to the seat in the shelter for Mrs Lee to collect.

Electricity was brought into the houses in around 1939. The engineers working here lodged with my mother-in-law. Before electricity we would use a range for cooking. Meals seemed to taste so much better then. Bread would cook to perfection and pies and cakes were always beautifully cooked. We used candles and lanterns for lighting. Water was piped into the houses in the 1950s and before this we had to fetch water from the tap in the road. Last thing at night families would go out to their nearest tap and fill up for the next morning.

When my daughter started school at Sparkwell in 1959 there was no bus to coincide with school time so all the mothers had to walk their children to school and back again. Thankfully it wasn't for too long as the children were provided with a school taxi. My daughter's headmistress at Sparkwell School was Mrs Paddon and the other teacher who taught the infant children was Mrs Ricketts.

Ivy Clague with sons Keith (left) and Edgar (right).

MEMORIES OF EDGAR CLAGUE

I was born in 1931 at No.2 Western Row, one of five brothers: Sid, Reg, Gerald and Keith. Our parents were Ivy and Bobby Clague. When my younger brother Keith was born we moved to Ivy Cottage which is next door to the village hut. Today, Ivy Cottage is owned by Mr and Mrs Brown. Our grandparents Bessie and Jimmy Lee (my mother's parents) lived in the cottage which is today known as 'Mousehole'.

As a young boy, I remember going down the 'hop way' which was the little lane between Rose Cottage and the stone building which was the butcher's shop to get bread from Spring Cottage. I remember it as the bakehouse and I am sure it was old Mrs Harris that used to bake the bread. She would give me the off-cut of the ends of the loaf to eat. Directly opposite the lane was the other lane leading to the fronts of Jubilee Cottages and South View Cottages – the lanes were known as 'up the hop way' and 'down the hop way'. Today Spring Cottage is owned by Mr and Mrs Evans and the old butcher's shop has been turned into a house called Morvah which is owned by Mr and Mrs

Edwards. As a youngster I recall when the end wall of Spring Cottage collapsed and fell down; this wall had the oven built into it. The cottage gets its name because there are three wells under the kitchen floor together with another one outside in the garden.

During the war there was a Mr and Mrs Pearn evacuated from Plymouth because of the bombing living in a temporary shack in the garden of Manor House. Apparently it was said they had 14 or 15 children. Mr Pearn accidentally shot his wife dead whilst he was cleaning his gun.

Ern Tucker, my friend Gerald's father, was Captain of the Hemerdon Football Team. Ern's parents were Jimmy and Polly Tucker of No.2 Western Row, Hemerdon. One year the lads dressed up Mrs Emma Penwill as the guy for bonfire night and sat her in a pram and wheeled her around the village singing 'guy guy guy, poke him in the eye, up the ladder and down the rope give us a penny to see the pope.' She was a good laugh and would do anything for a bit of fun for the children.

I delivered the newspapers to the villagers and still have the original paper-round list with all the names of the people who

lived in the village of Hemerdon at that time (see page 171). I would also deliver 300 papers to the American soldiers who were based at Hemerdon House during the war. They had a large camp on the lawns and they were all black soldiers. They were very kind, especially to the children down in Hemerdon Village. They would give us sweets and candy and also give us rides in their jeeps as well. When they were training the road between Hemerdon and Sparkwell was closed which meant that I couldn't get to school so I was sent to Plympton School.

The Americans would come down into the village to the Miners Arms and they would turn a skipping rope for the children to skip. They would stand my little brother Keith on the pub wall and give him sweets and crisps and sips of beer – even puffs of cigarettes to get him to sing. Keith was only about seven or eight years old then. He soon picked things up because he could sing 'Pistol Packin Ma Ma' all the way through. The Yanks thought this was wonderful and I remember one day he was standing on the wall singing, wearing a little toy gun in a holster around his waist.

My brother Keith and I delivered papers to Sid and Ada Farley who lived at Drakelands. They had a son George. Today it is the trout farm owned by Mr Henry Elford. Sid was tragically killed in an accident falling from a wagon full of hay. Ada was partially sighted and would catch Keith and myself to read all the war stories to her. We had a nickname for her which was 'Aunt Yappy'. She always made lovely dough buns though which was very often our reward for reading the stories. Their son George later had a market garden business at Boringdon Hill.

I remember my father was one of the gang of men who

went to Heybrook Bay to dismantle the old Army hut during the war which was then brought back to Hemerdon and put together like a jigsaw. Some of the men who accompanied him were Hedley Mumford, Ern Tucker and Jimmy Tucker.

Some field names I recall were Daddy Wallings Field, Iceland and Dock Park. Every field had a name.

My father ordered my long gold ringlets to be cut off when I was a young boy as he said I looked like a little girl. Everyone called me little Ivy. The ringlets were cut off and my name changed from Ivan to Edgar which is really my second name. Not many people know that.

One day passing by the Miners Arms garden hedge I heard voices. When I peeped in over I saw Archie Bawden digging a pit to bury Ned Honey's dog. Ned was the pub landlord. The dog was called Twister.

I could hear Archie Bawden reciting a little verse:

Ashes to ashes,
Dust to dust,
If the Lord won't have 'e,
The Devil must.

Ned Honey said 'I'm glad to see the back of that bugger.' That dog would bite anybody, I know because he had me a few times on the legs. It was no joke as I only had short trousers on. In fact back then boys left school wearing short trousers. By the time I had my first pair of long trousers both my brothers had worn them.

My Uncle Bill (my mother's brother) was in the Navy in 1918 during the First World War. He served on the vessel HMS Thunderer and he was also in the gun crew (see page 141, fourth photograph from the top, right-hand column of the page).

Sid and Muriel Clague outside No.4 Western Row.

Hemerdon Football Team, 1923. Left to right, back: ? Collings, George Mumford, Arnold Olver, ?, ?, ?, Bill Taylor, ?, Ned Honey, ?, ?, Dickie Munford; front: Lewis Bawden, Dick Perry, ?, Ern Tucker (Captain with ball between his feet), ?, ?.

Left: *Photograph of the darts team celebrating a win for the Miners Arms. Bottom front left is Ned Honey and next to him is Dick Mumford with his brother, George, far right kneeling. A young David Honey is second back on the left-hand side.*

Above right: *Mary Honey with all her trophies for tennis at the back of the Miners Arms.*

Above: *The pub in the 1960s.*

Inset: *David and Linda Honey.*

Right: *Ned Honey in his Home Guard uniform behind the pub.*

Far right: *Photo of Ned Honey at the back of the Miners Arms feeding his pigs and chickens.*

❧ THE MINERS ARMS & THE HONEY FAMILY ❧

Left: *Celebrations at the Miners Arms. Ned Honey pouring the drink with his son David, daughter Mary and customers looking on.*

Below: *The Honeys together for a family picnic near Hemerdon Ball.*

Below left: *Ned and Lily Honey with son David sitting on the wall and daughter Mary. Today David and his wife Linda carry on the pub business. They have two daughters – Janice and Kay.*

Bottom: *The Miners Arms in the 1930s.*

THE COOKE FAMILY AT SHERWELL

Bill, Don and Betty Cooke now reside at Sterts Farm, Hemerdon, after farming for many years at Sherwell Farm. Betty recounts:

Bill, born in 1927, was ten years old when he came to live at Sherwell Farm. Brother Don was born on 12 November 1932 and was four years old at the time. Our two sisters Barbara and Doreen also grew up at Sherwell. Our parents Leonard and Alice Cooke moved from Lew Down to take over the running of Sherwell Farm. Alice originally came from Plymstock and her father was a blacksmith there.
We can remember during the war, evacuees arriving in two lorry loads to the farm. They would arrive in the evening to escape the bombing of Plymouth and then they would go back in the morning. They would sleep in our barn. There were also three men who would sleep in a McVities Biscuit van.
Dad (Fred Sandy) drove a lorry for Matthews during the day but before he went to start his proper job he would drive the lorry from Lee Mill into the bus station and swap it for a bus. He would pick up a full load of mine workers and drive them out to Hemerdon Mine for their shift. Before he finished his lorry driving he would drive the bus out to the mine again and take them back into Plymouth. He then drove the lorry back to Lee Mill.

Above: *The Cooke family at Sherwell Farm. Back: twins Doreen and Don; centre: Bill and Barbara; front: parents Alice and Len Cooke.*

Right: *Don Cooke with Pleasant at Sherwell Farm.*

Below: *Bill, Betty and Don Cooke enjoying retirement at Sterts Farm.*

Bottom right: *Don and Bill Cooke saving hay.*

MEMORIES OF JACK LAMBSHEAD

I was born on 5 June l905, the second born out of the five brothers and my sister. My parents had a farm at Ilsington and I went to school at Newton Abbot. I lost my father when I was only 14 years of age – I had to grow up overnight working our farm and looking after the family for my mother as she was fully occupied caring for all the little ones. It's little wonder I suppose that farming is in my blood and if I could have my life over again I wouldn't choose to do anything else. It's hard work; all weathers, and I suppose I can put my arthritic shoulder down to the fact that during lambing and calving time it would mean going out getting soaked through many times and nipping home for a quick cup of tea and going back out again with the same damp coat. Not a clever thing to do really looking back.

I bought my farm at Highweek at Newton Abbot with monies left to me by my relations. I met my wife Marjorie and we married at North Tawton near Okehampton. We had our two children Jane and Anne there. Marjorie's daughter, Janet, my step-daughter, mainly lived at Bournemouth with an aunt.

In 1961 I bought Hemerdon Farm from Mr Alan Scott and moved the family into the farmhouse. My daughter Jane was very keen on horses and she had several horses when she was a youngster. Anne was never so keen though. I enjoyed dealing in horses and made quite a lot out of buying and selling them.

I can remember when we first moved here we were told stories that there were tunnels under the farm leading down across the fields to the old Newnham Farm. There is supposed to be silver buried in the tunnels so the story goes. There is a chapel in the

farmhouse that was once occupied by monks. I know when I first moved in there I found lots and lots of bees nests. The monks obviously made and sold the honey. The farm was called Priory Farm years ago.

Some of the fields I owned included Bull Field (Bayley Park Path Field), New Park, Calvert Well, Little Lowdamoor and Big Lowdamoor, Lower West Park and Higher West Park.

When Dick Mumford retired he lived in No.3 Western Row with his wife Ivy. Dick would drive my cattle lorry for me and we would go to Newton Abbot for the day every Wednesday. We would very often have a drink in the Jolly Sailor at Newton Abbot.

I owned No.3 Western Row for some years in the sixties and had alterations done, adding a second bedroom upstairs and a bathroom and toilet downstairs. My daughter Anne was going to

live there but she never did so I sold the cottage on. I also sold Hemerdon Farm Cottage, the tied cottage back in the 1970s.

Some of the labourers who helped me out on the farm included Arthur Rogers, Fred Bowden and Alan Swinbourne. They all lived in the tied farm cottage, Hemerdon Farm Cottage. When I first bought Hemerdon Farm I had 87 acres but I sold off 32 acres. During the early 1960s I sold the field between the pub and the phone box for the building of the three bungalows. Now I've retired from the farm and live in the first bungalow known as Highfields nearest to the Miners Arms. I can look out of my picture window on to the fields which I still own and watch the cattle and sheep. They are not my stock now but I rent the fields out to another farmer for grazing. I feel I can touch the farmhouse from here.

Jack leaving the Miners Arms with his family on 5 June 2000, after celebrating his 90th birthday. Sadly he died on 16 March 2001.

Monica's mother, Florrie (then Lee) at the age of 14.

Florrie Stancombe at home with Monica.

MEMORIES OF MONICA EXWORTHY (NÉE STANCOMBE)

I was born at No.4 Western Row, Hemerdon, in 1934. My parents were Jack and Florrie Stancombe. I had a brother called Maurice and we lived in the one-bedroom cottage. My mother was called Florrie Lee before she married. Her parents were Bessie and Jimmy Lee and they lived in No.1 Rose Cottage (today known as Mousehole). They had nine children altogether: Florrie, Ivy, Beattie, Gladys, William (Bill), Alf, Reg (who died of tuberculosis aged 18), Louis (who died aged 21 of tuberculosis), Georgina (who died aged approximately six years of tuberculosis) and another child (name unknown, who also died of tuberculosis).

My father kept four cows at the top of our garden and in the morning he would walk them down Hemerdon Lane to a field near Windwhistle where they would graze. Milking was done by hand and the milk was scalded and made into cream. My father also worked at Lee Moor Clayworks. I remember well the day one of our cows broke out of the shed at the top of the garden. It charged down the garden path and threw itself off the garden

bank straight in through the kitchen window of No.3 Western Row, our neighbour's house. Mrs Lilly Jones, poor lady, was elderly and we thought the shock of it would kill her. My father had to pay to replace the broken window. Annie Mearns (Mrs Jones' daughter) and grandson Lewellan also lived with her.

When I was a young child my mother worked for Captain Leonard Silverlock and his wife Freda at Carthew House. Mr Silverlock was Captain of the Mines. My mother did household chores for them. Mrs Silverlock's hobby was making model buildings of churches and houses. She used real building materials for the slate roofs and stone work for the walls. Some of the model buildings were of Elizabethan architecture. As a young child I was totally fascinated with them. I can remember they were situated up the driveway and they looked totally realistic sitting between shrubs and bushes. My mother also worked for Mrs Rhoda Palmer at Sterts Farm where she would clean the back scullery, etc. I can remember in the orchard there was an Anderson style air-raid shelter in front of the farmhouse.

My cousins that also grew up in the village were the Clague

brothers, Sid, Reg, Edgar, Gerald and Keith. We had a lovely family life in the village and I have lots of good memories.

During the war my brother Maurice became very friendly with two American soldiers, one was called Bruce and the other was called Vester Evans. They were based in a camp on the Woollcombes' estate at Hemerdon House. They came to see my brother one evening before they left to go to the Front Line. At the time I was in a tin bath in front of the fire having my bath when there was a knock at the door. I could hear my mum asking them in and I nearly died of shock when I looked up to see these two huge black American soldiers. They were smashing blokes and very kind. I remember they arrived with two huge tins of fruit salad for us. My brother kept in touch with Vester after the war right up until the time my brother died. It would seem Bruce was killed not long after they left here. I have kept their air-mail letters.

My father Jack and Bumble Mumford would play tricks on Mrs Bedford who lived at Hemerdon Farm Cottage. One day she was sitting in the living room and Bumble and my Dad climbed in over the garden hedge and hid behind a currant bush. They had a button attached to a piece of string (this was known as a titchy button). The button made a tapping noise on the window. Mrs Bedford said to her husband 'oh my Alb, I thought it was a dickie bird knocking to tell me my mother had died.'

Some of the old characters in the village had some really funny little sayings. Lizzie Mumford would say to the butcher 'Oh well, if I can't pay the Lord will.'

Another character was Archie Bawden who lived in Bawdens Cottage opposite the Miners Arms. I remember him saying 'my missis is so house proud her blows the dust out of the pot before her uses it.' Another time when the end wall of his cottage collapsed and fell out into the road he said 'caw bugger maid I thought me bed was going to end up in the road legs up.' When Archie and his wife had a lodger staying with them he had a huge appetite; Archie would tell his wife to 'fill him up this week mother, he won't need so much next.'

My playmates were Sheila Mumford and Brenda Sowden. I was very privileged when Mr Harry Rowe's grandchildren, Richard and Elizabeth Harwood, came to Lowdamoor as I was invited to tea several times and allowed to play with them in the grounds. Mr Rowe's daughter Muriel was a teacher at Sparkwell School and then she married Mr Harwood who was a dentist. I remember he had to take a tooth out for Sheila Mumford when she was little in the cottage. Sheila also had her ears pierced outside in the road with just a cork and a red-hot needle.

During the war the Americans closed the road between Hemerdon and Sparkwell for training. This meant that the children had to use a pass to get to school.

Mr and Mrs Bawden lived at Fosters Tenement (later known as Ploughlands) and Mr and Mrs Lewis Lock also lived there at some stage. They had a big black taxi which was nicknamed the Bottle Hill hearse.

In 1945 when I was 11 years old we moved to Bickfordtown Farm. My great-grandparents (my mother's father's father) lived in a little cottage on the moor. It was called Horniwinks. You could get to it by going over the little stream at Drakelands – it was not far past the farm on the same side.

All that is left of it now is a pile of stones. I believe the majority of the granite stone was used to build a barn at what is known as the Trout Farm. My grandparents, being the eldest in the village [being 83 and 78 years of age], received a surprise parcel of food from Princess Elizabeth when she married. The letter from Buckingham Palace reads:

Many kind friends overseas sent me gifts of food at the time of my wedding. I want to distribute it as best I can, and to share my good fortune with others. I therefore ask you to accept this parcel with my very best wishes.

Elizabeth

When my grandmother died, a tin of chicken soup that was kept back from the food parcel was given to my mother. Today I keep and treasure the tin of soup as a souvenir. I don't think I will ever be tempted to use the contents as the tin is very rusty and must be well and truly past the sell-by date!

Two models made by Mrs Silverlock, of a house and the church.

The Rowe family at Sterts Farm. Left to right, back: Harry, William, Annie, Jane Mary, Rhoda, Richard senr, Millie, Thomas, Richard junr; sitting: Joseph, Benjamin, George.

Rowe family gathering. Left to right from back: Harry, Benjamin, Alice (wife), Thomas, Rhoda, Richard junr; 2nd row: Fanny, Millie, Richard senr, Jane Mary (wife), Annie, Marion, William; children: Risdon, Eric and Reginald Stevens (children of Millie), Joseph, George, Richard, Nora and baby Daisy (children of Marion and William).

Winifred Bowden with her father Tom and her mother seated with baby brother Harold.

Alice and John Kingdom with granddaughter Rosie Couch at Smallhanger.

Rhoda Rowe (on her 21st birthday) whose family Winifred's father worked for at Sterts.

MEMORIES OF WINIFRED MUMFORD (NÉE BOWDEN)

I was born in Hemerdon in 1897 which now makes me 103 years of age. My parents were Tom and Mary (known as Annie Bowden). There were eight children altogether: Joseph, John, Frederick, Stan, Arnold, Harold, Annie Marie (known as Nan, who was housekeeper to Harry Rowe at Lowdamoor for 30 years) and myself. I am the eldest. My mother was called Bowden before she married. The Bawden family were another big family in Hemerdon village. Everyone seemed to marry within their own little communities back then. My father Tom worked for Joe Rowe at Sterts Farm so we had No.1 Jubilee Cottages as our home for a while because it was the tied cottage to the farm. We moved to No.4 Western Row later. My grandparents George and Maria Bowden lived at Muttram Cottage.

When I was about two years old we moved to Smallhanger. When it was time for me to go to school my mother had to walk me over the moors to Sparkwell School. It was bitterly cold in the winter time.

My father at this time was working for Arnold Olver and we lived in the farmhouse. My father also looked after the farm as well. He would walk to Plympton beside two big horses pulling three wagons of clay on tracks – he did this three times a day. The clay was sent by goods trains into Cattedown where it was transferred into boats to be sent either abroad or up the country.

I can remember if we needed to go to Plymouth we would have to walk from Smallhanger to Plympton to catch the train. It would cost 5d. return. I can also remember from St Mary's Bridge in Plympton there were no houses or shops at all between there and Crab Tree.

My husband was Hedley Mumford also of Hemerdon Village. He lived for a time at Spring Cottage and then his family moved to Ivy Cottage.

My niece Rosie Elliott (née Couch) was born at Hemerdon Farm Cottage (her father was a farm labourer at the time). Rosie recalls picking baskets full of whortleberries near Smallhanger. As a young child she would take them into Plymouth Market to be sold to the townspeople who loved them. The same with primroses.

Muttram Cottage, now Ploughlands (earlier known as Fosters Tenement). The property burnt down in the 1980s. Standing in front is Maria Bowden, Winifred's grandmother.

MEMORIES OF MRS MARY GUY (NÉE HONEY)

During the Second World War Adrian Palmer was a Lieutenant. They used to meet in Hemerdon Hut. He made them get up at 3a.m. one morning for an exercise – Adrian was a seed merchant. The farmers said that they would never buy any animal feed off him again! The only shooting they ever did was to shoot rabbits up on Hemerdon Ball. Tom Willcocks was also a seed merchant and used to deliver round the village in his lorry. He has the shop in Colebrook now.

Harry Rowe who lived at Lowdamoor used to catch the bus to church every Sunday morning. We used to see him walking through the village with his walking stick. He used to get a lift back with the Woollcombes or the Silverlocks who lived at Carthew. Humphrey Woollcombe used to come down to us after church to pick up his cream. Lily Honey (my mother) used to go most Sundays. My brother David used to sing in the choir and we would walk to Sunday School in the afternoon.

[We] used to ride our bikes as children, riding down to Windwhistle Wood and up to Jail Pond to swim. There was another pond further on towards the moors called Stockers but we were not allowed to swim there because it was very deep and therefore dangerous although I am not saying we never did! As children we used to play with Ronald and John Denny. Ronald married and lived at Galva Cottage and John moved to Sparkwell. We also played with Harry Rowe's grandchildren. Muriel, his daughter, had two children Richard and Elizabeth and they used to holiday with him.

We would take our shoes to be repaired at a cobbler's at Bottle Hill. I believe the house was on the hill near to the old quarry (today Newnham Car Spares occupy the quarry and it is a car breaking yard).

The butcher from Colebrook came round with a van. Gwen Perry used to drive the van as she worked for Ern Damerell. Ernie Pulleyblank took over the business and was married to Gwen's daughter Ruth. We also had a 'bread man' who used to deliver from Plympton. Also there was an ice cream van which came round every Sunday lunch time and a fish-and-chip van but I can't remember the day.

Beside Hemerdon Hut there used to be a little shop run by the Co-op, just a general village store.

Dick Perry used to deliver milk. He had a dairy in Underwood in Plympton. He always drove on the wrong side of the road because he said he could see what was coming the other way. He was very deaf so this was very dangerous and he was always in a hurry.

Mrs Clague who lived in the first cottage in Hemerdon used to clean for Harry Rowe as did Nan Bowden who lived in No.3 Western Row, Hemerdon.

Whist drives were held in Hemerdon Hut where the only heating was a cast-iron stove in the middle of the floor. Some people caught the bus down from Sparkwell and then the last bus home. We also had pictures in the hut. They were very noisy and the pictures were often 'starry' and had lines across them – apart from that they often broke down. Again, they had to finish before the last bus from the bus stop.

When Plymouth Argyle were playing at home Ned Honey (my father) always went with Bill Nicholson and a few others. Monday was market day at Plympton and Ned always went and several other farmers used to come back to the Miners rather the worse for wear – and then they got even worse. They used to play euchre in the afternoon, a game with dominoes.

Risdon Rowe, who lived at Hemerdon Farm, and also Sid Beable, who farmed at Lee Moor, used to hire out farm machinery. Sid Beable's farm is now filled in by the clay works. I remember the mines working and seeing all the buckets going round the cables and tipping out their rubbish on the dumps. We used to have a lot of lorries going through the village from there.

Farmers used a combine harvester for harvesting, a very noisy machine and [a] very dusty [one] which used to 'clank' its way up Ball Lane. We used to take tea and cider up to the men harvesting. All the farmers used to help each other out at harvesting time. We grew mangolds for feeding the cattle and used to go to the field picking mangolds and loading them on a cart and then riding home sitting on top behind the tractor.

'Old man Dickie Mumford' used to live in the end cottage (Elm Cottage) and his sons George, Bumble and Dick worked at the clay pits. He also had a daughter Kath who married Bill Nicholson who also worked at the clay pits.

My Uncle Ern Perry farmed at Sherwell which was owned by the Woollcombes. Uncle Ern's daughter Edie married Tim Rogers and when he left the Navy he became a postman and used to deliver in the village. He drove much too fast and Rex Palmer complained that he used to drive up to the door and heave the post out the window. He then used to call on us and have bread and cream for his breakfast.

Before we had a tractor we had a horse called Ginger who did all the ploughing, etc. I remember milking by hand and David and I used to take it in turns to fetch the cows from the *fields for milking before we went to school. We also killed our own pigs and poultry. Jack Martin used to cut them up for us. He used to work for Ern Damerell. We kept a lot of pigs and poultry as well as milking cows. We used to roll the milk churns out into the road to be collected by the milk lorry each day by 8a.m.*

I can just remember Grandma Honey who used to divide her time between her five children – Dorothy, Marjorie, Mabel, Elsie and Ned. She always wore long dark clothes and her hair was in a bun. Grandad Honey died before I was born.

Before my father bought The Miners off the Woollcombe

estate in 1947 we kept the barrels of beer in the tap room and served the beer from the doorway. The bar was always smokey from the fire and also cigarettes. It was mostly a men's pub until we bought a spirit licence. Then it was altered and David and Linda [see page 156] have altered it further since then.

MRS ANNIE LEE RECALLS

Mrs Lee remembers the doctors back years ago were Dr Stevens, Dr Stamp and his son Duncan Stamp. The practice was half way up the Ridgeway at Plympton. Dr Stamp senr would always arrive wearing a long black cape and black silk top hat. No one dared to breathe on his black case. If he ordered you to bed you went and God help you if he saw you out against his orders. Back years ago some operations were done on the dining room table in your own home by the doctor. There was no going off to hospital. The nearest hospitals were Plymouth Freedom Fields and Greenbank Hospital and people only were sent in there if they were dead or dying.

Both Mr and Mrs Lee also recall one Saturday afternoon around tea time when a terrible accident happened up at Drakelands where Mr Farley was killed after falling from his hay cart and breaking his neck. He was only in his late fifties. When their daughter Christine married she lived in No.1 Jubilee Cottages and later she moved next door into No.2. Both their grandchildren Mandy and Mark also grew up there.

Ann recalls the time Archie Bawden, one of the village characters, was asked by Mr George Woollcombe to come up to the estate and catch a rat that was being a menace there. Archie stated his terms and asked for a

penny a tail. Mr Woollcombe agreed to this thinking there was only the one rat. Archie being the character he was caught the rat in the cage which just happened to be pregnant. He let the rat have her young then presented the mother and her family to Mr Woollcombe who then had to cough up a penny for each tail.

Mr Woollcombe was not very happy about this at all because he thought he had been had and was on the brink of saying he would not be paying when Archie threatened to set the whole rat family free. Mr Woollcombe soon settled up.

Archie's brother Frederick married Russell's Aunty Emily. They moved to Gunnislake when they married and had a daughter Rosina. They both died at St Anne's Chapel, Gunnislake. The Lees can remember Fred applying for his driving licence when he was 84 and when asked what he wanted it for he replied 'I only want to get from pub to pub.'

On beautiful Sunday afternoons during the summer families would walk up to the Hemerdon Ball plantation for walks and to admire the view. When the war was on the trees were sawn down because this was a famous landmark and the Germans would be able to make accurate hits on Plymouth. Three decades on there are probably still people that remember the day Archie Bawden 'struck gold'. Mrs Lee recalled:

It was a Monday and it was a lovely sunny day in the month of June when I walked past the end of Archie's immaculate garden. He stood at the fence with a grin wider than a barn door. He was always happy and smiling, but this was happiness with a plus.

He held out a stone for me to look at and as I tried to work out what it was that I was holding, he exclaimed 'Cor, bugger maid I've struck gold'. I could see it had what appeared to be specks of gold running through it.

Being a Monday morning there were several neighbours pegging out washing and it was not long before the word had spread that Archie had found gold in his garden. He spent the rest of the day looking for more of the rocks but was unsuccessful, ruining his beautiful garden in the process. The 'fool's gold' certainly brightened up that Monday morning.

Archie Bawden with nephew Louis.

MR RUSSELL LEE RECALLS

I was born on the 19 March 1912 and raised at Penlee, Hemerdon. My mother Kate (née Penwill) came from a large family of eight who were also born and brought up in the village. The cottage was named Penlee after the first three letters from my mother's surname and my father's surname. Mother had four sisters: Emily, Mary, Thurza and Edith, and three brothers, William, Joseph and Samuel. My mother's parents Emma and William Penwill lived at No.2 Western Row, Hemerdon. My cousin Ron Penwill was born in No.1 Rose Cottage and later he moved with his sisters (Myrtle and Edith)) to Manor House. My father, Arthur Lee's parents were Tom and Sarah Lee – they lived at Drakelands. My grandmother's mother also lived with my grandparents. She was always known as Gran Garland. She was a large lady and weighed about 22 stone; she was always very jolly. She would sit all day in the greenhouse in the garden and spend it watching the miners going to and from work along the top road. She never let anybody do her ironing as she always insisted on folding it herself and sitting on it to get the creases out.

I liked it growing up in the village because I had my aunties and uncles all around and both sets of grandparents. I remember if I couldn't get some sweets off my mum I only had to nip down the hop way to see one of my aunts – they always spoilt me rotten.

As a young boy growing up my playmates were Sid Tucker, George Lee, Lewellen Meerns, Jim Mumford and Harold Elford. We all went to Sparkwell school and like all the other children from around the area would have to walk to school. At lunch time I would walk to the double gates outside the Woollcombes' estate and meet my mother who would arrive with a hot pasty for my dinner. Many a time I would end up throwing half my pasty away as I would be chased by the hunt's dogs and I thought if I threw my pasty they wouldn't chase me and bite me.

I remember one day at school Mrs James the headmistress went to open the high window in the classroom just above where I was sitting and the window fell down and landed on top of my head. I was really lucky to escape with just a sore head and bad bruising. It kept me off school for almost three weeks; I did try to stretch it out a bit longer but I couldn't fake my injuries any more so I was sent back to school.

Sid Tucker and myself would keep a watchful eye out of the school window for the hunt going by. When we saw the red jackets of the huntsmen riding by we would quickly put our hands up and say to our teacher 'can we step out Miss' (this usually meant that we wanted to be excused to go to the lavatory) but we would be gone like a flash up towards Cemetery Hill to watch the hounds riding across the moor.

It was such a sight on a bright autumn day to see all the huntsmen in their brilliant red jackets mounted on enormous horses with their pack of hounds running and darting each side of the horses. The head huntsman wore the bugle around his neck and would blow his tune to rally the dogs. To a couple of young boys this seemed so exciting. When the hunt party had gone we never went back to school – we would play around the top of Claymoor Lane until it was time to go home.

Mrs Hacker was the first lady to have a sweet shop in the village. Originally it was in her house at No.1 Jubilee Cottage but then she had a little shed building outside the house which was used as a shop for some time. My aunt Edith (née Penwill) married Alf Mumford and they started the village shop and ran it for many years until they retired and the shop was bought by the Co-op and finished in the mid fifties. The shop was situated next to the village hall.

Mr Tom Cannon from Plympton drove the Co-op bread van and Ern Damerell from Colebrook delivered meat and groceries. Most people kept their own pigs and chickens and the farms sold milk to the villagers. My parents kept fowls in a run at the top of the garden at Penlee and I remember my mum would say to me 'Russell go and ask your father to kill me a chicken.' I would run out into the garden and ask my father for the chicken, he would pick out a nice fat one and within a few minutes the fowl had its throat slit and I would have to help my father to pluck its feathers. Within no time it was sitting on the table roasted and ready for dinner.

We all grew our own vegetables and some families had an allotment in a field at the top of Back Lane. Next to this field was where the village sports day was held. This was a lovely day out for all the family. Walls Ice Cream was sent out on a three wheeled bike and it had on the box 'Stop Me And Buy One'. I can remember Bob Elford riding a beautiful brown horse called The Guiding Star around one of the fields up there. The horse belonged to Mr Arnold Olver.

As boys we would go badger hunting on the moors. This is banned now. If anyone is caught badger baiting now there is a very heavy fine for it. We would also catch rabbits along the railway line at Hemerdon Banks. Harold Elford was a crack shot with a catapult and would bring down rooks and crows. Some

Keith and Christine Lee with Jean who worked at the Co-op.

people had rook pie for their tea. Bill Taylor (Gwen and Doris' father) would take about half a dozen boys from the village up on the moors to Jail Pond near Stockers to teach us to swim. Most of the children from the village learnt how to swim in this pool. We would use a big plank of wood which we would put into the water and we would lie on it and use it as a float. We couldn't be bothered to take it away with us so we hid it in the bull rushes until next time. All the lessons never did me no good because I never did get the hang of it. We also amused ourselves playing football and marbles. We used to get a free marble out of the top of lemonade bottles back years ago.

When I was a young lad all the village children went to the chapel and I can remember Mr Clarence Abbot took the services for some time, then Mr Pengelly and then eventually Mr Foster. Sheila Mumford played the organ; she was excellent and she played by ear as she couldn't read any music. If we weren't paying attention and misbehaving Mr Abbot would send us to the back of the chapel and he also gave us something that we would have to remember for the next Sunday and sure enough when we turned up he would ask us to repeat what it was he had

told us the previous Sunday. This was one way of making sure we were listening and taking everything in. I was also in the choir at Sparkwell Church. My father was a tenor and both my children Christine and Keith were also in the choir. Keith was an altar boy.

My father was secretary of the village hall for many years and it was used for dances and card games and the football team met there. I can remember the football team was called Hemerdon United and they played in yellow and black stripe. It is a shame because there used to be a photograph of the village football team hanging in the hall but when it was broken into the photograph went missing. Also stolen was a silver plate that was won by the villagers at Sparkwell Fair for the best carnival float. I believe there may be another photograph of the football team hanging in the Miners Arms pub (see page 155).

When there was a dance in the hall Mr Gliddon (fiddler) and Mr Roberts both played violins; they both came up from Plympton and there was also Dolly Collins who was marvellous on the piano. Charlie Trott played the drums. He was only a young man but he could certainly play. He worked for my Uncle Bill Penwill at Manor House and lodged there as well. Mind you I'm not sure if Charlie Trott was his real name but we all knew him as that. They played really lively music and everybody danced the gay gordons, Boston two-step, polkas and waltzs. A special favourite that was sung was 'A Bird in A Gilded Cage'.

When the Second World War broke out I was enlisted into the Royal Air Force – I spent most of the war stationed in Cornwall. I married Ann Coombes before the war on 5 October 1938. It was our 60th wedding anniversary in 1998. Ann came from

St Maurice originally and we had a bungalow for a few years in Woodford Plympton. Our daughter Christine and son Keith were born there and when Christine was about five years old we moved back to Hemerdon. We agreed with my parents that we would move into Penlee and they would move up around the corner to Alma Cottage. When I came home from the war on leave Mrs Perry who lived in No.2 Jubilee Cottages would give me all the cream I wanted – she was very kind to me.

Larry Macbean was the boot maker who lived at Bottle Hill, the first cottage behind the quarry. He would make really lovely strong boots for the clay workers. You didn't wear out a pair of his boots in a hurry.

No.2 Rose Cottage was a tied cottage to Sterts Farm, as also was No.1 Jubilee Cottages. When I was a young lad Joe Rowe had Sterts Farm and in later years it passed to Rex Palmer then to his son Eric. The farm was rented from the Woollcombe family. Some families also collected milk from their farm as well. Our son Keith also worked for Rex Palmer at Sterts Farm for some time.

He is able to recall the names of some of the fields around the area of the village: Orchard, The Platt, Carthew, The Bull's Field, Galva, Sand Tip, Phillips, Quarry Field, Bus Stop, Three Corners, Pylon, Oakey, Icelands Nos 1, 2 and 3, Warrens, Big Charles, Cross Park, Plantation and Jubilee Field.

Right up until my eighties I would go up to the Woollcombe estate and saw down trees for clearance. I always used the old-fashioned bow saw.

Top: *Looking left with one's back to the bus stop.*
Centre: *Looking slightly to the right with one's back to the bus stop.*
Bottom: *Kerry Dobbs and Glen and Scot Taylor enjoying a day off because of the snow.*
View overlooking Plympton and Plymouth.

HEMERDON'S NEW VILLAGE HALL

The opening of the new hall took place on Friday 10 November 2000. Jane Lowney, daughter of Jack Lambshead, who donated the land upon which the old village hut stood and now the new hall stands, cut the ribbon and Father Freddy gave a short prayer and blessed the site.

The old village hut was a 1920s former First World War Army hut. It lasted remarkably well but a decision was taken a couple of years ago that it couldn't last much longer as the walls were leaning badly and the woodwork was rotten. It was decided to ask the villagers by way of a questionnaire whether they thought it would be worth while building a new hall. The response was an overwhelming 'yes'. Ideas for fund-raising events went into overdrive and fashion shows, garden parties, a '60s theme evening, cheese and wine evenings and a barbecue were held – which all helped enormously to pull in several thousand pounds towards the rebuilding effort.

The annual village ram roast held at the end of July usually makes around £2500. The stalls are set up in the car park of the Miners Arms. There are cake stalls, bric-a-brac, skittles, plate smashing, coconut shy, bottle stall, tossing the bale of hay, pony rides, bouncy castle, Punch and Judy, fortune telling, tug-of-war, face painting, candy floss, etc. The barbecuing of the ram always takes place in the centre of the car pack with the stalls around the edge. A massive mountain of hot dogs and burgers is also consumed. After dark when the stalls are sold out a local band provides music for dancing in the car park. Year on year this event has become ever more popular with people coming from miles around.

With a generous Council and National Lottery Grant the dream of the new hall was in sight. No longer would people have to make a dash to the outside loos – the new hall sports a ladies, gents and disabled toilets as well as a kitchenette for preparing food and which can also be used for serving drinks, etc. The new hall is also wider than the old one and has two walk-in cupboards which provide very useful storage space.

The Toddler Group meet weekly in the hall and whist drives are in full swing again but the quest for fund-raising continues; the next thing on the agenda is to replace the old tables and chairs.

Eileen and Bill Stevens celebrating their Golden Wedding Anniversary in August 2000.
Bill, now retired, was Principal Senior Manager at E.C.L.P. Lee Moor and Eileen trained as a fashion artist and worked in a studio in London.
Their children are:

John (born St Ives, Cornwall 1951)
Teresa (born Spain 1954)
Yvonne (born St Austell, Cornwall 1956)
Christopher (born Plymouth 1964).

Eileen and Bill moved from St Austell to Hemerdon in 1963. They live at Carthew which was originally built in 1908 for the Mine Manager of E.C.L.P.
Bill was Chairman of the old village hall for over 30 years and Eileen, whose hobby and passion is watercolour painting, has painted many works for raffle prizes at the village annual ram roast, which is held each July.
Eileen's paintings have helped to raise hundreds of pounds for the upkeep and repair of the old village hall and also for the past couple of years her paintings have raised huge amounts towards the building of the new village hall.
Many villagers have one of Eileen's paintings hanging proudly in their homes. She particularly enjoys painting old properties with lots of character.

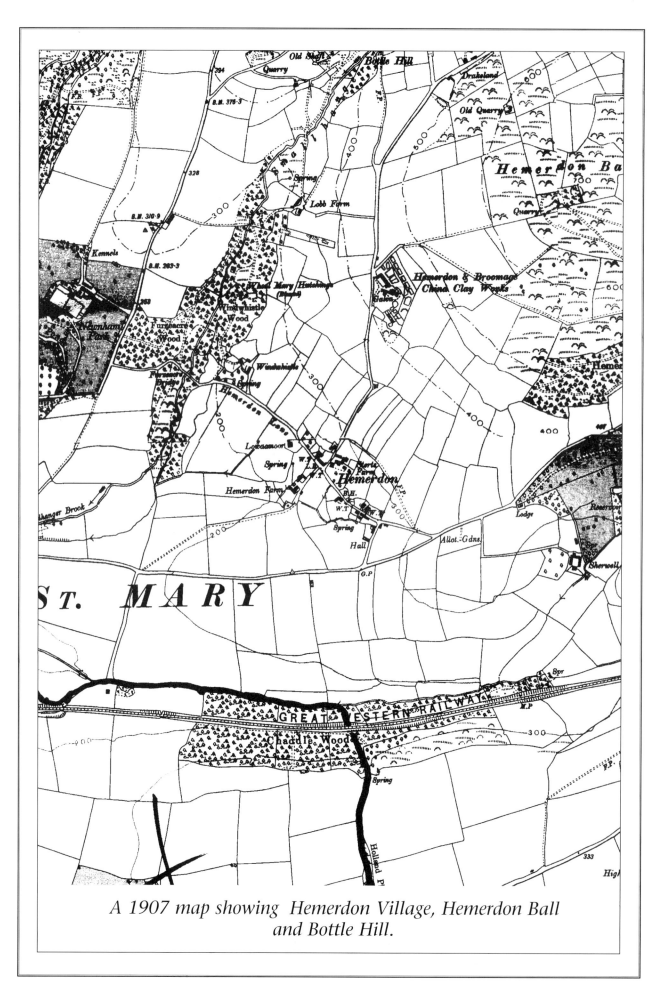

A 1907 map showing Hemerdon Village, Hemerdon Ball and Bottle Hill.

Edgar Clague's Sunday Paper Round for Hemerdon, 1939:

Mr and Mrs R. Clague
Mr and Mrs Joe Bawden
Mrs Simpson
Mr Arthur Lee
Mr and Mrs Paul
Mr and Mrs Perry
Mr and Mrs Tom Bowden
Mr and Mrs J Lee (grandfather)
Mr and Mrs Williams
Mr and Mrs Harris
Mr and Mrs Henry Lee
Mr and Mrs Sid Tucker
Mr and Mrs A. Bawden
Mr and Mrs N. Honey (Miners Arms)
Mr and Mrs R. Mumford
Mr and Mrs Jack Stancombe
Mrs Jones
Mr and Mrs Bill Mumford
Mr and Mrs Jack Hawke
Mr and Mrs Penwill
Mr and Mrs Bowstone
Mr and Mrs Harry Rowe
Mr R. Rowe

Mr J. Rower and Mrs Palmer
Mr and Mrs Paul
Mr and Mrs Lock
Mr and Mrs Silverlock
Mr and Mrs Jack Mumford
Mr and Mrs Nicholson
Mr and Mrs Tucker
Mr and Mrs Elford
Mrs Jenkins
Mrs Coles
Mr and Mrs L. Macbean
Mr and Mrs H. Lee
Mr and Mrs C. Miller
Mr and Mrs Farley
Mr G. Lee
Mr and Mrs F. Lee
Mr Luscombe
Mr and Mrs Olver
Mr and Mrs Philips

Edgar also delivered papers to USA soldiers during the war at Hemerdon House.

List of Families Recorded as Living in Hemerdon, Bottle Hill, Drakelands and Newnham area as at January 2001:

Armstrong	Denny	Lambshead (dec'd)	Schofield
Baldwin	Edwards	Martin	Sheldon
Berrystone	Elford	May	Smerdon
Birchall	Evans	Meen	Stacey
Bloom	Fellows	Milford	Stevens
Brown	Giblett	Mitchell	Styles
Bye	Grainger	Newsham	Tagert
Cobbold	Hart	Newton	Taylor
Collier	Hawkes	Parker	Vincent
Cooke	Hingston	Penwill	West
Daw	Honey	Phillips	Woollcombe

People who have Sadly Died Since research began on Hemerdon in October 1997:

Bessie Tucker (no relation to Sid Tucker)
Daisy Mumford
Sid Tucker
Adrian Palmer
Annie Lee
Jack Lambshead
Anne Lambshead, Jack's daughter

Above: *Winnie Mumford is* the oldest parishioner. *This photograph was taken on 31 March 2001. Winnie's 104th birthday was in July 2001.*

Above right: *Winnie's son, Norman in Scout uniform.*

Left: *Winifred Mumford with her husband Ed, who died at the tragically young age of 21 as a result of a motorbike accident.*

Subscribers

Mr and Mrs B. Allen, Lucas Wood
The Andrews family, Lower Venton Farm
Dorothy Barker, Castletown, Scotland
Jack and Sandra Barker, Lee Mill, Devon
Norman Barker, Saskatchewan, Canada
David E. Barker, Cornwood, Devon
Mrs E. Barnes, Walsall Wood, West Midlands
Mrs Doris Baskerville, Cornwood, Devon
Arthur Baskerville, Cornwood, Devon
Mrs M. Baskerville, Sparkwell, Devon
Dr Laurie Baxter, Lisa and Sarah Pobereskin,
    Sparkwell, Devon
Fred J. Bennett, Saltash, Cornwall
Tamsyn Blaikie, Lopwell House, Roborough,
    Devon
Dorothy Blandford (née Coombes), Torquay/
    formerly of Sparkwell, Devon
George Bone, Cape Town, South Africa
Jose Boon (née Trigger), Ivybridge, Devon
Neil, Suzanne, Kathryn, Jennifer and Samuel Boot,
    Venton, Sparkwell, Devon
Mrs M. Booth, Trowbridge
Mark and Margaret Brewer, Lee Mill, Devon
Mrs Nancy Bristow
K. J. Burrow, Bucks Cross, Devon
Anthea M. Carne, Sparkwell, Devon
Vi Clague and Janet Carowicz, Plymouth, Devon
Rosemary and Diana Carrington, Sparkwell,
    Devon
Ann Carter (née Stonehouse), Sparkwell, Devon
Mr and Mrs D. Cartlidge, Sparkwell, Devon
B. and M. S. Chudley, Venton, Devon
Mr and Mrs G. Chudley, Venton, Sparkwell, Devon
Bernard J. Chudley, Denstone, Staffordshire
Jonathan and Christine Chudley (née Vincent)
Mr and Mrs I. E. Clague, Plympton, Plymouth
E. S. and M. P. Clague, Plympton, Devon
Alan Stuart Clemo, Lutton, Devon
William Colborne-Mackrell, Beechwood,
    Sparkwell, Devon
Mr and Mrs E. Cole, Milton Keynes
Sylvia J. Collier, Sparkwell, Devon
Tony and Barbara Collier, Lucas Wood, Devon
Mr and Mrs K. Collings, Sparkwell, Devon
Neil Collings, Gulworthy, Devon
George Colton, Cornwood, Ivybridge, Devon
W. A. P. Conran, Bury St Edmunds
Betty Cooke, Hemerdon, Devon

Ann R. Cooper, late of Sparkwell, Devon
Mrs Mavis Cornish, Venton, Devon
Ashley E. Cox, Lutton, Devon
D. Crawford, Elfordleigh, Devon
C.D.C. and J.V. Crowley, Fursdon, Sparkwell,
    Devon
Gordon and Dorrie Cummings, Lucas Wood
Frank and Lynne Cummings, Sparkwell, Devon
Mr and Mrs Josh Dalton, Lucas Wood, Cornwood,
    Devon
Paul Dalton, Plympton, Devon
Freddie and Penelope Darwall, Ickford,
    Buckinghamshire
Jillian Davey
Mrs A. Davis, Plymouth, Devon
Paul and Liz Davis
Phyllis E. Davis (née Taylor), Sparkwell, Devon
Mr A. W. Daw, Plympton, Devon
Ellis Dawe and family
Revd Frederick G. Denman, Sparkwell, Devon
John and Lorraine Denny, Sparkwell, Devon
Barbara Devine, Cornwood, Devon
K. S. and C. F. Dobinson, Mount Pleasant, Devon
M. and E. Dobinson, Stone, Cornwood, Devon
Susan Donaldson (née Barker), Cornwood, Devon
Keith and Sue Downing
Graham and Kathryn Downing
Alison Louise Dunkley (née Stonehouse),
    Ivybridge, Devon
Marilyn and Dennis Ellicott, Sparkwell, Devon
M. and L. Elliott, Ivybridge, Devon
Rosemary L. Elliott, Sparkwell, Devon
Dawn Evans, Hemerdon, Devon
Val Evans, Bottle Hill, Plympton, Devon
Mr and Mrs Roy Exworthy, Sparkwell, Devon
Andrea Exworthy, Venton, Sparkwell, Devon
Veronica and Eric Exworthy, Venton, Sparkwell,
    Devon
Sally Fairman
Revd D. F. Farnham, Arundel, West Sussex
Nigel and Della Fellows (née Munro), formerly of
    Smallhanger and Claymoor
William H. Fisher, Wotter, Devon
Richard and Mary Ford
Bryan Foster, Plymouth, Devon
Susan Foster, Beechwood, Sparkwell, Devon
B. Friendship
Pat Friendship, South Brent, Devon

Olwen Gibson, Hemyock, Devon
Graham and Sue Goodanew, Cadleigh, Devon
Adrienne Gordon (née Kelly), Clophill, Beds.
Andrew Grainger, Hemerdon, Devon
Chris Dare and Judy Gray, Venton, Devon
Patricia M. Greenwood, Beaconsfield, Bucks.
John and Pat Grimes, Mount Pleasant, Sparkwell,
    Devon
W. R. Gulley, Sparkwell, Devon
David L. Gulley F.W.C.F., formerly of Mount
    Pleasant, Devon
Mary H. Guy (née Honey), Taunton, Somerset
Robert and Judy Hamar, Venton, Devon
Enid Hamlyn, Blacklands, Sparkwell, Devon
Mrs H. Harper, Sparkwell, Devon
Leonard Harris, Sparkwell, Devon
Robert J. Hart
Christine A. Hartley, Lee Mill, Devon
Nancy Hartley, Lee Mill, Devon
Mr and Mrs Jack Harvey, formerly of Smallhanger
    and Claymoor
Graham and Allison Hatcher (née James),
    Tavistock, Devon
Mary and David Hayward, Venton, Devon
Kate Heasman, Nottingham
Mr and Mrs H. Heighway
Derick and Enid Hext, formerly of Houndall Farm,
    Sparkwell, Devon
Sharon and Trevor Hext, Plympton, Devon
Michael and Trisha Hill, Plympton, Devon
Mr Harry Hill, Lee Mill, Devon
Mrs Sheila Hill, Plympton, Devon
J. Hill (née Stevens), Lee Mill, Devon
Derek Honey, Oxford
Mr and Mrs D. H. Honey, The Miners Arms,
    Hemerdon, Devon
Dr W. L. and Mrs H. S. Hooper, Sparkwell,
    Devon/Bournemouth
Stephen Hoskin, Polven, Caerhays, St Austell/
    formerly of Lower Venton
Marjorie Hosking, Plympton, Devon
Ivan Hurn, Dover, Kent
Dennis Hurn, Ivybridge, Devon
Mr R. Hurn, Plympton, Devon
Ruth and Tom Huxtable
Allan Huxtable
Dr Neil and Mrs Karen James-Pearson, Virginia,
    USA
Laity Jean and Roger, North Hill, Plymouth
Marcia V. Jeffery (née Bowden), Wadebridge,
    Cornwall
Kathleen F. Jenkins, Sparkwell, Devon
Mr and Mrs S. B. V. Johnson, Sparkwell, Devon
Marjorie Kerton
M. J. Kimberley, Kingsglen, Lee Mill Bridge, Devon
John Kingwell, Sparkwell, Devon
Andrew Kitts, Kirton, Lincolnshire
Peter Kitts, Box, Wiltshire
Bill Kitts, Sparkwell, Devon

John Knight, Beechcroft, Sparkwell, Devon
June Lapthorne, Higher Challonsleigh, Plympton,
    Devon
Mrs Gladys Lavers (née Lee), Plymouth, Devon
George Lee, Lee Moor, Devon
Linda Legg
Heather J. Lillecrapp, Plympton, Devon
Edwin and Jeannette Little, Brisbane, Australia
Edwin Little
Mr and Mrs Les Littlejohns, Hartland, Devon
Leonard and Phyllis Long, Venton, Devon
Carol Love, Yelverton, Devon
Jane Lowney (née Lambshead), Hemerdon, Devon
Laurence C. Lowry, Plympton, Devon
For all the Lowry family
J. E. Luckraft
Jean MacCormack (née Cummings), Bath
Lesley M. Masey, Sparkwell, Devon
Mary and Jim Masters, Dawlish, Devon
Mr R. May and D. Lake, Sparkwell, Devon
Tina Mears (née Tremain), Kingston, Devon
Mr and Mrs W. Miller, Plympton, Devon
Mr N. Miller, St Column Major, Cornwall
D. Molesworth, Hemerdon
Louise Moore (née Tremain), Crediton, Devon
Mrs Florrie Mudge, Sparkwell, Devon
Philip and Valerie Munro, formerly of
    Smallhanger and Claymoor
Julia M. Munsey, London N1
Mrs Elspeth Murdoch, Buchlyvie, Scotland
Trevor J. Nelder, Plympton, Plymouth, Devon
Mrs J. Netherton
Mrs J. J. M. Newton
Elisabeth Nicol (née Carter), formerly
    Claymoor/now London
Sheila Palmer, Treen, Elfordleigh, Devon
Miss Romaine Palmer OBE, Plympton, Devon
Sue and Geoff Pearn, Smithaleigh, Devon
Alan E. Pearse
Dr and Mrs Geoffrey Perham, Sparkwell, Devon
Mrs K. Phillips, Wembly
Jill V. Phillips, Sparkwell, Devon
John and Allison Phillips, East Gosford, Australia
Vanessa Philp, Sparkwell, Devon
Pat Philp, Sparkwell, Devon
Yvonne Pinder (née Nelder), Blandford, Dorset
Kenneth Pledger, Plymouth, Devon
Brenda and Brian Priestley, Sparkwell, Devon
Audrey Prizeman, Plymouth, Devon
Frederick C. Quest, Sparkwell, Devon
Joyce Reed
Harold Reed, Ermington, Ivybridge, Devon
Mr and Mrs W. Roberts, Waterlooville, Hants.
Mr and Mrs D. Root, Lee Mill
David and Betty Ruttledge, Amesbury, Wiltshire
Lt Cdr F. W. Sadler RN (Ret'd), Cheltenham, Glos.
W. Salter, Ermington, Devon
Frank and Jessie Sercombe
John and Caroline Serpell, Yealmpton, Devon

SUBSCRIBERS

Charles and Sylvia Serpell, Sparkwell Farm, Sparkwell, Devon
Mr and Mrs R. Serpell
Mr C. Serpell, Higher Baccamore Farm, Sparkwell, Devon
Paula Serpell, Plympton, Devon
Pamela J. Shephard, Halesowen, Worcs.
Jennifer Shingleton, Yealmpton, Devon
Freda M. Short, Tavistock, Devon
Richard and Kay Silverlock, St Austell, Cornwall
Bob and Norma Skelley
Cynthia M. Skelton (née Serpell), Isle of Sheppey
George E. Small, Sparkwell, Devon
John E. Small, Lee Moor, Devon
Mrs K. Smith, Sparkwell, Devon
Travey B. I. Smith, Lee Mill, Devon
Jane Snowling (née Barker), Sidmouth, Devon
Sparkwell Golf Course
Mr and Mrs A. Spear, Kent
Mrs J. Stacey, Taunton, Somerset
Mrs B. Stancombe, Lutton, Devon
Rita Stevenson (née Hosking), Mary Tavy, Devon
Andrew J. Stonehouse, Sparkwell, Devon
Robert Stonehouse, Sparkwell, Devon
Jennifer Sturdy (née Thorrington), Plymouth
Mario, Coral, Emily and Edward Styles, Hemerdon, Devon
The Symons family, Venton Cottage 1948–49
Bob and Frances Tagert, Hemerdon, Devon
Mrs E. Taylor, Sparkwell, Devon
Charles and Dorothy Taylor, Plymstock, Plymouth, Devon

The Thomson family, Marks Bridge, Cornwood, Devon
Graham Thorne, Maldon, Essex
Mr and Mrs W. Thorrington, Sparkwell, Devon
David Thorrington, Plympton, Devon
Joyce A. Traynor, Crosby, Liverpool
Ann and Peter Tremain, Sparkwell, Devon
Daisy M. Trevarthen (née Elford), formerly of Hemerdon, Devon
Richard Trigger, Plympton, Devon
Gerald Tucker, Sparkwell, Devon
Mrs Joan M. Tucker, Sparkwell, Devon
Becky Tucker, Cornwood, Devon
Penry C. Turpin, Mount Pleasant
Mr and Mrs Upham (née Trethewey),
John and Kim Vane, Bottle Hill, Sparkwell, Devon
Paul A. Verran, Sparkwell, Devon
Stella Vincent (née Collings), Ontario, Canada
Betty and Dick Walke, Horrabridge, Devon
John F. W. Walling, Newton Abbot, Devon
The Watts family, Collaford Farm, Plympton, Devon
Peter and Wendy Wellington, Ivybridge, Devon
Glenys and David Wickstead, Plympton, Devon
Mrs C. Willcocks
Jean Williams, Choakford, Sparkwell, Devon
Rob and Julie Willis, Colebrook, Devon
Robert and Helen Wood
Sheila Wooldridge (née Long), Plympton, Devon
J. H. G. Woollcombe, Hemerdon
A. P. and J. D. Wotton

*The last celebration to take place in the
village before this volume went to print:
the Diamond Wedding Anniversary of
Mr and Mrs Thorrington, 28 June 2001.*

ALSO AVAILABLE IN THE SERIES

The Book of Addiscombe • Various
Book of Bampton • Caroline Seward
Book of Bickington • Stuart Hands
The Book of Blandford Forum • Various
The Book of Brixham • Frank Pearce
The Parish Book of Cerne Abbas • Vale & Vale
The Book of Chittlehampton • Various
The Book of Constantine • Moore & Trethowan
The Book of Cornwood and Lutton • Various
The Book of Creech St Michael • June Small
The Book of Cullompton • Various
The Book of Grampound with Creed • Bane & Oliver
The Book of Hayling Island and Langstone • Rogers
The Book of Helston • Jenkin with Carter
The Book of Hemyock • Clist & Dracott
The Book of High Bickington • Avril Stone
The Book of Ilsington • Dick Wills
The Book of Lamerton • Ann Cole and Friends
Lanner, A Cornish Mining Parish • Scharron
Schwartz & Roger Parker
The Book of Loddiswell • Various
The Book of Lustleigh • Tim Hall
The Book of Manaton • Various
The Book of Meavy • Pauline Hemery
The Book of Morchard Bishop • Jeff Kingaby
Minehead with Alcombe • Binding & Stevens
The Book of North Newton • Robins & Robins
The Book of Pimperne • Compiled by Jean Coull
The Book of Plymtree • Tony Eames
The Book of Porlock • Denis Corner
Postbridge – The Heart of Dartmoor • Reg Bellamy
The Book of Priddy • Various
The Book of Rattery • Various
The Book of South Stoke • Various
South Tawton and South Zeal with Sticklepath • Roy
and Ursula Radford
The Book of Stourton Caundle • Philip Knott
The Book of Swanage • Rodney Legg
The Book of Torbay • Frank Pearce
Uncle Tom Cobley and All • Stephen Woods
The Book of Watchet • Compiled by David Banks
The Book of West Huntspill • Various
Widecombe-in-the-Moor • Stephen Woods
The Book of Williton • Michael Williams
Woodbury • Roger Stokes
The Book of Woolmer Green • Various

SOME OF THE MANY FORTHCOMING TITLES

The Book of Addiscombe, Vol. II • Various
The Book of Barnstaple • Avril Stone
The Book of Bridestowe • R. Cann
The Book of Buckland Monochorum • Hemery
The Book of Carshalton • Stella Wilks
The Book of Chagford • Ian Rice
*The Book of Chittlehamholt with
Warkleigh & Satterleigh* • Richard Lethbridge
*The Book of Chittlehamholt with
The Book of Colney Heath • Bryan Lilley
The Book of Down St Mary • Various
*The Book of Dulverton
with Brushford, Bury & Exebridge* • Various
The Book of Dunster • Hilary Binding
The Book of Hurn • Margaret Phipps
The Book of Lulworth • Rodney Legg
The Book of Markyate • Richard Hogg
The Book of Mawnan Smith • Various
The Book of Newdigate • John Callcut
The Book of Newton Abbot • Ian Rice
The Book of North Tawton • Various
The Book of Northlew with Ashbury • Various
The Book of Peter Tavy • Various
The Book of Publow with Pensford • Various
*The Book of Sampford Courtenay
with Honeychurch* • Stephanie Pouya
The Book of Staverton • Pete Lavis
The Book of Studland • Rodney Legg
The Book of Wythall • Val Lewis

For details of any of the above titles or if you are interested in writing your own community history, please contact: Community Histories Editor, Halsgrove House, Lower Moor Way, Tiverton Business Park, Tiverton, Devon EX16 6SS, England, e-mail: naomic@halsgrove.com

In order to include as many historic photographs as possible in this volume, a printed index is not included. However, the Community History Series is currently being indexed by Genuki. For further information and indexes to volumes in the series, please visit:
http://www.cs.ncl.ac.uk/genuki/DEV/indexingproject.html